Negation in Gapping

OXFORD STUDIES IN THEORETICAL LINGUISTICS

GENERAL EDITORS: David Adger, *Queen Mary College London*; Hagit Borer, *University of Southern California*

ADVISORY EDITORS: Stephen Anderson, *Yale University*; Daniel Büring, *University of California, Los Angeles*; Nomi Erteschik-Shir, *Ben-Gurion University*; Donka Farkas, *University of California, Santa Cruz*; Angelika Kratzer, *University of Massachusetts, Amherst*; Andrew Nevins, *Harvard University*; Christopher Potts, *University of Massachusetts, Amherst*; Barry Schein, *University of Southern California*; Peter Svenonius, *University of Tromsø*; Moira Yip, *University College London*

RECENT TITLES

PUBLISHED IN ASSOCIATION WITH THE SERIES
The Oxford Handbook of Linguistic Interfaces
edited by Gillian Ramchand and Charles Reiss

For a complete list of titles published and in preparation for the series, see pp. 267–8.

Negation in Gapping

SOPHIE REPP

OXFORD
UNIVERSITY PRESS

OXFORD
UNIVERSITY PRESS

Great Clarendon Street, Oxford OX2 6DP

Oxford University Press is a department of the University of Oxford.
It furthers the University's objective of excellence in research, scholarship,
and education by publishing worldwide in

Oxford New York

Auckland Cape Town Dar es Salaam Hong Kong Karachi
Kuala Lumpur Madrid Melbourne Mexico City Nairobi
New Delhi Shanghai Taipei Toronto

With offices in

Argentina Austria Brazil Chile Czech Republic France Greece
Guatemala Hungary Italy Japan Poland Portugal Singapore
South Korea Switzerland Thailand Turkey Ukraine Vietnam

Oxford is a registered trade mark of Oxford University Press
in the UK and in certain other countries

Published in the United States
by Oxford University Press Inc., New York

© Sophie Repp 2009

The moral rights of the author have been asserted
Database right Oxford University Press (maker)

First published 2009

British Library Cataloguing in Publication Data
Data available

Library of Congress Cataloging in Publication Data
Data available

Typeset by SPI Publisher Services, Pondicherry, India
Printed in Great Britain
on acid-free paper by
the MPG Books Group

ISBN 978-0-19-954360-1 (Hbk.)
ISBN 978-0-19-954361-8 (Pbk.)

1 3 5 7 9 10 8 6 4 2

Contents

General Preface

The theoretical focus of this series is on the interfaces between subcomponents of the human grammatical system and the closely related area of the interfaces between the different subdisciplines of linguistics. The notion of 'interface' has become central in grammatical theory (for instance, in Chomsky's recent Minimalist Program) and in linguistic practice: work on the interfaces between syntax and semantics, syntax and morphology, phonology and phonetics, etc. has led to a deeper understanding of particular linguistic phenomena and of the architecture of the linguistic component of the mind/brain.

The series covers interfaces between core components of grammar, including syntax/morphology, syntax/semantics, syntax/phonology, syntax/pragmatics, morphology/phonology, phonology/phonetics, phonetics/speech processing, semantics/pragmatics, intonation/discourse structure as well as issues in the way that the systems of grammar involving these interface areas are acquired and deployed in use (including language acquisition, language dysfunction, and language processing). It demonstrates, we hope, that proper understandings of particular linguistic phenomena, languages, language groups, or inter-language variations all require reference to interfaces.

The series is open to work by linguists of all theoretical persuasions and schools of thought. A main requirement is that authors should write so as to be understood by colleagues in related subfields of linguistics and by scholars in cognate disciplines.

In this volume Sophie Repp uses the behaviour of negation in gapping sentences as a probe into the interaction between the syntactic computation and the interface systems. She shows that certain principles of the interpretation of conjunction are crucial to understanding apparently core syntactic and semantic facts, and argues that a true understanding of the phenomenon requires a theory which details the interaction of syntactic and non-syntactic processes and constraints.

David Adger
Hagit Borer

Acknowledgements

This book is a revised version of my doctoral dissertation, which I filed in September 2005 at the Humboldt University, Berlin. Therefore I want to thank especially my three supervisors Chris Wilder, Manfred Krifka, and Gisbert Fanselow. Chris as a great specialist in ellipsis helped to me look for the right questions and to recognize intriguing problems at a time when I was quite new to the field. I benefited enormously from Manfred's very careful reading of the chapters as I developed them, his many insightful comments and discussion of the implications of my analyses. The study has improved considerably with his help. When Chris had left Berlin, Gisbert, I am glad, also agreed to come on board for my supervision, discussed many syntactic details with me and always reminded me not to forget the great picture over all the little details.

For long discussions of data and theories, I would like to thank especially Andreas Haida, who met up with me time and again and never grew tired of discussing yet another twist to a problem, yet another curious set of data, and very happily and critically commented on what I had written. The book in its present form would not be what it is without the careful reading and very constructive criticism of Katharina Hartmann and Jason Merchant, who reviewed the book for publication. Both of them insisted on a clear explication of my ideas and stringent argumentation which I hope to have supplied. Both of them also were happy to discuss my work beyond the reviewing stage, for which I would like to thank them as well.

I have also benefited greatly from meetings with my colleagues in the Berlin-Potsdam linguistics community, including the DFG-funded graduate school 'Economy and Complexity in Language', where I started, as well as the DFG-funded Collaborative Research Centre on information structure, where I am a researcher at present, and the Centre for General Linguistics (ZAS). I thank especially Ewald Lang, Holden Härtl, Stefan Hinterwimmer, Roland Hinterhölzl, Ljudmila Geist, Greg Kobele, as well as Márcela Adamíkova, Joanna Błaszczak, Philippa Cook, Cornelia Endriss, Caroline Féry, Werner Frey, Silke Hamann, Thomas Holder, and Sue Olsen. In the wider world, I received very valuable comments from and could discuss my work with Petra Hendriks, Kyle Johnson, Jennifer Spenader, Carla Umbach, Susanne Winkler as well as audiences in Cologne, Edinburgh, Manchester, Oslo, Ottawa, Stockholm, and Tübingen.

For generously helping me with native speaker judgements, I would like to thank especially Márcela Adamíkova, Jeroen Aspeslagh, Joanna Błaszczak, Dirk Bürger, Doreen Bryant, Philippa Cook, Leen Croenen, Nicole Dehé, Eva Engels, Sachiko Hara-Francke, Andreas Haida, Silke Hamann, Stefan Hinterwimmer, Claes Hvilsted-Olsen, Ljudmila Geist, Beata Gyuris, Holden Härtl, Geert van Hout, Nick Hubble, Keri Jones, Jessica Jones, Judith de Jong, Kris Lauwerijs, Leman Mutlu, Robert Schuster, Ichiko Takashima-Gitschmann, Chris Wright, Yuko Yoshida, and many others. For assisting me with formatting and references, I would like to thank Christian Krause.

Parts of Chapter 4 appeared as Repp (2006) and are reproduced with kind permission from Springer Science and Business Media.

The book is dedicated to a certain film maker, who thinks that linguistics is a crazy subject.

Sophie Repp

List of Abbreviations

ACC	accusative
Agr	agreement
AgrP	agreement phrase
ATB	across-the-board
ConP	conjunction phrase
CORR	correction
CP	COMP (complementizer) phrase
CSC	coordinate structure constraint
CT	contrastive topic
DAT	dative
DP	determiner phrase
DUR	durative
E-feature	ellipsis-feature
EPP	extended projection principle
FEM	feminine
FocP	focus phrase
FP	functional projection
H	high
HPSG	head-driven phrase structure grammar
IP	inflection phrase
L	low
LF	logical form
MASC	masculine
NEG	negative
NegP	negation phrase
NOM	nominative
NP	noun phrase

NPI	negative polarity item
PART	particle
PBC	principle of balanced contrast
PERF	perfective
PF	phonetic form
PolP	polarity phrase
Pol_1P	polarity phrase 1
Pol_2P	polarity phrase 2
Pos	positive
PPI	positive polarity item
PredP	predicate phrase
REFL	reflexive
RNR	right node raising
Spec	specifier
SUBJ	subject
TOP	topic
TP	tense phrase
vP	light V-phrase
VP	verb phrase
VPE	verb phrase ellipsis
\	falling accent
/	rising accent

1

Introduction

1.1 The problem and outline of the book

This book investigates the behaviour of the negation in gapping, which will be shown to be of a rather changeable nature. Attention will focus on gapping sentences that contain a negative marker in the first conjunct, which in the second conjunct is—or seems to be—elided. In such sentences, the negation can be interpreted in three different ways. In some environments, the second conjunct, just like the first, is interpreted as negative. An example for this is given in (1.1a). Such cases can be considered the default case in ellipsis in general: what is elided in the second conjunct, is taken to be identical to an antecedent in the first conjunct. In (1.1a), this is *hasn't got*. I shall call such readings **distributed scope** readings. In other environments, the negation scopes over the whole coordination, that is the negation takes **wide scope**. This is illustrated in (1.1b). There are special conditions on the intonational realization of this reading. For (1.1b) to be felicitous, it must be read as a single intonational phrase without a pause between the conjuncts. In addition, there must be an accent on the auxiliary. In the default distributed scope reading, on the other hand, the two conjuncts are realized as two individual intonational phrases, the verb is deaccented and the contrast pairs are highlighted by accents. I shall come back to the details of this later. Note that a wide scope reading is also available for (1.1a) if read with the appropriate intonation. Conversely, (1.1b) cannot receive a distributed scope reading even if the intonation is the appropriate one. The difference between (1.1a) and (1.1b) is that in the latter only the auxiliary and the negation are elided whereas the former also elides the main verb. It seems that auxiliary gapping only allows a wide scope reading (Johnson 1996/2003). A third possibility for the interpretation of the negation in the first conjunct is what I shall call here **narrow scope**. This means that the second conjunct is interpreted as positive. This is the case in (1.1c) and (1.1d). The intonation here roughly corresponds to that of the distributed scope readings, that is there are two individual intonational phrases.

(1.1)   a. Pete hasn't got a video and John _[1] a DVD.
           = [It is not the case that Pete has a video] and [it is not the case that
           John has a DVD].

       b. Pete didn't clean the whole flat and John _ laze around all after-
           noon.
           = It is not the case that [Pete cleaned the whole flat and John lazed
           around all afternoon].

       c. Pete wasn't called by Vanessa but John _ by Jessie.
           = [It is not the case that Pete was called by Vanessa] but [it is the
           case that John was called by Jessie].

       d. Pete wasn't called by Vanessa and John only _ by Jessie.
           = [It is not the case that Pete was called by Vanessa] and [it is the
           case that John was only called by Jessie].

Thus, we have three options to interpret the negation in a gapping sentence:

(1.2)   READINGS OF THE NEGATION IN GAPPING SENTENCES

       a. distributed scope of the negation: $(\neg A) \wedge (\neg B)$

       b. wide scope of the negation: $\neg(A \wedge B)$

       c. narrow scope of the negation: $(\neg A) \wedge (B)$

All these readings at the surface have a negative marker in the first conjunct,
which is, or seems to be, elided in the second conjunct along with the finite
verb.

   I will show that the factors which influence the interpretation of the negation are manifold. Apart from intonational factors, they include the contents
of the gap (finite main verb, finite modal/auxiliary with or without non-
finite main verb, negative polarity items); the type of coordinator used (*and*,
but);[2] the contextual requirements of certain semantic operators in the second
conjunct (*only, even*) and the kind of negation involved (propositional or
speech-act-level).

   Most of the negation data so far have only been discussed for English—if
they have been discussed at all. In this study, I shall examine in depth evidence

---

[1] A note on notation: I will mark gapped material with an underscore in examples where the
position of the (sometimes discontinuous) gap is relevant. In examples where the formal details of
the gapped material are important I will present the gapped material in the gap position and mark it
with strikethrough. Otherwise, I will not mark the gap explicitly. In the English translations, I only use
gapping sentences if these are grammatical and if they do not run the risk of obscuring the intended
reading.
[2] This is the full set of conjunctions I will consider.

from German as well as English. In addition, I shall draw attention to similarities and differences with other languages, for example Dutch, Japanese, Polish, Russian, and Slovak. These languages do not all behave alike in the interaction of gapping and negation. In German or Dutch, for instance, we observe that the distributed scope readings are best obtained if the negative marker actually is uttered in the second conjunct.[3] Eliding it produces a degraded result as is shown for German below:

(1.3) a. Max hat das Buch nicht gelesen und Martha die Zeitschrift
           Max has the book not   read   and Martha the journal
           ~~??nicht.~~

           ~~not~~

       b. Max hat das Buch nicht gelesen und Martha nicht die Zeitschrift.
           'Max didn't read the book and Martha didn't read the magazine.'

The findings I present in this study are important for the theory of gapping because none of the accounts that have been suggested in the literature are equipped to deal with all the data I discuss. I will show this in detail in Section 1.3. The obstacles are obvious in a theory that considers copying or deletion of some sort or other as the central mechanism behind gapping. Should the negation be copied in one case (distributed scope readings) but not in the other (narrow scope readings)? How can the wide scope readings be accounted for in a deletion or copying account? Why would main verb gapping differ from auxiliary gapping when it comes to negation? Theories that have been developed to deal with the wide scope readings, and which assume gapping to be the coordination of smaller conjuncts (such as TP or vP) face difficulties when it comes to the narrow scope readings: these theories assume the contents of the gap and structure of the gap to be such that a narrow scope reading cannot be accommodated.

In the present study, I propose a copying account for gapping, where copying is implemented as sideward movement (Nunes 1995, 2004). I argue that the conjuncts in the case of the distributed scope readings and the narrow scope readings are ordinary full clauses. Only the wide scope readings have (slightly) smaller conjuncts with the negation scoping over them. For the narrow scope readings I suggest that there is no negation in the second conjunct, instead there is a positive morpheme. My argument will proceed as follows.

Chapter 1 serves as a general introduction. I present some well-known features of gapping and discuss the three types of theories that have been

---

[3] If uttered, the negative marker appears in a different position from the one it would take in a non-elliptic structure, compare (1.3a) versus (1.3b) in the main text. I shall not discuss this issue.

proposed for gapping: deletion and copying accounts, small conjunct analyses, and sharing approaches. The discussion should provide an impression of the theoretical possibilities as well as the merits and the shortcomings of existing accounts of gapping when it comes to the negation data. Chapter 1 ends with a sketch of my own proposal.

Chapter 2 investigates the distributed scope readings (case (1.1a)). We already saw in (1.3) above that German is more restricted than English in its ability to interpret the negation in the second conjunct if that negation is elided. I shall discuss the syntax of English versus German clausal negation and propose that syntactic differences between the two languages are responsible for their divergent behaviour in gapping. The main argument makes use of the status of adjuncts (German negation) versus heads (English negation). I propose a **copying hypothesis for gapping** which says that gapping is derived by copying material from the first conjunct to the second conjunct by way of sideward movement after the phonology of the first conjunct has been spelt out. Only material required to build a convergent derivation from the impoverished numeration of conjunct 2, which only contains the remnants of the gapping conjunct, is copied. This includes sentential functional projections and their complements. Adjuncts are not copied because they are not required in the above sense, which means that in German the negation is not copied whereas in English it is. Combined with the semantic-pragmatic principle of balanced contrast introduced in Chapter 3, as well as the finding that the negation in the wide scope readings is a different type of negation than in the other readings (Chapter 4), this proposal can account for the negation data.

Chapter 3 investigates the narrow scope readings and the various environments they occur in. First, I look at gapping with German *aber* (which I call contrastive *but*) and argue for an account of the conjunction which takes its information-structural sensitivity into account. Contrastive *but* interacts with contrastive topics and foci, with the negation in the first conjunct being one such focus. The second conjunct provides the appropriate focus alternative, that is positive polarity. A short section on *and* shows that similarly to *aber* this conjunction can also signal contrast. More specifically, in addition to the neutral kind of contrast usually found in gapping, it also occurs in coordinations that have implicative, or attitudinal, commentary-laden readings. I show that such readings are not available in gapping and formulate the **principle of balanced contrast** (**PBC**) for gapping with *and*, which says that both conjuncts must make the same kind of contribution to a discourse topic. This principle forms an important part in the analysis of auxiliary

gapping as well as gapping with focus particles in the second conjunct, also
to be discussed in Chapter 3. For auxiliary gapping, I show that the reason
why this subtype of gapping never occurs with distributed readings is that
the second conjunct introduces a whole new *v*P, which comes with its own
polarity information (on the level of the event). This is by default positive.
A distributed reading—copying of the negation from the first conjunct—is
precluded. A narrow scope reading can arise if the PBC is obeyed, which I will
demonstrate will require the negation of the first conjunct to be interpreted as
predicate negation ($\approx$ a negatively described event). For gapping with focus
particles in the second conjunct, I show that the positive polarity of the second
conjunct here is determined by the context-sensitive semantics of the focus
particles. We find that it is the reading which obeys the PBC that emerges in
gapping.

Chapter 4, which is based on Repp (2006), investigates those gapping cases
where the negation operates on the speech act level, which I call **illocutionary negation**. The presence of such a negation can produce a narrow scope
reading (corrections with German *sondern*, corrective *but*) or a wide scope
reading. I show that gapping with a wide scope reading of the negation has
particular discourse, syntactic, and intonational characteristics from which
I conclude that declaratives with a wide scope reading must be denials, and
that interrogatives with a wide scope reading must involve so-called outer
negation, both of which are instances of illocutionary negation. This has
repercussions for the syntactic analysis of the two kinds of readings. The
wide scope readings are the coordination of smaller conjuncts than the distributed and narrow scope readings, neither of which involve illocutionary
negation.

Chapter 5 delivers a new semantic definition of gapping. It investigates the
issue of finiteness and shows that gapping does not necessarily involve the
elision of the finite verb. Rather, it is the referential anchoring of a sentence
which is elided in the second conjunct of a gapping sentence, and this can also
be expressed by other elements in a sentence (e.g. complementizers).

Chapter 6 summarizes the findings and analyses from the previous chapters, and concludes.

1.2 Some basic features of gapping

Gapping is a type of ellipsis which in English as well as in other head-initial
languages elides the finite verb in the second conjunct, and which in strictly
head-final languages like Japanese or Korean, elides the finite verb in the first

conjunct (Ross 1970).[4] Example (1.4a) illustrates this for English, where the finite verb *gave* is elided in the second conjunct. Example (1.4b) shows that in Korean the finite verb *cwuessta* ('gave') is elided in the first conjunct. In head-final languages where the finite verb can also take a non-final position, as is the case in the V2 languages German or Dutch, gapping elides the finite verb in the second conjunct (see (1.4c) for a German example).[5]

(1.4)   a.   John gave Mary a flower and Bill _ Sue a book.

    b.   John-i   Mary-eykey Kkoch-ul   (*Korean*; J.-S. Kim 1997: 178)
       John-NOM   Mary-DAT   flower-ACC

       _   kuliko Bill-i   Sue-eykey Chayk-ul cwuessta.
       ~~gave~~ and   Bill-NOM   Sue-DAT   book-ACC gave

    c.   John gab Mary eine Blume und Bill _   Sue ein Buch.
       John gave Mary a   flower and Bill ~~gave~~ Sue a   book
                                       (*German*)

Throughout, I shall use the following terms for the description of gapping sentences. The elided material in the second conjunct is the *gap* and the corresponding identical material in the first conjunct is the gap's *antecedent*. The remaining overt material in the second conjunct are the *remnants* and the corresponding constituents in the first conjunct, their *correlates*. Remnants and correlates together are the *contrast pairs*.

Along with the verb, other material such as direct or indirect objects can be omitted as well. In (1.5), the indirect object is elided in addition to the verb:

(1.5)   John gave Mary a flower and Bill _ Sue_.

In the case of verbal complexes, it is sufficient to elide only the finite verb and have other, non-finite verbs contrast with each other. Examples (1.6a)–(1.6c) illustrate this for the gapping of modals and auxiliaries. In (1.6a), an infinitive is left behind and in (1.6b) and (1.6c), participles:

---

[4] In some accounts (e.g. Kuno 1978; Saito 1987), it is assumed that gapping in Japanese and Korean is actually right node raising (RNR), where RNR is assumed to be a true raising operation rather than phonological form deletion as is assumed in more recent accounts, e.g. by Hartmann (2000) or Wilder (1994, 1995).

[5] In German, we find verb-final structures, such as (i) below, where the verb is elided in the first conjunct. These are cases of RNR (see Hartmann 2000 for a detailed analysis of RNR):

(i)   Max sagt dass die Jungs drinnen _   und die Mädchen draußen spielen.
    Max says that the boys inside ~~play~~ and the girls   outside play
    'Max says that the boys are playing inside, and the girls, outside.'

(1.6)   a.   He may stay inside and she _ go to the beach.   (Sag 1980: 198)

       b.   Max   hat   abgewaschen   und   Maria   _   die   Treppe
           Max   has   washed.the.dishes   and   Maria   ~~has~~   the   stairs
           gekehrt.
           swept
           'Max washed the dishes and Mary swept the stairs.'

       c.   Er   ist   verhaftet   worden   und   sie   _   freigelassen   _.
           He   is   arrested   been   and   she   ~~is~~ released   ~~been~~
           'He was arrested and she, released.'

In the introductory section, I mentioned that whether an auxiliary or a main verb is gapped interacts with the interpretation of the negation in gapping. I give an account of this in Chapter 3.

There are always at least two contrast pairs in gapping. If the elision of the finite verb and additional material leaves only one contrast between the two conjuncts, as for instance in (1.7), the result is usually referred to as *stripping* or *bare argument ellipsis*. This type of ellipsis usually comes with an extra polarity element (*too, not*):

(1.7)   John put the sugar on the table, and the salt too.

Whether stripping is a subtype of gapping or not is controversial. I shall not be concerned with stripping in this study, see for example Winkler (2005) and the references cited therein.

The restrictions operating on gapping include almost all levels of linguistic analysis: they concern information-structural, prosodic, semantic, as well syntactic aspects. These restrictions determine the semantic relation between the conjuncts, the identity of gap and antecedent, and the syntax and semantics of the contrast pairs. First, observe that gapping is restricted to coordinations and comparatives.[6] In coordinations, it is best with *and* or *or* (Jackendoff 1971), but the conjunctive use of *then* also seems acceptable (Johnson 1996/2003). In English, *but* is problematic in most environments,[7] for example (1.8a), although there are some curious exceptions. For

---

[6] I shall ignore comparatives because they are subject to additional restrictions, which I cannot discuss here.

[7] For speakers who accept pseudogapping, (1.8a) can be expressed using this ellipsis type:

(i)   John ate rice but Jim did potatoes.

Hoeksema (2006) conducted a corpus study of gapping and pseudogapping in English and found that pseudogapping combines more often with *but* than with *and* whereas for gapping it is the other way round. It seems that the two ellipsis types display different kinds of contrast. Indeed, when confronted with a gapping sentence that contains contrastive *but*, speakers of English often report that there is 'not enough contrast' that would warrant the use of the conjunction. For further discussion of the choice between pseudogapping and gapping, also see Agbayani and Zoerner (2004).

instance, if adjuncts (including the agent in passives) are contrasted along with the subjects as in (1.8b), the use of *but* becomes acceptable (Chris Wilder, p.c.). Likewise, if the second conjunct contains some sort of negation as in (1.8c), *but* can be used (J. Camacho cited in Johnson 1996/2003: 20). Johnson (ibid.) also points out that gapping can involve the conjunction *nor*, see (1.8d).

(1.8)   a.   #John ate rice but Jim potatoes.

   b.   The Beatles played on Monday but Elvis on Tuesday.

   c.   Sam ate something but Mittie nothing.

   d.   Mary hasn't a car, nor Sally a garage.

German accepts contrastive *but—aber—*in all environments. It also accepts *dann* ('then') and variants of it, such as *und daraufhin* ('and then, as a consequence'), as well as complex coordinators like *sowohl-als auch* ('both-and'), *weder-noch* ('neither-nor'). The peculiar behaviour of *but* in English finds parallels in other languages, such as Polish, where the conjunction which normally expresses the meaning of English *but—ale—*, cannot be used in gapping. Instead, the conjunction *a* must be used, which is a conjunction that expresses a contrast 'greater' than simple *and—i*.

   As for the identity of gap and antecedent, we find that the elided verb must be semantically identical to its overt antecedent, which includes the categories of tense, aspect, and mood. For tense, this is illustrated in (1.9a), where the first conjunct requires a past tense interpretation and the second conjunct, a future interpretation. Gapping is ungrammatical in this case. Example (1.9b) illustrates the same for aspect in Russian: the first conjunct has imperfective aspect and the second conjunct, perfective aspect. Again, the result is ungrammatical:

(1.9)   a.   * The boy played with a toy car yesterday, and the girl ~~will play~~ with a doll tomorrow.

   b.   * Wtchera   ja   pisala   pismo dwa tchasa, a   ty
        yesterday I   wrote.DUR letter   2   hours, but   you
        ~~napisala~~   ~~pismo~~ za dri tchasa.
        wrote.PERF ~~letter~~ in 3   hours
        'Yesterday I wrote a letter for 2 hours but you wrote a letter in
        3 hours.'   (*Russian*)

Non-semantic features of gap and antecedent do not have to be identical. It is not necessary to have identical person, number, and gender features on the elided verb and its antecedent. In other words, φ-features are irrelevant. In (1.10a), the antecedent verb is singular whereas the elided verb is plural. In (1.10b), the gender features on antecedent verb (feminine) and gapped verb (masculine) are different:

(1.10) a. He was drinking wine and the others ~~were drinking~~ beer.

      b. Mat'   poimal-a   pticu, a   syn ~~poimal~~   sobaku.
         mother caught-FEM bird, and son ~~caught-MASC~~ dog.
         'The mother caught the bird and the son the dog.'   (*Russian*)

Note in this connection that polarity is a meaningful category, so the polarities of the first and second conjuncts should always be the same. The existence of narrow scope readings therefore is quite unexpected.

    Another important question in the study of gapping has been the question of what makes good remnants. The first thing to be observed is that the remnants must contrast 'appropriately' with their correlates in the antecedent clause. Appropriate contrast can be established between elements of a well-defined alternative set, such sets being, for instance, different locations, different times, different agents, etc. Contrasting elements from different sets, such as from a set of times and a set of locations is not appropriate in this sense and results in ungrammaticality:

(1.11) * The boy played in the afternoon and the girl in the barn.

Note that to contrast appropriately, it can be quite sufficient if there is referential contrast between a remnant and its correlate (Hartmann 2000). On the surface, remnant and correlate can be the same (see (1.12a)), but only for certain types of DPs, such as specific indefinites (see (1.12a) versus (1.12b)), and only in the pre-gap position (see (1.12c)). For discussion of this phenomenon, see Hinterwimmer and Repp (2008).

(1.12) a. One student called the director and one student the dean.

      b. *A student called the director and a student the dean.

      c. *The director called one student and the dean one student.

    Next to appropriate contrast, the notion of structural parallelism of remnants and correlates has played an important role in the analysis of gapping. It is not necessary that the syntactic category of a remnant and its correlate are the same. What is important is that the remnant fit the requirements of the elided verb, which means that, for instance, in copular constructions the correlate can be an adjectival predicate whereas the remnant is a nominal predicate, compare (1.13a):

(1.13)   a.   We consider Leslie rather foolish, and Lou a complete idiot.

                                                      (Sag *et al.* 1985: 160)

        b.   Die Gladbacher   bestimmten nach der Halbzeit
             the Gladbach.team dominated after the half.time
             zwar   das Spiel, die Hamburger   weiter das
             admittedly the game the Hamburg.team further the
             Ergebnis.   (Winkler 1997*b*: 32).[8]
             result
             'The Gladbach team did dominate the game after half-time but the
             Hamburg team still decided the result.'

        c.   Max ist nur stolz   aufs   Land,   Peter aber   schon
             Max is just proud of.the country Peter however already
             ein richtiger Nationalist.
             a   outright nationalist
             'Max is just proud of his country but Peter is an outright nation-
             alist.'

Active-passive alteration is disallowed (in contrast to some instances of VP ellipsis):

(1.14)   * The budget cuts might be defended publicly by the chancellor, and
          the president ~~might defend publicly~~ her labor policies.

                                              (Johnson 1996/2003: 24)

Furthermore, the size of the remnants has been of considerable interest in the analysis of gapping. Hankamer (1973) formulated the *major constituent condition*, which says that remnants must be major constituents where a 'major constituent of a given sentence S_0 is a constituent either immediately dominated by S_0 or immediately dominated by VP, which is immediately dominated by S_0' (Hankamer 1973: fn. 2). The proposal is supported by examples like the following:

(1.15)   a.   * John came up with evidence against that proposal and Max with
             arguments in support of.

        b.   * Tim verlegt die Rohre über den Putz   und Max die
             Tim installs the pipes on   the plaster and Max the
             Kabel unter.
             cables under
             'Tim is installing the pipes on the plaster and Max is installing
             the cables under the plaster.'   (Hartmann 2000: 149)

---

[8] *Zwar* has no equivalent in the elliptical clause.

As (1.15) illustrates it is impossible to have only prepositions as remnants even though semantically that would make sense. Prepositions are not major constituents. On the other hand, it is possible to have just the particle of a particle verb as a remnant as the following examples show. Particles are not major constituents either (but see Hartmann 2000 for a proposal on this):

(1.16) a. Der eine ging nach Bremen, der andere von dort weg.
            the one went to   Bremen the other   from there away
            'One of them went to Bremen, the other left the place.'

                                                    (Winkler 1997b: 32)

        b. Peter looked up and John down.

It is usually assumed that gapping is island-sensitive, that is that the remnants in the elliptic clause may not be contained in a syntactic island. Neijt (1979) was the first to discuss this in detail. In (1.17), the remnant is situated in an embedded clause that constitutes a *wh*-island, here marked by square brackets. The sentence is ungrammatical (no matter whether the matrix verb is elided or not):

(1.17) * Pete knows which boy bought a toy car
          and John (knows) [which boy bought a ball].

It seems that the major constituent condition would capture a case like (1.17). On the other hand, there are cases which do seem to violate islands. Consider the two minimal variants of (1.17) in (1.18), which show that one of the remnants can be situated in a *wh*-island if the *wh*-phrase is also a remnant (the remnants and correlates require heavy stress here).

(1.18) a. Pete knows which boy bought a toy car and John [which girl a baby doll].

        b. Pete knows which boy bought which toy car
            and John [which girl which baby doll].

Pesetsky (1982) discusses subject–object asymmetries in sentences with *wh*-islands which he compares to *wh*-in-situ effects. It seems that embedded objects are contrasted more easily than embedded subjects:

(1.19) a. ?This man knows why you eat spaghetti, and that man, maccaroni.

        b. *This man knows why spaghetti makes you sick and that man maccaroni.

        c. He asked where I bought the maccaroni and where the spaghetti.

        d. *He asked where the spaghetti was sold and where the maccaroni.

                                                (Pesetsky 1982: 644–6)

Coppock (2001) shows that the Left Branch Condition, illustrated in (1.20a), does not seem to pose a problem for gapping, see (1.20b):

(1.20)   a.   * [How tall] did the Lakers hire [t a forward]?

         b.   I make too strong an espresso, and Fred too weak.

Other islands, like the sentential subject constraint (see (1.21)) or adjunct islands (see (1.22)) are completely out. This calls for a detailed analysis of gapping with different kinds of islands.

(1.21)   *That Alfonse ate the rice is fantastic and [~~that~~ Harry ~~ate~~ the beans] ~~is fantastic~~.   (Neijt 1979: 24)

(1.22)   a.   *Dr Smith will be mad if Abby talks to the teacher
              and Dr Miller ~~will be mad~~ [~~if Abby talks~~ to the headmaster].

         b.   *Dr Smith will be mad if Abby talks to the teacher
              and Dr Miller ~~will be mad~~ [{if / ~~if~~ } Susan ~~talks~~ to the headmaster].

Although the status of islands in gapping is not well understood it seems clear that gapping is clearly different from other ellipsis types such as sluicing. Sluicing can violate a wide range of islands (Chung *et al.* 1995; Fortin 2007; Merchant 2001; Ross 1969).[9] Example (1.23a) is a sluicing example with an adjunct island which is similar to the gapping example in (1.22). Example (1.23b) is the ungrammatical non-elliptic counterpart of (1.23a).

(1.23)   a.   Ben will be mad if Abby talks to one of the teachers, but she couldn't remember which.   (Merchant 2001: 88)

         b.   *Ben will be mad if Abby talks to one of the teachers, but she couldn't remember which (of the teachers) Ben will be mad [if she talks to $t_{\text{which of the teachers}}$].

As a matter of fact, gapping actually disallows some embedding structures which are not islands, such as complement *that*-clauses (e.g. Koutsoudas 1971; Hankamer 1979; Johnson 1996/2003; Wilder 1994; Williams 1997):[10]

(1.24)   * Jim claimed that Alan went to the ballgame and John ~~claimed that Alan went~~ to the movies.

---

[9]   VP-ellipsis or fragment answers also are subject to islands. For accounts of this difference between sluicing on the one hand and VP ellipsis on the other, see e.g. Fox and Lasnik (2003) and Merchant (2008). For the island sensitivity of fragment answers, see Merchant (2004).

[10]   Such sentences improve if matrix subject and embedded subject are co-referent (Merchant, p.c.).

(i)   Jim said that he called his mum and John ~~said that he called~~ his dad.

Gapping in embedding structures with embedded non-finite clauses is more readily available. The following examples contain control structures (1.25a, 1.25b), raising structures (1.25c) and small clauses (1.25d). In all these cases, one remnant occurs in the matrix clause whereas the other occurs in the non-finite embedded clause. According to Hankamer's (1979) major constituent condition, they should all be impossible since the remnant in the embedded clause is neither immediately dominated by S_0 or the VP which is immediately dominated by S_0:

(1.25)   a.   Max versprach Whiskey mitzubringen, und Peter Wein.
             Max promised whiskey to.bring   and Peter wine
             'Max promised to bring whiskey and Peter wine.'

                                                       (Lee 1998: 122)

       b.   John tried to buy beer and Bill fried chicken.   (Neijt 1979: 52)

       c.   John seems to be happy and Mary unhappy.

       d.   I consider Liz fond of chocolates and Sam of pies.

                                              (Johnson 1996/2003: 21)

We see that the whole question of embedding in gapping structures is quite intricate. Island constraints do not seem to be the right sort of constraints: they are too strict for some cases and too lax for others. Nor does the major constituent condition make the right predictions. I shall not discuss these issues to a great extent in this book and generally leave them for future research. One aspect that I will discuss in some detail, however (see Chapter 5), is the following: it is perfectly possible to have gapping in a coordination of embedded clauses. In this case, however, the complementizer must be left out along with the verb (Fiengo 1974; Hartmann 2000; Wilder 1995, 1996):

(1.26)   Jim claimed that Alan went to the ballgame and (*that) John ~~went~~ to the movies.

The last feature of gapping I would like to mention in this introduction is the intonation of gapping, which has received increased attention in recent years. Carlson (2001*a*, 2001*b*), Féry and Hartmann (2005), and Winkler (2005) approach this feature of gapping experimentally. In run-of-the mill gapping (which includes the distributed scope readings), see example (1.27) from Féry and Hartmann (2005) for an illustration,[11] non-clause-final correlates and

---

[11] The tones are described in the notation of the tone sequence model (for American English, e.g. Beckman and Pierrehumbert 1986; Pierrehumbert 1980; for German, e.g. Féry 1993, 2001; Grice *et al.* 2005; Uhmann 1991 and many others).

remnants are marked by a rising pitch accent and clause-final correlates and remnants, with falling accents. The shape of the accents in the first conjunct can vary depending on the left context. In some cases they can be left out. The accents in the second conjunct, however, are obligatory. The verb typically is deaccented. As for phrasing, Féry and Hartmann (2005) found that the two conjuncts are separated by a clear intonational phrase break. The first conjunct is usually marked by a high boundary tone although low boundary tones appear too. The second conjunct is reliably marked by register down-step.

(1.27)   What kind of toys are Anna and Maria making for their sons?
Anna bastelt ihrer Enkelin   ein Segelboot
Anna makes   her   granddaughter a   sailing.boat
L* H   L* H   H* L H%
und Maria ihrem Sohn ein Müllauto.
and Maria her   son   a   rubbish.van
      L* H   L* H   H* L L%
'Anna makes her granddaughter a sailing boat and Maria her son a garbage truck'.   (Féry and Hartmann 2005: 107–8)

Carlson (2001*a*, 2001*b*), who investigates gapping and the ellipsis type of left peripheral deletion in English, observes that the intonation to some extent can disambiguate sentences that are ambiguous between these two structures. Left peripheral deletion is an ellipsis type where material in the left periphery of the second conjunct is elided. Carlson found that in sentences with three potential correlates for two remnants such as (1.28), the intonation given in (1.28a), where the subjects carry a rising accent and the object of the first clause does not carry any accent, makes hearers interpret the sentence more often as gapping than the intonation given in (1.28b). In the latter case, the object of the first clause carries a rising accent. Note, however, that the preferred reading in sentences such as (1.28a) still is left peripheral deletion (more than 50 per cent), which Carlson explains in terms of processing economy. Semantic parallelism between the conjuncts (using contrasts that have more content than proper names) is more effective in disambiguating the two ellipsis forms than intonation, see (1.28c):[12]

---

[12] In languages with morphological case marking such as German such ambiguities do not arise if the case marking is unambiguous.

(1.28) a. BOB insulted the guests during DINNER
            L* H   H* L–H%
            and SAM ~~insulted the guests~~ during the DANCE.
                L* H   H* L–L%

        b. BOB insulted the GUESTS during DINNER and ~~Bob insulted~~
            H*   L* H   H* L–H%
            SAM during the DANCE.
            L* H   H* L–L%

        c. The BOY gave the camel some GRASS and the GIRL ~~gave the camel~~
            some HAY.

These examples illustrate that contrast formation is very important in gapping. This obviously interacts with the information structure of gapping. I shall come back to this in the next section.

The intonation pattern typical of the wide scope readings is quite different from the one discussed above, as was first noted by Oehrle (1987) and Siegel (1987). Winkler (2005) investigated this issue experimentally and found that in the wide scope readings, the finite verb carries the strongest accent in the coordination, the conjuncts are not separated by an intonational phrase boundary, and the accents on the contrast pairs are somewhat weaker than in the distributed scope readings, or even are optional (also in the second conjunct). The boundary tone at the end can also be low. Example (1.29) illustrates:

(1.29) Leon CAN'T eat CAVIAR and Anna BEANS.   (Winkler 2005: 200)
        (H*) H* +L   H* +L H⁻ (H*) H* +L H%

I shall come back to this issue in more detail in Chapter 4. The intonation of the narrow scope readings has not been investigated so far and will be described in Chapter 3.

1.3 Theories of gapping

There are three major types of theories that have been suggested for the analysis of gapping. They can be roughly divided into (i) deletion and copying accounts, (ii) accounts that assume gapping to be the coordination of conjuncts smaller than clause-level, that is *v*Ps or TPs, and (iii) three-dimensional or sharing accounts. In this section, I review some representatives of these approaches to give readers unfamiliar with gapping research a good overview of the field. Every subsection will end with an examination of the relative suitability of each type of account to handle the negation facts sketched in the introductory section. So readers already familiar with the literature on gapping are kindly asked to go directly to the end of the respective sections.

1.3.1 *Deletion and copying approaches*

Deletion or copying is probably the most intuitive approach to ellipsis in general. So just as we would expect, deletion and copying accounts are widely available for gapping as well. Deletion accounts assume that syntactic structure is built up and then deleted in an additional syntactic transformation, which results in an empty structure with lexical material missing or, alternatively, in the deletion of phonological material only. Accounts of this sort are, for example, those by Hankamer (1973, 1979), Hartmann (2000), Jackendoff (1971), Neijt (1979), Ross (1970), Sag (1976), Stillings (1975), van Oirsouw (1987, 1993). Yet another way to view deletion is to assume that phonological insertion happens late in the derivation, as is done in the framework of Distributed Morphology (Halle and Marantz 1993), and that ellipsis applies before this step with the consequence that neither syntactic nor phonological structure is deleted but that phonological material is not inserted (Klein 1993; Wilder 1995).

Another dimension along which deletion accounts differ is the kinds of elements that are assumed to be deleted. There are those accounts which delete larger constituents such as *v*Ps or TPs, from which the remnants have been removed beforehand so that a partially empty *v*P or TP is deleted (e.g. Abe and Hoshi 1997, 1999; Coppock 2001; Jayaseelan 1990; J.-S. Kim 1997; Larson 1990; Lin 2002; Reinhart 1991; Sohn 1994; van den Wyngærd 1998). And there are those accounts which assume that smaller elements (e.g. verbs) are deleted directly (most of those in the previous paragraph).

Copying and interpretive accounts are more interested in the interpretation of the elided string in the second conjunct by way of copying material from an identical antecedent in the first conjunct, although they also restrict the occurrence of empty structure itself. Such accounts have been proposed for instance by Chao (1988), Lee (1998), or Wasow (1979). In what follows, I first look at a few representatives of the 'simple' deletion and copying accounts, that is those without movement of the remnants from some larger, to-be-deleted constituent, and after that, I turn to accounts that combine deletion or copying with remnant movement.

1.3.1.1 *'Simple' deletion*   Hartmann (2000) and Wilder (1995, 1996) are recent accounts that assume deletion without movement. Hartmann (2000)

combines information-structural aspects with other grammatical factors. Wilder (1995, 1996) examines very thoroughly the morpho-syntactic and phonological licensing conditions of gapping and other types of ellipsis without recourse to information structure; I start with his proposal.

Wilder (1995, 1996) identifies gapping as an instance of a more general ellipsis type: *forward deletion*, which also includes, for example, left peripheral deletion, see (1.28) above and (1.30a) below, as well as stripping, ((1.7) above, and (1.30b) below).

(1.30) a. John bribed his sister with some chocolate and _ his brother with a new toy car.

  b. John bribed his sister with some chocolate and _ his brother _, too.

Forward deletion is different, on the one hand, from *backward deletion* (= right node raising) and, on the other, from VP ellipsis, NP ellipsis, and sluicing. Wilder suggests that forward deletion is licensed at Logical Form, and observes that at that level, the ellipsis site and antecedent must be content-identical. This accounts for the semantic identity of gap and antecedent we observed to be necessary in gapping (also see e.g. Neijt 1979 and Sag 1976). Identity conditions on morpho-syntactic and phonological content Wilder finds to be of a mixed nature in forward deletion. Sometimes both morpho-syntactic and phonological identity are required and sometimes only one of them has to apply.[13] Wilder proposes that forward deletion 'arise[s] through the base-generation of formless elements that surface as gaps in PF [phonetic form]. Within the minimalist model, [this] can be implemented by adopting the "split lexicon" hypothesis, with form-insertion applying at Spell-Out' (Wilder 1995: 103). In other words, the lexical entry is not necessarily an undividable

---

[13] The German example in (i) below, for instance, is ungrammatical because the reflexive pronoun in the first conjunct takes accusative case (*mich*) but its elided counterpart in the second conjunct takes dative case (*mir*). Example (ii), on the other hand, is fine and the reason for this seems to be that even though the case asymmetry persists phonological identity is given:

(i) * Ich soll   mich   erholen und ~~ich soll~~   ~~mir~~   was   gönnen.
   I   should REFL.ACC relax   and ~~I   should REFL.DAT~~ something give.a.treat
   'I should relax and give myself a treat.'   (Wilder 1995: 98)

(ii) Sie soll   sich   erholen und ~~sie soll~~   ~~sich~~   was   gönnen.
   she should REFL.ACC relax   and ~~she should REFL.DAT~~ something give.a.treat
   'She should relax and give herself a treat.'   (*ibid.*)

Both of these examples are instances of left peripheral deletion. Wilder does not give examples of this sort that clearly are instances of gapping. Indeed, Wesche (1995) suggests that phonological identity plays a role in left peripheral deletion but not in gapping. This makes a unified analysis of the two ellipsis types doubtful.

unit of three types of information—semantic, syntactic, phonological—but the information types are associated with each other and can play separate roles at different points during the derivation. This allows for late phonological insertion and does not require the assumption of a deletion process.[14] Semantic interpretation, on the other hand, is easily ensured. Note that the flexibility I noted with respect to the agreement of the finite verbs in the two conjuncts (example (1.10)), which is an instance of morpho-syntactic non-identity, is accounted for because agreement is irrelevant at Logical Form (LF).

In addition to the condition on content identity at LF, Wilder sets up two syntactic conditions: the *head condition* and a version of the major constituent condition (see above). The head condition says that 'an ellipsis site may not be c-commanded by an overt (non-deleted) head in its domain (= conjunct)' (Wilder 1995: 74). This accounts for the obligatory deletion of the finite verb in C /I /V before the deletion of other material c-commanded by it, as well as the deletion of the complementizer in C when this c-commands the gapped verb (recall (1.26)). Finally, there is also a context identity condition at LF: the antecedent must stand in the same hierarchical relation to its conjunct as the ellipsis site, which is basically a parallelism constraint.

It is not quite clear whether the unitary treatment of all types of forward deletion can be maintained in this way. There are reasons to believe that left peripheral deletion might be different from gapping because it is more sensitive to phonological identity (see note 13), or that yet other forms of forward ellipsis (NP-ellipsis, subject gaps) might also require different conditions from gapping because of differing syntactic restrictions (see e.g. Büring and Hartmann 1998; Hartmann 2000). However, these concerns are not vital in the present discussion. I am only interested in the predictions for gapping and these seem to be largely adequate. Note, however, that the negation facts do not receive an easy explanation in this account. I shall discuss this in conjunction with an evaluation of Hartmann's (2000) theory of gapping.

Hartmann (2000) proposes that gapping is largely determined by conditions operating at the interface between syntax and prosody. The gapping process itself is assumed to be phonological deletion. The first of Hartmann's conditions is the *finite-first condition*, which says that 'the finite (part of the) verb is obligatorily left out in a non-first conjunct' (2000: 156). Building on the

---

[14] An interesting psycholinguistic study in this respect is Schmitt (1997), who conducted an experimental study on the production of gapping and found that semantic information is active at the gap site during production but phonological information is not.

observation that complementizers also have to be gapped in gapping ((1.26) above), and the assumption that the finite verb and the complementizer are associated with the assertion of a sentence, where assertion relates to claiming the truth of a proposition (Höhle 1988; Jacobs 1984; Klein 1998), Hartmann extends this condition to the claim that it is the assertion that is dropped in gapping. I discuss this issue in Chapter 5, where I argue that Hartmann's suggestion cannot be upheld.

The other main condition Hartmann proposes is the *maximal contrast principle*, which says that the number of contrasting remnant-correlate pairs must be maximized. Contrast pairs are related to phonological phrases, that is to say, each remnant (and to a lesser extent each correlate) must be related to a pitch accent heading a phonological phrase. Non-contrasting elements must be elided. Syntactically, Hartmann subscribes to Hankamer's (1979) major constituent condition.

Hartmann (2000) establishes a strong connection between deaccenting and gapping, and shows how the information structure of a coordination interacts with the availability of deletion. Thus, she takes seriously the requirements on the prosodic realization of the gapping remnants on the one hand, and of the gapped verb on the other. Hartmann argues that it is not possible to have an accented verb in the first conjunct and elide its counterpart in the second conjunct. In out-of-the-blue unergative constructions in German, for instance, the verb typically attracts the main pitch accent, see (1.31a) (Uhmann 1991). In unaccusative sentences, on the other hand, the subject carries the main accent, see (1.31b) ('\' marks a falling accent):

(1.31)   What's happening?   (slightly changed from Hartmann 2000: 171 f.)

   a.   Hans \TANZT.
        Hans   dances
        'Hans is dancing.'

   b.   \HANS kommt.
        Hans   comes
        'Hans is coming.'

Hartmann shows that gapping is not possible with unergative verbs (the result really is a stripping structure, which Hartmann takes to be a subcase of gapping, Hartmann, p.c.):

(1.32)   *Hans \TANZT und Klaus.
         Hans dances and Klaus
         'Hans is dancing and Klaus (is dancing).'

Note that if the context provides for narrow focus gapping becomes possible. This supports Hartmann's generalization ('/' marks a rising accent):

(1.33)   Who's dancing?
/Hans tanzt und \Klaus.

Merits, problems, and the negation facts. Hartmann (2000) and Wilder (1995, 1996) provide very valuable insights for the analysis of gapping. We shall see throughout this study that prosody, contrast formation, and more generally, information structuring, which are central in Hartmann's account, are vital in the analysis of gapping sentences with negation, too. Also, Wilder's head condition makes exactly the right predictions for gapping, and his observations concerning morpho-syntactic identity must feature in any analysis of the ellipsis type.

With respect to the negation facts, both accounts are able to handle the distributed scope readings because they represent the default case in accounts that consider gapping as deletion under identity. The cross-linguistic differences between, for example, English and German, however, are unexpected. As for the wide scope readings, note that even though Hartmann does not consider them her account predicts that the negative marker in these cases is not gapped because it is accented. This is precisely what previous accounts of wide scope readings have assumed and this is what I assume in this study as well: the negation in these cases is not gapped but scopes over the entire coordination. On the other hand, Hartmann's account predicts that the negation, if accented, should contrast with the polarity of the other conjunct. This is obviously not the case in the wide scope readings (but we shall see that some of the narrow scope readings behave in just this way). Both in Hartmann's proposal and in Wilder's it is quite unclear how the narrow scope readings come about as these cannot be captured via deletion under identity. I argue in Chapter 3 that the polarity in the narrow scope readings is different in the two conjuncts and that the positive polarity in the second conjunct is silent. This is quite unexpected in both of these theories. Finally, differences between main verb gapping and auxiliary gapping are completely unexpected in both accounts.

What is somewhat unclear in deletion accounts in general is how the identity between the two conjuncts is actually ascertained. Is there a moment in the derivation when the two conjuncts are compared with each other? How could this be done? Syntactic matching operations (like feature matching) are quite different from the kind of matching that would be required in a gapping coordination. Merchant (2001) proposes a PF deletion theory of ellipsis, more specifically, sluicing, where this problems is overcome. The identity requirement he poses is a semantic one (a condition on mutual entailment of the two conjuncts, which takes their focus structure into account, viz. e-givenness, see Merchant 2001: 31). Thus, while he argues for a fully present syntactic structure in the second conjunct, this structure does not have to be compared for identity to that of the first conjunct. I shall argue in Chapter 2 that even this kind of approach cannot capture the negation data in gapping, see Section 2.3 for detailed discussion.

1.3.1.2 *Copying* The copying accounts I would like to review here, Lee (1998) and Chao (1988), are very different from more traditional accounts of ellipsis and illustrate the variedness of the gapping theories that have been put forward. Lee (1998) is an HPSG-account of gapping and other types of ellipsis that like Hartmann's (2000) deletion approach also takes into account information-structural aspects. I just summarize the basic ideas here without going into the details of the formalism. The central operation in Lee's proposal for any ellipsis type[15] is *default inheritance*. Default inheritance basically means that the first conjunct serves as a kind of prototype for the second conjunct. The second conjunct inherits all those syntactic and semantic (*synsem*) values from the former that have no counterpart in that second conjunct (in HPSG terminology, all those attribute-value-pairs which are left undefined in the second conjunct). Via the algorithm of Carpenter's (1993) *sceptical default unification* (see Lee 1998: 69 ff. for details), the gap in the elliptical conjunct is filled with a corresponding antecedent, so that the gap becomes a kind of anaphor.

Since a default inheritance of synsem values is not restrictive enough for the specific constraints that the individual ellipsis types have, Lee proposes type-specific restrictions. For gapping, this includes a version of the major constituent condition and a restriction on parallelism, which—roughly—requires the conjuncts to be parallel in terms of the subcategorization requirements of the verb, theta-role assignment to the remnants, and information structure. Information-structural parallelism of two phrases obtains if the context assigns to the two phrases in question foci that contain contrastive accents. For the gapping of other material along with the verb, such as NPs,[16] Lee operates with the notion of 'active discourse referents' from centering theory (Grosz *et al.* 1995). It is the most active discourse referent which must be the source for the inheritance mechanism for an NP that is elided together with the verb. Lee assumes that phonological

---

[15] Lee does not examine Right Node Raising.

[16] Lee treats the elision of the verb plus NP as a combination of two different ellipsis processes: 'V-ellipsis' and 'NP ellipsis'.

values are not inherited in gapping, thus accommodating the agreement facts.

Like Lee (1998), Chao (1988) is interested in the reconstruction of the meaning structure of the second conjunct. She rejects deletion as a mechanism to derive ellipsis for various reasons I shall not go into here. As an alternative to deletion, Chao proposes to extend the X-bar schema by 'defective structures' in which the heads are not instantiated and where the head projections are optional:

(1.34) $X'' \rightarrow$ (Spec) $(X' \sim) Y^*$
          $X' \sim \rightarrow Y^*$

This allows for projections with chains of complements, adjuncts and/or a specifier whereas the head can remain empty. Here is an example of a second conjunct consisting of a subject and an object, thus missing the verb:

(1.35)   Bill saw Susan and John Mary.

In order to avoid over-generation, a licensing condition determines that the top node must be clausal and all other nodes must be a normal or a semantic projection (i.e. no functional projection). In a second step then, the elliptic clause must be 'e-constructed' at LF, which is done by copying parallel material from previous discourse, that is from the first conjunct. This account is tainted with a number of problems, as Klein (1993) points out. The most obvious is the question of case assignment in the second conjunct, which is not provided for if the head is absent. For further criticism and discussion, see Klein (1993) and also Merchant (2001).

Merits, problems, and the negation facts. Copying accounts face similar difficulties to those pointed out for the deletion accounts above. It is quite unclear how the different readings come about, how the negation could be 'prevented' from copying into the second conjunct or how it could be made to take wide scope. Nevertheless, as I shall argue in Section 2.3, a copying account can best look after the explanatory desiderata arising with the negation data. The details of the copying mechanism are (of course) what matters.

1.3.1.3 *Deletion and copying with movement*   There are several kinds of objectives behind the idea of combining deletion/copying with remnant movement. One is to move material out of a phrasal constituent which subsequently can be copied, or deleted under identity with a corresponding phrasal constituent in the other conjunct. This way, the problem of non-constituency encountered in gapping can be avoided: gapping seems to afflict an element which is not a phrasal constituent: V /I /C. If, however, a larger constituent, say a vP or a TP, is elided this problem is shunned. In addition, a certain parallelism with the derivation of other ellipsis types such as VP-ellipsis or sluicing (= IP-ellipsis) can be achieved. Another motivation for assuming remnant movement is the possibility of modelling the information-structural aspects of gapping. The idea is that the remnant phrases are foci, or topics and foci, and therefore move to an information-structurally designated position outside the vP. This makes possible the deletion of a constituent—the vP—which after the remnants have left only contains given material. There are other empirical facts which speak for a remnant movement analysis, which I shall mention as we go along.

One of the first to suggest a deletion account with movement of the remnants was Jayaseelan (1990). Jayaseelan assumes that English gapping involves rightward, heavy NP shift type movement of VP-internal material, and subsequent deletion of the then empty lowest IP (the subject moves to the left). For an illustration, consider (1.36). In (1.36), the subject moves to the left to adjoin to IP (= S) and the object moves to the right and also adjoins to IP. The lowest IP is now empty except for the verb, and can be deleted:

(1.36)   John shot the wolf and Mary the rabbit.
[IP John$_1$ [IP [IP t$_1$ shot t$_2$] the wolf$_2$]] and [IP Mary [IP [IP e] the rabbit]].

The rationale behind the application of heavy NP shift type movement to gapping is the focusing of the remnants, which Jayaseelan takes to be an indication for gapping remnants to be 'heavy in some sense' (1990: 65). Therefore, they are bound to behave like heavy NPs and can be extraposed. Jayaseelan also finds a number of parallels between heavy NP shift and gapping (such as a prohibition on preposition stranding).[17] Note, however, that not everything

---

[17] It is one of the major goals of Abe and Hoshi (1995, 1997) to explain some preposition stranding differences between English and Japanese simple clauses versus gapping sentences, respectively. For criticism of Abe and Hoshi (1995, 1997), see J.-S. Kim (1997).

that can be a remnant in gapping can also be shifted as a heavy NP. Pronouns are a case in point. They cannot undergo heavy NP shift (see (1.37a) versus (1.37b)) but they can be gapped:

(1.37) a. I introduced to my friend a colleague I had been working with for years.

  b. *I introduced to my mother him / HIM.

  c. JOHN talked to HER and BILL to HIM.

This undermines the idea that heavy NP shift is the type of movement that is involved in gapping.

Jayaseelan's (1990) idea that gapping can be related to the movement of 'heavy', or focused phrases is also pursued by Abe and Hoshi (1997, 1999), J.-S. Kim (1997), and van den Wyngærd (1998),[18] with Abe and Hoshi (1997, 1999) and J.-S. Kim (1997) paying special attention to typological variation. Abe and Hoshi (1997, 1999) argue that whereas English gapping involves leftward and rightward movement, Japanese gapping (and gapping in head-final languages in general) only involves leftward movement. They combine Jayaseelan's account with Saito's (1985) condition on adjunction sites, which requires that an element adjoin to that side of a category which is opposite the head, where the head of XP is X′ and the head of X′ is X. In (1.38), which shows the patterns for English, YP is the adjoining phrase:

(1.38) a.   b.

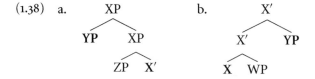

The idea for English gapping is that it only allows the structure in (1.38b), that is right adjunction of the object DP. The (a)-case is ruled out on the strength of a crossing constraint which says that one contrasted element (YP) should not cross another contrasted element (ZP) (Pesetsky 1982). For specifier-initial, head-final languages like Japanese, where both X′ and X occur on the right, Saito's condition on adjunction sites predicts general left adjunction. Abe and Hoshi (1997) argue with a number of tests that Japanese gapping indeed involves (only) leftward movement. Thus, the Japanese version of the English (1.36) above looks as follows:

---

[18] Van den Wyngærd (1998) actually is a small conjunct coordination account. Such accounts will be discussed in the next section.

(1.39)   John-wa   ookami-wo, sosite Mary-wa   usagi-wo   utta.
            John-TOP wolf-ACC,   and   Mary-NOM rabbit-ACC shot.
            'John shot the wolf and Mary the rabbit.'
            [[$_{I'}$ John-wa [$_{I'}$ ookami-wo [$_{I'}$ e]]], sosite [$_{I'}$ Mary-wa [usagi-wo$_1$ [$_{I'}$ t$_1$
            utta]]]]   *(Japanese)*

In (1.39), the object is moved to the left and adjoined to I'. I' can then be copied/deleted (Abe and Hoshi assume copying).

J.-S. Kim (1997) agrees with the direction of the remnant movements in English versus Japanese as suggested by Abe and Hoshi but assumes that the type of movement involved is focus movement. The remnants move to a Focus Phrase (FocP), which is situated above TP. After this, TP is deleted. Kim suggests that Korean, which like Japanese is a verb-final language with backwards gapping, involves leftward focus movement. English gapping, on the other hand is assumed to involve leftward movement only of the subject, which is independent of gapping and arises from the fulfilment of the EPP. The other focused phrase[19] moves rightward to Spec,FocP, which Kim assumes to be to the right of Foc'.

Merits, problems, and the negation facts. The accounts we just saw implement the gist of the major constituent condition as a function of movement.[20] Focus movement as such is a controversial issue. Association (of focus particles and the like) with focus, for instance, has been argued since Anderson (1972) and Jackendoff (1972) not to respect island constraints (but see Drubig 1994 and Krifka 2006 for the possibility of an alternative view). From Section 1.2 we know that islands are not a clear-cut thing in gapping and that the whole issue of where the remnants can occur in gapping is highly complex. I cannot discuss this issue here. In my own proposal I will assume that there is topic and focus movement although nothing hinges on that idea.

The negation data do not receive an explanation in the focus movement accounts any more than they do in the 'simple' deletion and copying accounts. Since the negative marker is elided we must assume either that it is deleted with the emptied vP or TP, or that it is copied from the vP/TP of the previous

---

[19] Kim assumes that English gapping in general only involves two remnants, a claim that was around especially in the early days of gapping theory. However, as Kuno (1976) has shown, even English gapping allows more than three remnants in the right discourse context.

[20] The movement accounts can easily handle the case of particle remnants, recall example (1.16a) above. (i) shows that particles can move to the German forefield position:

(i)   Weg   ging er von   Bremen.
     Away(=PART) went he from Bremen
     'Away he went from Bremen.'

conjunct. This requires identity between the two conjuncts, which poses the same problems as in the non-movement accounts.

1.3.2 *Gapping as small conjunct coordination: taking the negation into account*

The first small conjunct accounts were especially 'made' for some of the negation data, that is the wide scope versus the distributed scope readings of the negation. They were a late arrival in the analysis of gapping mainly because of the typical clause-medial position of the gap (at least in English), which precludes an easy identification of smaller conjuncts than TPs/CPs that could be conjoined. Also, the occurrence as gapping remnants of elements that normally are assumed to occur in the C-domain (e.g. *wh*-phrases, topicalized phrases) makes a small conjunct analysis problematic. There are various versions of the small conjunct analysis. Siegel (1984, 1987) provided the original observations about, and a first analysis of the wide scope reading of the negation in gapping in terms of categorial grammar.[21] A quite influential account, which combines a small conjunct analysis with across-the board movement is proposed in several papers by Johnson (1994, 1996/2003, 2000, 2006). Small conjuncts have also been combined with deletion (Coppock 2001). Most recently, sideward movement has entered the arena (Agbayani and Zoerner 2004; Winkler 2005). I shall not look at all these proposals here. I will spend some time on Johnson (1996/2003) as it covers the greatest subset of the data investigated in this book (Section 1.3.2.1). I shall also look at Winkler (2005), which is meant to cover differences between English and German, which are also part of the issues discussed here (Section 1.3.2.2). To get started, though, let me pay credit to the first to have discussed the wide scope readings.

Siegel (1984, 1987) observed that negation in English can take wide scope over the whole coordination in gapping, also see Oehrle (1987).[22] The following case of auxiliary gapping, which only allows the wide scope reading—both of the negation and the modal verb—is from Siegel (1984):

(1.40)   John can't eat caviar and Mary eat beans.[23]   (Siegel 1984: 524)

In Siegel (1987), it is suggested that gapping is a coordination of tenseless clauses and that tensed elements like modals or auxiliaries (with or without

---

[21] Also see Steedman (1990) for an account of gapping in categorial grammar.

[22] Oehrle (1987) investigates the Boolean properties of negative gapping sentences, which I have to ignore here.

[23] Most of my informants reject this kind of sentence with the repeated main verb in the second conjunct.

negation) are added to the coordination as a whole. Adopting a slightly revised version of Bach's (1983) categorial grammar, Siegel (1987) analyses a sentence like (1.40), as follows (details omitted):

(1.41)   John can't eat caviar and Mary eat beans

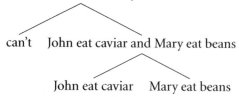

The proper position of the auxiliary in the clause is realized by an insertion rule. Note that no ellipsis is involved in this derivation. This is different in the following example, which—depending on the intonation (see Section 1.1)—is ambiguous between a distributed and a wide scope reading:

(1.42)   John can't eat caviar and Mary beans.

Siegel suggests that the ambiguity arises because there are two analyses available. One analysis of (1.42) is a coordination of the sort shown in (1.41) where, in addition, the tenseless main verb is elided. This is the wide scope reading. The other analysis is a coordination of tensed clauses with the elision both of the tensed auxiliary and of the tenseless main verb, which results in the distributed scope reading.

1.3.2.1 *Across-the-board predicate shift and reconstruction*   The idea that gapping can be the coordination of conjuncts smaller than TP or CP is also advocated by Johnson (1994, 1996/2003, 2000, 2006).[24] Johnson combines small conjunct coordination with across-the-board (ATB-) movement and scrambling. He rejects 'ellipsis' (which he takes to be deletion) altogether as a possible operation in the derivation of gapping. The reason for this is that he finds crucial differences between constructions which he takes to be clear instances of ellipsis (VP ellipsis and pseudogapping) on the one hand, and gapping on the other.[25] For other applications of ATB-movement to gapping, see Zoerner and Agbayani (2000), López and Winkler (2003), and Paul (1999).

Johnson assumes that negative gapping sentences are coordinations of *v*Ps (non-negative gapping) or TPs (negative gapping). I shall only discuss the

---

[24] Johnson developed his ideas in a number of (partly unpublished) papers, which differ (sometimes considerably) in their details. I use the (1996/2003) paper because it covers most of the data that are central in the present study.

[25] Note, however, that it is not at all clear what the ellipsis process in VP ellipsis should look like. Some researchers reject a deletion account and treat VP ellipsis more like a proform or anaphor rather than the outcome of a syntactic deletion process (e.g. Hardt 1993; Kempson *et al.* 1999; Lobeck 1995; López 1995).

latter case here. In Johnson's analysis, the TP is situated below AgrP and PredP (for predicate phrase; see Zwart 1993), so that the inflectional domain is structured AgrP-PredP-TP. The derivation of gapping proceeds as illustrated in (1.43).[26] The remnants (*his guest, kumquats*) and their correlates (*Ward, natto*) scramble out of their respective TPs to a higher position, which Johnson uncommittedly calls XP. Having been emptied of the contrastive material, the TPs in the two conjuncts are identical and can be predicate-shifted[27] across-the-board to PredP, which is outside the coordination. Furthermore, the subject of the first conjunct (*Ward*), in fulfilment of the Extended Projection Principle (EPP), and in violation of the coordinate structure constraint,[28] moves up to Spec,AgrP.[29] Finally, the auxiliary-negation-complex moves to Agr.

(1.43)   Ward won't prepare natto and his guest kumquats

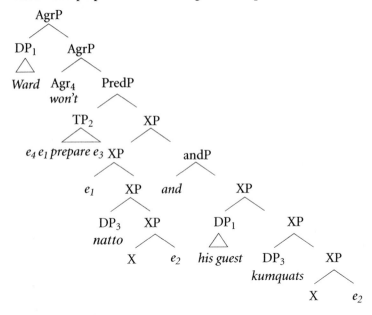

---

[26] Note that 'e' are unpronounced copies.

[27] Predicate shift was first proposed in the analysis of verbal complexes in Dutch, German, and Hungarian, e.g. Hinterhölzl (1999), Koopman and Szabolcsi (2000), Zwart (1993, 1997).

[28] Johnson argues that the CSC only applies to A′—but not A-movement. Also see Lin (2001).

[29] There is a problem with the nominative case assignment to the subject of the second conjunct, which Johnson (1996/2003) discusses in detail. Also, as already noted by Siegel (1987), the subject of the second conjunct in a gapping sentence can be accusative:

(i)   We can't eat caviar and him eat beans. (Siegel 1987: 61)

Also see Zoerner (1995) for case assignment in coordinations of this sort.

With a two-copy chain it is possible to interpret the higher or the lower copy. Looking at the ATB-predicate-shifted TPs, we find that the higher copy of the chain is situated outside the coordination whereas the lower copies are situated inside the two conjuncts. This opens up the possibility of interpreting the negation in these two different positions. Interpreting the higher copy yields wide scope, interpreting the lower copies yields distributed scope. Extending proposals by Takano (1995) and Heycock (1995), Johnson assumes that it is only in the case of ATB-moved predicates (TPs and *v*Ps) or positive indefinites that the lower copies are interpreted. This generalization captures the fact that combined finite verb + main verb gaps reconstruct: they are a predicate. Auxiliary/modal gapping with negation, on the other hand, does not receive a distributed scope reading: in a sentence like (1.44), only the auxiliary-negation complex, which is not a predicate, moves ATB:

(1.44)   Ward won't prepare natto and his guest eat kumquats

(Johnson 1996/2003: 69)

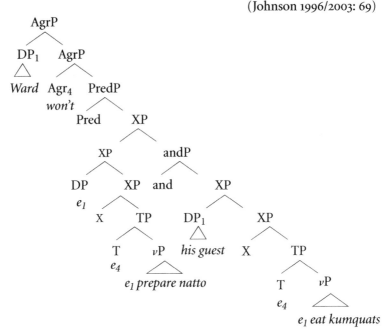

The TPs or *v*Ps are not and cannot be shifted ATB: if *v*P were ATB-moved the auxiliary would not be part of it. If TP were ATB-moved the main verb would be part of it because it cannot scramble out of *v*P individually. The result

would be a combined finite verb + main verb gap rather than an auxiliary gap.[30]

Merits, problems, and the negation facts. As I said before, Johnson's account has been quite influential. One of the reasons for its success apart from the wide scope facts was that in its earlier stages it involved ATB-movement of the verbs alone, which predicted that gapping would be absent in languages that do not have verb movement such as Chinese. Gapping is indeed a lot more restricted in Chinese than it is in English or German. Nevertheless, it does not seem to be completely absent in that language. Gapping in Chinese can occur in coordinations without a conjunction (which expresses the meaning of *and*, Paul 1999) or with the conjunction *wo* ('while', N. Zhang 1997). Disjunction (with the conjunction *haishi*) is ruled out (Paul 1999), although stripping in an *either–or* construction seems good (M.-D. Li 1988). Also, contrasts must involve numeral classifiers (*three* versus *four*), contrastive demonstratives (*this* versus *that*), or temporal complements (for more details cf. for instance Chao 1988; M.-D. Li 1988; Y.-H. A. Li 1998; Paul 1999; Tang 2001; N. Zhang 1997).[31] Many of these restrictions concern the proper formation of contrast. I argue in Chapter 3 that gapping is very sensitive to the particular kind of contrast involved, and that this interacts with the semantics of various conjunctions. Thus, it may well be that the limitation of Chinese gapping has both syntactic and semantic-pragmatic reasons.

Another prediction of Johnson's (1996/2003) account is that gapping is less restricted in languages with scrambling than in languages without. Johnson suggests that this seems to be borne out for German when compared with English. Furthermore, López and Winkler (2003) note that ATB-movement of the verbal complex to the inflectional domain accounts for the fact that in Japanese or Korean gapping is backwards because in these languages the head is located to the right of its complements so that the

---

[30] Since predicate shift is central to Johnson's account of gapping, he suggests that in auxiliary gapping, predicate shift only applies to the TP of the first conjunct. The underlying assumption is that predicate shift is obligatory in the sense that some feature of Pred needs to be satisfied and this can be done by moving a predicate ATB or by a simple move from the nearest, i.e. the first conjunct. It is unclear though, what happens to the matching predicate feature on the predicate in the second conjunct.

[31]
   (i)   * Zhangsan xihuan pingguo, Lisi juzi.   (Tang 2001: 201)
         Zhangsan like   apple,   Lisi orange
         'Zhangsan likes apples and Lisi oranges.'

   (ii)   Zhangsan chi-le   san-ge   pingguo, Lisi si-ge   juzi.   (Li 1998: 41)
         Zhangsan eat-Perf three-Cl apple   Lisi four-Cl orange
         'Zhangsan ate three apples and Lisi four oranges.'

movement would have to be to the right. This certainly is an interesting outcome. Finally, the assumption of ATB-movement predicts that gapping should only be possible in coordinations and not in subordinations. This is what we find. In Chapter 5, I propose an alternative account of this restriction.

On the problem side, Johnson's account cannot deal with all the negation facts, most notably, it cannot deal with the narrow scope facts. ATB-movement requires the two TPs to be alike. The negation can either be interpreted above the coordination (= wide scope) or inside both conjuncts (= distributed scope) but it cannot scope over the first conjunct only. Also, the finding that auxiliary gapping, depending on the contrast relation between the conjuncts and the discourse context, can sometimes receive a narrow scope reading (see Chapter 3), is unexpected under this account. Finally, the fact that the wide scope readings have quite different syntactic, intonational, and pragmatic restrictions from the other readings (see Chapter 4) cannot be accounted for.

1.3.2.2 *Sideward movement and derivation in phases* In Winkler's (2005) small conjunct account, the gapping coordination is derived through sideward movement (Nunes 1995, 2001, 2004; Nunes and Uriagereka 2000). Sideward movement is a Minimalist copy-and-merge process which copies constituents and merges them with unconnected, independently merged syntactic objects. It is a repair mechanism that is applied if a derivation is in danger of crashing, and has been applied for instance in the analysis of parasitic gaps and standard ATB-movement (Nunes 1995, 2004). Winkler (2005) assumes that sideward movement is part of the derivation of gapping sentences. She proposes that in gapping, the vP of the right conjunct, which the contrastive remnants have left through movement to an A-bar position (López and Winkler 2003), is copied, moves sideward, and merges with the correlates of the (as yet unconnected) first conjunct. An example is given in (1.45). In (1.45), the relevant vP is vP$_3$, which has been emptied of the remnants *Leon* and *Hanna*, then is copied and merges with the correlates *Manny* and *Anna* in the first conjunct. Subsequently, the subject of the first conjunct moves to Spec,TP, to fulfil the EPP (step 2.1 in (1.45)); the vP in the first conjunct is preposed (scrambled) for word order reasons (Kayne 1994; step 2.2). Then the vPs of the first and second conjunct are merged (step 2.3). Finally, the lower copies of the vP-chain are deleted as an instance of chain reduction (marked by strikethrough, see Section 2.3 for more on this).

(1.45)   Manny loves Anna and Leo Hanna.

Step 1: Sideward movement

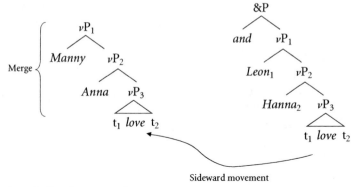

Sideward movement

Step 2: Further operations

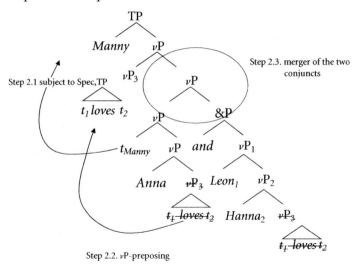

Step 2.2. vP-preposing

Winkler combines the syntactic derivation shown in (1.45) with proposals for the semantic, information-structural, and prosodic aspects of gapping, especially in view of the wide versus distributed scope negation facts. She explains the difference in prosody between the two readings as a function of the size of the phases that are made available by LF to be sent to PF. She proposes that in the wide scope cases, the highest *v*P, that is the one that contains both conjuncts, constitutes a phase and therefore is sent to the interface of syntax and prosodic structure. In the distributed case, the lower *v*Ps are individual phases and are sent off individually. This then results in the respective intonation patterns. Thus, derivation in phases gives us the mapping with PF.

What is unclear, however, is how the distributed scope facts are derived from the syntactic derivation given in (1.45). As the negation usually (and also by Winkler) is assumed to be situated above *v*P, it remains a mystery how the distributed reading is derived at LF.

For German gapping, Winkler (2005) proposes that it involves the coordination of ΣPs. A ΣP is a functional phrase that hosts the negation/affirmative features of a clause (Laka 1990). Winkler bases her suggestion on the observation that in German, the elision of the negative marker is felt to be marginal and that speakers prefer to repeat the negative marker in the elliptic conjunct (also see Section 1.1):

(1.46) Ich glaube, dass Leon nicht Klavier spielen kann und Peter
        I   think   that Leon not   piano   play   can   and Peter
        *(nicht) Gitarre.
          not   guitar
        'I think that Leon can't play the piano and Peter (can't play) the guitar.'
                                              (Winkler 2005: 215)

Winkler (2005) further observes that a wide scope reading of the negation is particularly difficult to obtain in German and needs some 'anchor for the cumulative reading' (ibid.). Such an anchor can, for instance, be an adverb that identifies the conjuncts as parts of one complex event, such as *gleichzeitig* ('at the same time'):

(1.47) CONTEXT: I don't believe this:
        Leon kann nicht Kaviar essen und Anna *(gleichzeitig)
        Leon can   not   caviar eat   and Anna   at.the.same.time
        Bohnen.
        beans
        'Leon can't eat caviar and at the same time, Anna beans.'

While this is true, one would still want to account for the fact that this sentence does actually receive a wide scope interpretation: if wide scope is to be derived from the syntactic structure, why would that be different in a gapping construction that contains an additional adverb? Winkler does not answer this question. In Chapter 4, I shall argue that the context has a decisive role to play in the interpretation of the wide scope readings, which also has repercussions for their syntactic structure.

Merits, problems, and the negation facts. Winkler's account of gapping in terms of sideward movement combined with restrictions at the interfaces avoids some of the difficulties of Johnson's (1996/2003) ATB-movement proposal (e.g. violation of the CSC). On the other hand, it loses some of its advantages (restriction of gapping to coordination). Importantly, however, it remains unsatisfactory in several respects concerning the negation data. Two of these just have been mentioned: for English, the structure designed to capture the wide scope facts is extended to the distributed scope environments without sufficient amendments; for German, the wide scope reading is not accounted for. In addition to this, the contrast between English and German in the acceptance of gapping with negation does not fall out of the account if all the negation data in German are taken into account: in the next chapter we shall see that there are cases where German seems quite happy with gapping involving negation, which makes the ΣP-coordination analysis unlikely. Also, why should German gapping actually be the coordination of ΣPs whereas English gapping is the coordination of *v*Ps or TPs? Finally, while Winkler's account is equipped to deal with the narrow scope readings in German—the two conjoined ΣPs can have different values (negative in the first conjunct, positive in the second conjunct)—for English, which also has narrow scope readings, this option is not available, and the analysis of these readings is quite unclear.

In general, I would like to argue that the small conjunct accounts, despite their merits, face some important difficulties. As I already mentioned in the introduction to this section, the very assumption of small conjuncts is problematic in the light of gapping sentences which involve (or seem to involve) the coordination of CPs:

(1.48) a. When did John arrive and when Mary?

b. Why did John go by train and why Mary by car?

(1.49) Mittags gab es für die Kinder ein Konzert und abends für
at.noon give it for the children a concert and at.night for
die Erwachsenen.
the grown.ups
'At noon there was a concert for the children and at night for the grown-ups.'

Examples (1.48) and (1.49) show that elements which are usually assumed to occur in Spec, CP, such as *wh*-words or topicalized phrases, can be contrasted in a gapping construction. This problem is approached by López and Winkler (2003) as well as Winkler (2005), who suggest that there is an intermediary position for focused/topicalized phrases in Spec,*v*P, which in gapping is the final landing site of the *wh*-word or focused phrase.[32] This seems to be a good solution to the puzzle of apparent CP-coordination. Still, as it has been argued that some *wh*-phrases, such as *why*, are not moved to CP, but are base-generated in that position (e.g. Hegarty 1991; Law 1993; Murasugui 1992; Reinhart 1998; Rizzi 1990), the problem cannot be considered as completely settled: as (1.48b) above illustrates, *why* makes an acceptable remnant in gapping. In the chapters to come I argue that the distributed scope and the narrow scope readings are best considered coordinations of large conjuncts (CPs). The wide scope reading is a coordination of smaller conjuncts but not of the sort envisaged by Johnson (1996/2003) or Winkler (2005).

1.3.3 *Sharing approaches*

A third type of theory that has been proposed for gapping is sharing theories, which come in different shapes. There are three-dimensional structure, multiple dominance, and factorization theories and they have been proposed, for example, by Goodall (1987), Grootveld (1994), Moltmann (1992*a*, 1992*b*), Muadz (1991), Wesche (1995), and Williams (1977, 1978). In a shared structure, the first and second conjuncts are mapped onto one and the same tree. Certain elements in that tree are shared by both conjuncts: those that occur in only one conjunct. Others are not shared: the contrast pairs. The contrasting elements occur in the tree as literally branching off the two-dimensional structure (see (1.50), the coordinator is adjoined to the second conjunct), or in an ordered list, see (1.51). I am giving a simplified syntax here for better readability.

(1.50)   John met Sue and Mary Bill.   (after Moltmann 1992*a*)

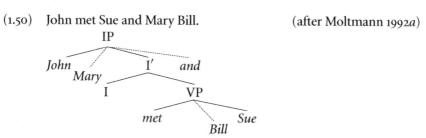

---

[32] Evidence for such an intermediary position comes from sentences like the following (Chomsky 1995, 2000; Fox 1999, 2000):

(i)   [Which of the papers that he$_i$ wrote for Mrs Brown] did every student$_i$ get her$_j$ to grade t?

The *wh*-phrase must reconstruct so that the pronoun *he* can get bound, i.e. is c-commanded by its binder, *every student*. However, reconstruction to the base position *t* violates the binding principle because the pronoun *her* then c-commands *Mrs Brown*. Thus, it is argued that the *wh*-phrase must reconstruct to a position lower than the subject and higher than the object, such as the edge of *v*P.

(1.51)   John met Sue and Mary Bill.   (after Wesche 1995)

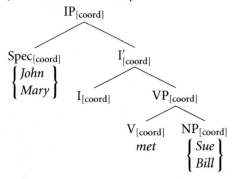

The name *multiple dominance theory* comes from the possibility of having a node dominated by several mother nodes. This can best be seen in a representation of the ellipsis type of right node raising (also see Wilder 1999). In (1.52), the NP node of the shared element is dominated by the VPs of both conjuncts (again this is a simplified version):

(1.52)   John met and Sue saw this man.   (Moltmann 1992*b*: 267)

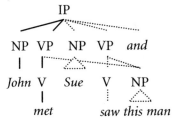

Shared structures in general, it has been proposed are generated through the union of simple phrase markers (Goodall 1987), through rules that directly produce such structures (Muadz 1991; Wesche 1995), or certain admissibility conditions (Moltmann 1992*a*). Within the Minimalist Program, sharing has also been advocated to account for phenomena other than gapping, for example ATB-movement of *wh*-phrases or the derivation of adjuncts. For instance, the operations pair merge (Chomsky 2001) and parallel merge (Citko 2005) produce shared structures. The details are not important here.

The most obvious challenges for sharing approaches next to the syntactic restrictions are linearization, semantic interpretation, and asymmetries between the conjuncts. I cannot possibly go into the details of these here but let us look at a few examples to get a rough idea of how such puzzles are solved. For linearization, special linearization rules are usually formulated. Moltmann (1992*a*), for instance, proposes for gapping (simplified) that all but one of the elements dominated by a splitting node (= a node that branches into three dimensions) follow everything else in the sentence. The relative ordering between elements that branch off at different splitting nodes must be preserved. The rules ensure that from a structure such as (1.53), it is not (1.53b) that is linearized but (1.53a).

(1.53)

```
                       John              Mary
                        /                 /
        IP-and    NP          met    NP
                        \                 \
                       Bill              Sue
```

    a.   John met Mary and Bill Sue.

    b.   * John met Mary and Sue Bill.

Wesche (1995: 130) formulates the following rule for gapping: 'first linearize the elements of the first line including all of the involved Factors [= shared elements] ..., then the remaining elements line by line, connecting the lines by the given conjunction.' The problem with these rules is that they do not follow from anything. At best, they are descriptive rules of what is happening.

As for the semantic interpretation of gapping in a shared tree, it is mostly assumed that both conjuncts are large conjuncts (clauses) and that each one of them is interpreted individually. The shared element is assumed to be present in each one of them. Moltmann specifically assumes the construal of so-called m-planes, which are 'the syntactic basis for semantic interpretation' (1992a: 39), that is their function is similar to LF. They are different from LF, however, in that they can come in different sizes, for example as CPs or NPs. Their size depends on the scope of the coordinator, which is fixed by syntactic conditions. For gapping, Moltmann assumes that each conjunct is a full clause (IP) and that it is interpreted as such.

Merits, problems, and the negation facts. An advantage of the sharing approaches according to Moltmann (1992b) is that conjuncts (or parts of them) on the one hand seem to act as a unit and, on the other hand, are independent of each other. Also, the theories capture the much-observed parallelism between conjuncts in a straightforward way. Finally, they can very naturally account for the coordinate structure constraint and ATB-movement.

The flexible conjunct size proposed by Moltmann (1992a) obviously gives us a handle on the wide scope negation data because we can assume that—similarly to the small conjunct analyses discussed in the previous section—the coordinator in these cases takes smaller scope, so that the negation can scope over whatever else there is in the two conjuncts. I will not try to formulate this here but it is clear that this should generally be possible. The narrow scope readings, in contrast, do not seem to be easily accommodated in the sharing approaches. If both conjuncts are anchored in the same tree, it is difficult to model asymmetries between the conjuncts which arise in the shared parts, that is the parts that occur in only one conjunct. Note that this also holds for the non-identity of non-semantic features in gap and antecedent. Wesche (1995) deals with the non-identity of agreement features between first and second conjunct by assuming the generation of a shared finite verb, which, however, can have multiple feature lists. Another problem of the sharing approaches is that they do not offer an explanation for the differences between German and English gapping with negation. It is quite unclear why one language should be more permissive in this respect than the other. Likewise, the different readings associated with main verb versus auxiliary gapping remain a puzzle.

1.4 Summary and sketch of the proposal

The previous section provided an overview of the theories that have been suggested for the analysis of gapping. Although some of the theories were shown to be very successful in the explanation of many of the characteristics that have been identified for gapping—the various requirements on the identity of gap and antecedent, the information–structural set-up or the restrictions on the syntactic structure—the negation data do not receive a completely satisfactory account in any of them. The proposal I make tries to fill this gap. It is a copying account combined with a semantic–pragmatic principle (the principle of balanced contrast, see Chapter 3), which requires the two conjuncts in gapping to be balanced. Furthermore, it makes differentiated structural assumptions for the distributed and narrow versus the wide scope readings.

There are two sets of data that make me favour a copying account over any of the other accounts discussed above. The first are the differences between languages with a negative marker that is a head and languages where the negative marker is an adjunct. As I will discuss at length in Chapter 2, in languages with adjunct negation it is more difficult to interpret the second conjunct with a distributed scope reading. The second set of data is the behaviour of gapping in the context of certain negative polarity items in a language like German, which is a language with adjunct negation. Example (1.54), where the verbal complex that is gapped in the second conjunct, *ausstehen können* ('can stand'), is a negative polarity item (NPI), is impeccable with a distributed reading:

(1.54)   Paul kann den russischen Film nicht ausstehen und Maria den
         Paul can   the   Russian   film   not   stand   and   Maria the
         französischen.
         French
         'Paul can't stand the Russian film and Maria French one.'

These two sets of data show that the behaviour of the negation in gapping
is very particular in even more respects than 'just' scope. This sets gapping
apart from other ellipsis types. In sluicing or right node raising, for instance,[33]
a distributed reading (i.e. the actual default ($\neg$A) & ($\neg$B)) is unproblematic
even if the negative marker is an adjunct (as in German):

(1.55)   SLUICING
         Peter hat eine der   Mäuse nicht gefangen, aber er
         Peter has one of.the mice   not   caught   but   he
         verschweigt,   welche   ~~der~~   ~~Mäuse er~~ ~~nicht gefangen hat.~~
         keep.quiet.about which.one ~~of.the~~ ~~mice~~   ~~he~~ ~~not~~   ~~caught~~   ~~has~~
         'Peter didn't catch one of the mice but he keeps quiet about which one
         he didn't catch.'

(1.56)   RIGHT NODE RAISING
         Peter hat einen der   Hamster ~~nicht~~ ~~gefangen,~~ und Maria hat
         Peter has one   of.the hamster not   caught   and Maria has
         eine der   Mäuse nicht gefangen.
         one of.the mice   not   caught
         'Peter didn't catch one of the hamsters and Maria didn't catch one of
         the mice.'

I therefore assume that gapping is distinct from sluicing or right node raising,
which have both received very insightful accounts in terms of deletion (e.g.
Merchant 2001 for sluicing, Hartmann 2000 for right node raising, the details
for the two ellipsis types differ).

     I propose that the second conjunct in gapping is derived by copying from
the first conjunct after the phonology of the first conjunct has been spelt
out. The copying mechanism is implemented in terms of sideward movement
(Nunes 1995, 2004). An important assumption in my copying account is that
the numeration of the gapping conjunct only contains the remnants, that
is material that is visible at PF. Since it is impossible to build a convergent
structure from such a numeration, material from the first conjunct needs to
be copied. Crucially, only the copying of material that is *required* to build a

---

[33] VP ellipsis is not relevant here as the negation is situated above the ellipsis site.

convergent structure is copied so that sentential functional projections are copied whereas adjuncts are not. The positive reading of the second conjunct that results from the syntactic derivation in languages with adjunct negation clashes with the requirements imposed on gapping by the principle of balanced contrast to be proposed in Chapter 3. Therefore, distributed readings with an elided adjunct negation are unacceptable, whereas those with an elided head negation are acceptable. The NPI data ((1.54)) also fall out from this analysis. The details are spelt out in Chapter 2.

The different scope readings of the negation receive the following structural analyses in my account. The distributed and the narrow scope readings are coordinations of large conjuncts (with a split CP), where a narrow scope reading is realized by a positive morpheme in the second conjunct. So for instance, the narrow scope sentence in (1.57a) has the (simplified) LF given in (1.57b) (for StrengthP, see Chapter 4). Note that the surface word order differs. Shaded material is present at LF but not pronounced at PF.

(1.57) a. Hans hat das Buch nicht gekauft, aber Maria die
            Hans has the book not   bought but Maria the
            Zeitschrift.
            magazine
            'Hans didn't buy the book but Mary bought the magazine.'

        b.

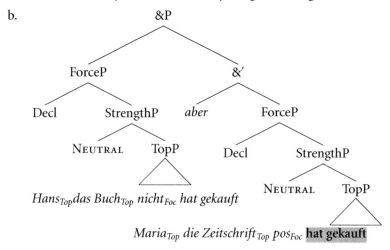

I argue for this kind of structure for the narrow scope readings in Chapter 3. The distributed scope readings look similar but with the negation copied.

The wide scope readings differ from the above in that they are small conjunct coordinations. Thus, I do not collapse them with the other readings as earlier accounts did. Wide scope readings are small conjuncts, and the other readings, large conjuncts. The reason for this is that the negation in the former is different from that in the latter—illocutionary negation versus propositional negation (see Chapter 4)—which is reflected in different structural positions for the negation at LF. A wide scope sentence such as (1.58a) has the LF in (1.58b):

(1.58) a. Max liest NICHT das Buch und Maria die Zeitung.
Max reads not   the book and Maria the paper
'It is not the case [that Max is reading the book and Mary the paper].'

b.

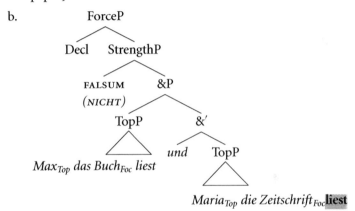

The difference with the other readings is that there is only one ForceP and one StrengthP. Strength hosts operators that modify the force of an utterance, amongst which is illocutionary negation. I argue for this structure in Chapter 4.

The auxiliary gapping cases will be discussed in Chapter 3 because contrary to previous claims they can receive a narrow scope reading. The differences with other narrow scope readings concern the contrast pairs involved (whole *v*Ps rather than objects for the non-subject contrast pair) and the kind of negation present (predicate negation rather than propositional negation), whose syntactic representation for the purposes of this introduction can be considered as more or less the same as that of propositional negation.

2

The syntax of clausal negation: The distributed scope readings in main verb gapping

This chapter investigates those gapping sentences where the negation takes distributed scope:

(2.1)   distributed scope of the negation: $(\neg A) \wedge (\neg B)$

The main question I shall be concerned with is why German seems to be more reluctant than English to produce such a reading if the negative marker is left out in the second conjunct:

(2.2)   a.   Max didn't read the book and Martha the magazine.

      b.   Max hat das Buch nicht gelesen und Martha [??](nicht) die
          Max has the book not read and Martha not the
          Zeitschrift.[1]
          magazine

Not all English speakers accept sentences like (2.2a) as perfect.[2] Importantly, German speakers overwhelmingly reject (2.2b), although an appropriate context might improve the sentence for some.[3] The intuitive reason why German

---

[1] The negative marker in the German sentence takes different positions in the two conjuncts. I will leave this matter unexplored.

[2] Ross (1970: 250) marks the following as ungrammatical:

(i)   I didn't eat fish, Bill rice and Harry roast beef.

Similarly, Jackendoff (1971: ex. 14) and Sag (1976: 143) find gapping with negation problematic. Other authors, like Siegel (1984, 1987), Oehrle (1987) and Johnson (1996/2003) judge it to be good. The many native speakers (mainly of British and Irish English) that I consulted, confirmed the latter judgement.

[3]   (i)   CONTEXT: Every teacher told some of the pupils to stay in the class room:

      [?]Bartz hat einige Fünftklässler nicht rausgeschickt und Meyer einige Sechstklässler.
      Bartz has some 5th.graders not sent.outside and Meyer some 6th.graders
      'Bartz didn't send some of the 5th graders outside and Meyer some of the 6th graders.'

speakers reject sentences such as (2.2b) is that the second conjunct dangles between a negative and a positive reading.

I demonstrate later (Section 2.1.3) that the difference between English and German carries over to other languages 'like English' and other languages 'like German'. It is a difference of syntactic category: the former have a negative marker that is a head and the latter have a negative marker that is an adverb. I argue that it is this categorial difference which is responsible for the difference in acceptability, and argue for the following hypothesis about the syntactic derivation of gapping:

(2.3)   THE COPYING HYPOTHESIS FOR GAPPING
Gapping is derived by copying material from the first conjunct to the second conjunct by way of sideward movement after the phonology of the first conjunct has been spelt out. Only material required to build a convergent derivation from the impoverished numeration of conjunct 2, which only contains the remnants of the gapping conjunct, is copied. This includes sentential functional projections and their complements. Adjuncts are not copied because they are not required in this sense.

The details of the copying process and its consequences for the interpretation of gapping will be spelt out in Section 2.3.

By way of introduction, consider the following data, which do not quite seem to match the English-versus-German picture I have drawn so far. The reluctance in German main verb gapping to leave out the negation in the second conjunct is not the same in all environments. Conversely, English is not always happy to make do without the negation. So far, I have only looked at clausal negation, which is expressed by *not* or reduced *n't* in English, and by *nicht* in German. If we look at other adverbial negative markers in German, we still find that they cannot be left out in the second conjunct. This is illustrated for temporal *niemals* ('never') in (2.4a). The English version is given in (2.4b), which is just as marginal as its German counterpart:

(2.4)   a.   ??Der kleine Max hat niemals Geige gespielt und der kleine
              the   little   Max has never   violin played and the little
              Johann Klavier.
              John   piano

         b.   ??Little Max never played the violin and little John the piano.

Thus in English, there seems to be a difference between clausal negation expressed by *not/n't* on the one hand, and adverbs like *never* on the other. In Section 2.1, I argue that English *not/n't* is a head whereas German *nicht* is an adjunct. German *niemals* and English *never* are quite clearly adjuncts.[4] Given the hypothesis in (2.3) then, it is not really surprising that these adjuncts should behave in a way similar to German *nicht*.

Next, consider some examples where German gapping is perfectly happy with the elision of the negative marker *nicht*. This happens for instance if the gapped verb is a negative polarity item, that is, if that verb must be licensed by a negation (or another licensor). In (2.5a), the verbal complex *ausstehen können* ('can stand') is an NPI, and in (2.5b), the verbal complex *sich träumen lassen* ('would have dreamt of') is. The examples are perfect.

(2.5) a. Paul kann den russischen Film nicht ausstehen und Maria
           Paul can the Russian   film not   stand   and Maria
           den französischen.
           the French
           'Paul can't stand the Russian film and Maria the French one.'

       b. Paul hat sich die Reise   in den Himalaya nicht träumen
           Paul has REFL the journey to the Himalayas not   dream
           lassen und Maria die Reise   in den Jemen.
           let   and Maria the journey to the Yemen
           'Paul wouldn't have dreamt of travelling to the Himalayas and
           Mary of travelling to Yemen.'

I conclude from this that Winkler's (2005) proposal for German, which I discussed in Chapter 1 and according to which German is the coordination of ΣPs, is robbed of one of its major arguments. If German indeed were the coordination of ΣPs it should not be possible to leave the negative marker out in the distributed readings. Example (2.5) shows that in NPI contexts this is very well possible. Obviously, we now face a new puzzle. The negation in gapping is even more capricious than it might have seemed at first. The answer to this puzzle will be (see Section 2.3) that the negative marker in the NPI environments must be copied because it needs to license the negation-dependent verbal complex.

There are obviously other ways of marking the negation in English and German than the markers *not* or *nicht* or the adverbs mentioned above, for example *no/kein*, *nobody/niemand*. Space does not permit me to discuss these here and the following brief remarks are all I will say about them (except for a few words in Section 2.1.2). *No* and *kein* are fusions of the negation with an indefinite determiner. When used in gapping, they cannot be left out in the second conjunct:

---

[4] I am not subscribing to the analysis by Cinque (1999) and others, according to which adjuncts come in functional projections, also see Section 2.3 on this.

(2.6) a. Max hat keine Äpfel gegessen und Martha *(keine)
           Max has no   apples eaten   and Martha no
           Kirschen.
           cherries

       b. Max ate no apples and Martha *(no) cherries.

The negative marker in these cases incorporates the indefinite determiner belonging to the remnant. In this sense, it may come as no surprise that *no* and *kein* cannot be elided: they contain part of a remnant. Still, these markers deserve some discussion as the exact nature and place in the derivation of the 'fusion' is debated. Syntactically, there might be a clausal negation present in the structure that combines with the non-negative indefinite determiner (see Section 2.1.2). Semantically, there is evidence from scope interactions with modals that would favour such an analysis (e.g. Penka and Von Stechow 2001).

Negative quantifiers like *niemand/nobody* and *nichts/nothing*, which can be considered fusions of the negation with an indefinite pronoun, behave somewhat curiously when gapped. In the following sentence, gapping *niemand* produces the bizarre interpretation that a person by the name of *niemand* was seen by father and son:

(2.7) *Der Vater hat niemanden auf der Brücke gesehen und der
        the father has nobody   on   the bridge seen   and the
        Sohn hinterm   Haus.
        son   behind.the house
        'The father saw nobody on the bridge and the son behind the house.'

The reasons for this effect are unclear to me.

This chapter is organized as follows. Section 2.1 discusses the syntactic realization of clausal negation in English (2.1.1) and German (2.1.2). Section 2.2 investigates syntactic differences between adjuncts on the one hand, and heads and arguments on the other (2.2.1), and it examines in greater detail the behaviour of adjuncts in gapping (2.2.2). Section 2.3 spells out my proposal for the syntax of gapping, which is summarized in the copying hypothesis in (2.3) above.

2.1 Clausal negation in English and German

Clausal negation is the negation of the proposition corresponding to the whole clause. It is expressed in a number of different ways in the world's languages (see e.g. Dahl 1979; Jacobs 1991; Payne 1985) but in the last fifteen years or so, the idea that clausal negation can be represented syntactically as a functional projection has been widely accepted. Nevertheless, it is still assumed that there might be differences between languages so that some languages might lack a Negation Phrase and realize clausal negation in a different way. The first proposals for a NegP came from Kitagawa (1986) for Japanese, Kayne (1989*b*) for French and Italian, and Pollock (1989) for French and English. The assumption of a NegP yields certain advantages, such as the provision of specifier and head positions that can be used in the licensing of operators through the specifier–head relation, or in the licensing of negative concord (e.g. Haegeman 1995; Zanuttini 1997; Acquaviva 1997). In addition, the assumption of a NegP has proved fruitful in the analysis of certain category-related effects. For instance, it is usually expected that a negative head blocks the movement of other heads in the clause, whereas a negative specifier interferes with the movement of XP-categories (cf. Zanuttini 2000 for a summary).

NegP is usually assumed to be part of the I-domain of a language, although other positions have been suggested as well. Lasnik (1972), building on Klima (1964), proposes that the negation is situated in C and according to Haegeman (1995, 2000), [neg] is generated in its own projection NegP and then moves to a focus position in C to take clausal scope. For the present purposes, it is sufficient to assume that clausal negation—whether NegP or not—must be interpreted at least above vP so that all arguments of the clause can occur in its scope (cf. Acquaviva 1995).

It is often assumed that the negation is not necessarily at home in a NegP but in a polarity phrase (PolP), that is in a phrase that not only houses negative but also positive polarity. We encountered this in Chapter 1 in the shape of Laka's (1990) ΣP used by Winkler (2005). Similar suggestions have been made, for instance, by Culicover (1991) or Haftka (1994).

2.1.1 *English*

In English, clausal negation is expressed by *not*, which needs the support of an auxiliary (*do, have*) or a modal (*can, may*), which it follows. The auxiliary and negation can occur in contracted form:

(2.8)   a.   *John cried not.

        b.   John {did not / didn't} cry.

As already mentioned above, there are other ways to express clausal negation in English, which I will not discuss here.

Klima (1964) is the seminal study on clausal (and also non-clausal) negation in English. He proposes that the negation is represented by the abstract constituent *neg*, which he introduces to capture the fact that negation can be expressed in many different ways but still has the same interpretation. For clausal negation, Klima suggests that *neg* is dominated by *S*, alongside with *wh*, the subject nominal and the predicate. In other words, it is situated in what today would be considered the C-domain. This position on the one hand reflects certain similarities between questions and *neg* (e.g. the triggering of subject–auxiliary inversion and the licensing of negative polarity items), and on the other hand, it enables *neg* to take scope over the whole clause. The actual surface position *neg* takes is then realized by transformational rules.

The idea of a NegP for English was first introduced by Pollock (1989). Pollock (1989) investigates the behaviour of verbs with respect to negation and adverbs, and forwards the Split-Infl-Hypothesis, according to which the I-domain is split into several projections: TP, NegP and AgrP. This division is proposed on the basis of comparative data in English and French, which according to Pollock differ with respect to their movement options to these various projections. With respect to the categorial status of the negative marker versus adverbs, the following data are pertinent. For French, (2.9a) and (2.9b) demonstrate that auxiliaries can move before the negation in non-finite clauses. Main verbs, in contrast, cannot, compare (2.9c) versus (2.9d). Examples (2.9e) and (2.9f) show that the situation is different for adverbs: main verbs can move across adverbs.

(2.9) a. Ne pas être heureux...   b. N'être pas heureux...
           ne not be   happy   *ne* be not happy

       c. Ne pas sembler heureux... d. *Ne sembler pas hereux...
           ne not seem   happy   *ne* seem   not happy

       e. Souvent paraître triste... f. Paraître souvent triste...
           often   to.look sad   to.look often   sad

For English, the following data show that a negative adverb (*never*) can occur above a finite main verb whereas *not* cannot:

(2.10) a. John isn't singing.

        b. *John not sings.

        c. John never sings.

Pollock takes all this to be evidence that the negation is not the same as an adverb, that is to say that adverbs and negation do not occur in the same structural position. He proposes the existence of a NegP, situated between TP and AgrP. I shall not review the detailed arguments for the workings of this NegP here, suffice it to say that Pollock takes NegP to be an inherent barrier for verb movement whereas adverbs cannot form such a barrier because they are not maximal projections (for details also see Pollock 1997). Pollock's (1989) basic idea that there is a NegP in the English IP has been quite successful.[5] It is usually assumed that the negation has the status of the head in the NegP[6] mainly because main verbs cannot move across it, thus being subject to the head movement constraint (Travis 1984). Auxiliaries, which can move across the negation, require a special proviso.[7]

What other evidence is there for a head versus a specifier analysis of the negation in English? The first thing to be observed is that the regular marker *not* and its contracted form *n't* have actually been claimed to be quite different. The main reason for this is that their distribution is not always the same:

(2.11) a. John has probably (not/* n't) heard the news.

b. John probably has (not/n't) heard the news.

Obviously, *n't* as a reduced phonological form needs to attach to some carrier. It seems that this carrier must be an auxiliary or a modal. For *not*, even though it needs *do*-support as such, no such adjacency condition holds. It has been suggested by Zwicky and Pullum (1983) that *n't* actually is an affix—rather than a clitic—for a variety of reasons. It attaches only to particular hosts (finite auxiliaries) and not to others (main verbs, nouns, etc.). There are arbitrary gaps in the set of combinations that are possible (*mayn't*, *amn't*). There are morpho-phonological idiosyncrasies (*ain't*) as well as semantic idiosyncrasies (*mustn't* = must>not>P, *can't* = not>can>P). Aux+*n't* can be affected by syntactic operations (see below). Reduced *n't* cannot attach to clitics (**I'dn't be doing this*). The marker *not* obviously is not assumed to be an affix (although Kayne (1989a) toys with the idea).

What does this imply for the syntax of these elements? Several authors have argued that *n't* should be a head, and *not*, a specifier (e.g. Haegeman 1995; Haegeman and Guéron 1999; Kayne 1989a; Zeijlstra 2004). Others have suggested that *n't* should already be part of the verb coming out of the lexicon

---

[5] For a highly critical position, see Baker (1991) and, for a reply, Pollock (1997).

[6] Pollock (1989) himself, although favouring a head analysis for English negation, does not categorically exclude a specifier analysis. This latter option is rejected by Ernst (1992) on principle. He argues that *not* has the semantic features of a head: it is obligatory and it is the semantic centre of the phrase. Yet this objection is usually considered a necessary compromise of the analysis.

[7] Such as proposed by Chomsky (1991), who says that the auxiliary's trace in Agr can be deleted after feature checking because it is not relevant at LF.

(e.g. Kim and Sag 2002; Rupp 2003; Sag to appear). For the first position, consider the following example with two negative markers:[8]

(2.12)   He couldn't not have accepted.

Kayne (1989a) points out that for a structure like (2.12) one can either assume that it contains two negative heads, or, alternatively, that *not* is not a head but a specifier whereas *n't* is a head. He suggests that *not* might be either the specifier of the NegP or of some other category. Observe, however, that contracted *couldn't* in (2.12) can easily be replaced by *could not* and nothing much changes. In other words, the difference in form between *n't* and *not* is not decisive here.

Haegeman (1995) and Haegeman and Guéron (1999) also hold the opinion that *n't* should be a head, and *not*, a specifier. They investigate polarity questions and observe that *n't* moves along with the auxiliary to C (which is where the auxiliary is generally assumed to move in subject–auxiliary inversion in questions). The full form *not*, in contrast, does not move together with the auxiliary:

(2.13)   a.   Didn't you try?

       b.   *Did not you try?

       c.   Did you not try?

The idea is that *do* originates in T, which in Haegeman (1995) is situated under NegP, and on its way up, picks up the affix in Neg. If *not* is in the specifier of NegP it is not expected to move along with the auxiliary. This analysis, however, is not compelling if we assume the order of functional projections originally proposed by Pollock (1989), that is TP-NegP. The auxiliary and the negative head in this case would simply be adjacent and since *n't* requires adjacency with an auxiliary, it must move along with it to C. As *not* does not require that adjacency, it will stay in situ: its movement would not be motivated.[9]

Some further evidence for a specifier analysis of English *not* was brought up by Rizzi (1990). In (2.14b) and (2.14c) (the examples are from Haegeman and Guéron 1999), the adjunct *why* cannot be construed with the embedded clause but only with the matrix clause.

---

[8]   The scope relations in (2.12) are n't > could > not.

[9]   Haegeman (1995) herself cites some counterexamples to the above analysis:

(i)   Does not John come too?

(ii)   Is not history a social science? (Quirk *et al.* 1985: 809)

Note that these examples contain so-called *outer* negation, which I shall discuss in detail in Chapter 4, where I will show that outer negation is different from ordinary clausal negation.

(2.14)   a.   Why did you say [$_{CP}$ t$_{why}$ that [$_{IP}$ John was fired t$_{why}$?]]

   b.   *Why did you say [$_{CP}$ when [$_{IP}$ John was fired t$_{why}$?]]

   c.   *Why did you not say [$_{CP}$ t$_{why}$ that [$_{IP}$ John was fired t$_{why}$?]]

Assuming that movement of the *wh*-adjunct must proceed cyclically through the available specifier positions, we see that in (2.14b), *when* in Spec,CP blocks movement to Spec,CP of the matrix clause. For (2.14c), it is assumed that Spec,NegP is occupied by *not*. Consequently, *why*, which on its way to the specifier of an A-bar position needs to move through Spec,NegP, which also is an A-bar position, cannot do so and the structure is ruled out (Relativized Minimality, Rizzi 1990). The marker *not* creates a weak island. As the same structure with *n't* instead of *not* is just as ungrammatical, it is assumed that if the head of NegP is filled with *n't*, its specifier has the feature [+NEG]. This blocks movement through Spec,CP. Similarly, Ouhalla (1990) assumes that the specifier of NegP generally hosts an empty operator if the negative marker itself is a head (also see Acquaviva 1997; Haegeman 1995; Rizzi 1994; Rowlett 1998).

   This position is problematic in several respects. First, the effects observed in (2.14) seem to depend on the particular matrix verb used (Sprouse 2003). Thus, whereas (2.15a) and (2.15b) allow both a matrix and an embedded reading of *why*, (2.16a) and (2.16b) only allow a matrix reading:

(2.15)   a.   [Why did you think [t that John was fired?]]

   b.   [Why did you not think [t that John was fired?]]

(2.16)   a.   [Why did you know [*t that John was fired?]

   b.   [Why didn't you know [*t that John was fired?]

Thus, it seems unlikely that the effects are exclusively due to the syntax of negation. Second, the approach of an obligatorily filled specifier in NegP makes the distinction between head and specifier in terms of movement virtually impossible. If the presence of a head automatically blocks the specifier as a landing site it becomes more difficult to argue for a category to be a specifier: *not* might also just sit in Neg with the specifier hosting an empty operator. It seems then that the weak island data in (2.14) do not really tell us much about where *not* is: it might simply be the empty operator that blocks the movement.[10] Furthermore, the effects in (2.14) might generally be accounted

---

[10] The idea that the specifier always hosts a negative operator has been endorsed especially in the NEG-criterion approach proposed by Haegeman and Zanuttini (1991); also see e.g. Acquaviva (1997),

for in semantic terms (in addition to the observed matrix verb dependency). Citing Szabolcsi and Zwarts (1993),[11] Błaszczak (2001) points out that despite the different ways in which languages encode negation, weak island effects are quite pervasive cross-linguistically and concludes that a semantic theory might be more appropriate. There have been other accounts of negative islands, some more semantic, some more syntactic (see e.g. Beck 1995; Rullman 1995). I cannot discuss these theories here. What I conclude from the aforesaid for the present purposes is that the evidence for a specifier position for *not* is very far from being decisive.

Let us next look at some more evidence for the head position of English *not*. Rupp (2003) investigates imperatives that have a very similar surface structure to the polarity questions shown in (2.13) above. The surface similarity to questions is only apparent, though: imperatives have quite a different structure.[12] Here are some imperatives with negation:

(2.17)   a.   Don't you try again.

      b.   *Do not you try again.

      c.   *Do you not try again.

      d.   Do not try again.

We see that, as in questions, *not* cannot occur together with the auxiliary *do* before the subject. Rupp (2003) argues that the auxiliary in imperatives is situated in I, and that the subject is situated in a functional projection (FP) between I and V (e.g. AspP). Thus, the underlying clause structure is IP-NegP-FP-VP. According to Rupp (2003), (2.17c) is ungrammatical because there is no landing site for the subject between NegP and I:

(2.18)   [$_{IP}$ do [$_{NegP}$ not [$_{FP}$ you [$_{VP}$ try again]]]]
              ⌐————?————⌐

Example (2.17b) is ungrammatical for reasons of case assignment: if the subject does not take its usual position in Spec,IP some special proviso is required

Haegeman (1995), and Rowlett (1998). For critical discussion of the NEG-criterion, see e.g. Rullmann (1998) or Kato (2000).

[11] Szabolcsi and Zwarts (1993) argue that weak island violations are semantically incoherent because an operator tries to operate in an inappropriate denotation domain.

[12] The structure of imperatives is very controversial and I cannot summarize or discuss the debate around these constructions here. For recent analyses, also in connection with negation, cf. for instance Beukema and Coopmans (1989), Han (2000, 2001), Han and Lee (2007), Platzak and Rosengren (1998), Potsdam (1998), Rivero (1994), Rivero and Terzi (1995), Zanuttini (1994, 1997), S. Zhang (1991), Zeijlstra (2006).

for the assignment of nominative case and the establishment of agreement. Following Chomsky (1995), Rupp argues that the relevant constellation is the adjacency between FP and I. This adjacency is disrupted if another head intervenes. This is the case with Neg in (2.17b).

For *don't* in (2.17a), Rupp assumes that it is a lexical unit coming directly from the lexicon. This position has been existent in the study of imperatives for some time. Yet whereas most earlier accounts assume that *don't* is inserted directly under C (e.g. Beukema and Coopmans 1989; Henry 1995; Zanuttini 1991), Rupp (2003) suggests that it appears in I. This ensures the adjacency between I and FP: Neg does not intervene.

The assumption that *n't* actually comes as part of a lexical entry fits the affix analysis mentioned above quite well. On the other hand, it seems like an unnecessary complication of the theory of negation. Rupp points out that we no longer would have the same LF representation for semantically equivalent sentences—those with *don't* and those with *do not*. Note, however, that negative affixes can be considered heads depending on how inflectional affixes are assumed to merge with the verb. Zeijlstra (2004) argues that a process where they are picked up as a result of movement is compatible with a head analysis. Alternatively, if the negative affix is already part of the verb, Zeijlstra argues, the verb carries an uninterpretable negative feature which it must discharge. As far as I know, the idea of a unitary lexical element has not been pursued with great zest for other sentence types apart from the imperative[13] in English and I shall not investigate this issue here any further. For the analysis of the gapping data, the question of whether the negation is part of a verbal head or a head in its own right is inconsequential.

There is one last aspect in the study of English negation that has been considered as relevant for the distinction between heads, specifiers, and adjuncts. It has been claimed that there actually are two different *not* (apart from the adverbial *not* of constituent negation), the difference being their sensitivity to tense. Zanuttini (1996) proposes that NegP itself is dependent on the presence of TP: it subcategorizes for TP as a complement. The head of NegP can be *n't* or *not*. What she calls adverbial *not*, in contrast, is not dependent on the presence of a TP. The evidence Zanuttini (1996) adduces to support her position is twofold. First, she highlights the old observation that the negation in its contracted form always attaches to the finite auxiliary and not to nonfinite verbs. It seems to link up with temporal features. Second, she shows that the negation behaves differently in subjunctives as compared to indicative

---

[13] But see Kim and Sag (2002) and Sag (to appear) who make a similar proposal for the negation in finite sentences.

clauses. Example (2.19) shows that aux-supported *n't/not* is ungrammatical in subjunctives:

(2.19)   a.   I insist that she not stay.   (Zanuttini 1996: 196)

      b.   *I insist that she don't/doesn't/does not stay.

Zanuttini assumes subjunctives to have an impoverished I domain. More precisely, she takes these structures to have no TP.[14] The idea is then that only the adverbial TP-independent negative marker *not* can occur in subjunctives.

However, (2.19) only really shows that subjunctives do not support *do*-insertion in T. It does not show that there should be no NegP: *not* could still be related to NegP with NegP being independent of TP. The fact that *n't* does not occur in subjunctives simply follows from the absence of an auxiliary and thereby the absence of a host to which *n't* can attach. Note that other proposals for the structure of subjunctives assume that they do have a TP (IP) albeit a different one from the TP in declaratives. For instance, Baltin (1993), Lasnik (1995), Potsdam (1997), and Roberts (1985) assume that the head of the TP in subjunctives is a morphologically-independent zero modal. Thus, we could still say that NegP is related to (zero) tense.

Consider in this respect subjunctives involving VP ellipsis. Such data are investigated for instance in Baltin (1993), Lobeck (1995), and Potsdam (1997). VP ellipsis is generally thought to be licensed by a head, usually the finite auxiliary in T. Obviously, we have just seen that subjunctives do not have a fully functional TP. What does this mean for VP ellipsis? Consider the following data from Potsdam (1997):

(2.20)   a.   *Kim needs to be there but it is imperative that the other organiz-ers don't_.

      b.   *Kim needn't be there but it is imperative that the other organizers _.

      c.   Kim needs to be there but it is better that the other organizers not _.[15]

      d.   *Kim needs to be there but it is better that the other organizers too.

Example (2.20a) illustrates that it is not possible to have a finite auxiliary in subjunctive VP ellipsis. Sentence (2.20b) shows that neither is it possible

---

[14] The tense features are determined by the matrix clause of a subjunctive-selecting matrix verb and are therefore situated in the complementizer in C.

[15] Potsdam notes that examples of this sort have a rather stylized flavour but nevertheless are grammatical.

to have nothing. In (2.20c), we see that it is possible to have *not* license the ellipsis site. This is not possible for *too* ((2.20d)). The conclusion to be drawn from this is that the negation in subjunctives must be a head: it can license VP ellipsis (Baltin 1993; Lobeck 1995; Potsdam 1997).[16]

Potsdam (1997) explicitly rejects the idea that *not* can be an adverbial adjunct in these constructions because neither constituent negation (which is usually assumed to be adverbial) nor left-adjoined adverbs can precede the ellipsis site in VPE (Baker 1971; Ernst 1992; Johnson 1988; Kim and Sag 2002; Sag 1978). Examples (2.21a) and (2.21b) show this for constituent negation versus clausal negation, respectively, (2.21c) is an example with an adverb:

(2.21) a. *Some of the students have been studying but some have been not _.

        b. Some of the students have been studying but some have not _.

        c. *The maid was sweeping the dust under the rug and I was just _ too.

So far, the evidence clearly points towards a head analysis for English negation. The evidence brought forward for a specifier analysis did not sustain scrutiny. There is one piece of evidence that is clearly problematic for a head analysis. This is the *why not* test put forward by Merchant (2006). Merchant argues that if the negative marker in a language is a phrase (usually adverbial) it can occur in the construction *why not?*, see (2.22). If it is a head it cannot, see (2.23):

(2.22) a. warum nicht?   *warum nein?   (*German*)

        b. waarom niet?   *waarom nee?   (*Dutch*)

        c. shida anu?   *shida ey?   (*Tsez*)

(2.23) a. *giati dhen?   giati oxi?   (*Greek*)

        b. *perchè non?   perchè no?   (*Italian*)
            'why not?'   'why no?'

English obviously groups with the first set of languages. I would like to argue here that English in comparison to German and other languages with an adverbial negation has moved further in what is known as the Jesperson cycle

---

[16] Potsdam observes in a footnote (fn. 5), that some data are problematic for the head-licensing account:

(i) *We can't count on Josh to be waiting for us at the airport so we request that you be _ instead.

be as a head should license the ellipsis site but it does not. Potsdam assumes that the head-licensing condition is necessary but not sufficient.

(Jesperson 1917). In their earlier stages, both German and English had a pre-verbal negative marker (German *en* and English *ni*), which got strengthened by an additional postverbal marker in later stages (*niet* and *noght/nott*) so that a situation quite similar to modern day French *ne pas* arose. The preverbal, clitic-like markers in German and English got lost (cf. the loss of preverbal *ne* in spoken French) and both languages ended up with the 'stronger', originally postverbal marker, *nicht* and *not*. English has developed further in the cycle, as is also argued by Zeijlstra (2004). Zeijlstra points out that in colloquial style, *not* is increasingly taken over by *n't*, which always has to attach to finite *do*, as I discussed above. He suggests that *n't* can be considered a preverbal marker, which typically is a head, even though on the surface it is postverbal. This is the next stage in the Jesperson cycle (which has come full circle now). Also, certain varieties of English (e.g. African American English) are negative concord languages, which, as is also argued by Zeijlstra (2004) and Zanuttini (2000), typically are languages where the clausal negative marker is a head. Despite the differences between *n't* and *not* in the environments discussed above, I would like to suggest that both markers (if they are considered different markers) have moved away from the adverbial stage they used to have in earlier stages of English and now have acquired head properties. The fact that *not* groups with adverbial languages in the *why not?* test can be considered a relict from an earlier stage.

2.1.2 *German*

Clausal negation in German is realized by the word *nicht*.

(2.24)   Hans hat nicht geweint.
         Hans has not   cried
         'Hans did not cry.'

As before, I shall restrict my discussion to this marker and ignore other realizations of the negation. The opinions on German *nicht* are manifold. It has been argued that it should be the head of a NegP, or its specifier, or that there should be no NegP at all and that *nicht* should simply be an adverb. Traditionally, it has been assumed that *nicht* in German is a kind of adverb that is left-adjoined to the VP (Bartsch and Venneman 1972). Yet Jacobs (1982) argues that *nicht* must be a category separate from adverbs[17] because it cannot occur in the forefield of a German V2-clause, a position where other adverbs can occur freely, and which is typically used to test phrasehood (also cf. Haftka 1994):

[17] He settles for an analysis of *nicht* as an adsentential element.

(2.25) {Ständig   / Wahrscheinlich / *Nicht}   (Jacobs 1982: 144)
        continuously probably   not
        bewundert Luise Peter.
        admires   Luise Peter
        '{Luise admires Peter all the time. / Luise probably admires Peter. /
        Luise does not admire Peter.}'

The differences in (2.25) are strong yet I suspect that the reason behind this
might be the lack of motivation—in terms of information structure—for
placing the negative marker in the forefield position. It is quite possible to
have *nicht* modified by an intensifier (which is typically accented) in Spec,CP:

(2.26) \GAR nicht bewundert Luise Peter.
        at.all not admires   Luise Peter
        'Not at all does Luise admire Peter.'

Such a sentence can be uttered in a situation where it is at issue how much
Peter was admired by Luise.

   The first to apply the NegP analysis to German was Grewendorf (1990).
Following a proposal by Lehmann (1974) for a position of the negation to the
right of the verb in German, Grewendorf assumes that the NegP in German is
adjoined to the right of VP,[18] or, alternatively to the right of TP:

(2.27)

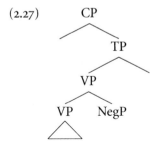

Grewendorf rejects the more traditional idea that the negation occupies a
position to the left of VP because *nicht* in German often takes a position
directly before the verb but not before the verb's arguments:

(2.28) weil   Peter dem Jungen das Buch   (Grewendorf 1990: 70)
        because Peter the boy   the book
        nicht gab
        not   gave
        'because Peter didn't give the book to the boy'

---

[18] I am using VP and *v*P interchangeably in this section as in some of the older accounts there was
no *v*P. Eventually, I take the negation to be an adjunct to *v*P.

Note, however, that most of his criticism, which mainly concerns the faculta-tive character of scrambling, is no longer valid in view of more recent devel-opments in the syntactic analysis of scrambling (also see Büring 1994 on the following). If we follow Diesing (1992) in assuming that the VP is the domain of existential closure and if we assume further that subjects are generated VP-internally (Koopman and Sportiche 1991), data such as (2.28) receive a natural explanation if the negative marker is positioned to the left of the VP:

(2.29)   weil Peter dem Jungen das Buch nicht [$_{VP}$ t$_{Peter}$ t$_{dem Jungen}$ t$_{das Buch}$ gab]

The definite DPs have scrambled out of the VP. That way, they leave the domain of existential closure. If indefinites are involved we find that their position with respect to the negation (usually) coincides with the strong and weak readings of indefinites:

(2.30)   a.   weil   ein Republikaner einem Grünen
             because a   republican   a   member.of.green.party
             nicht hilft
             not   helps
             'because republicans don't help a member of the Green party'

        b.   damit nicht ein Republikaner einem Grünen
             so   not   a   republican   a   member.of.green.party
             helfen muss.
             help   must
             'so we don't end up with a republican having to help a member of
             the Green party'   (Grewendorf 1990: 79)

In (2.30a), the indefinites are positioned to the left of the negation and receive a generic reading. In (2.30b), the indefinites are to the right of the negation and are interpreted existentially. Existential indefinite DPs typically merge with clausal negation to *kein* + *NP*, if, on the surface, they are adjacent to it (but see Chapter 4 for exceptions and their analysis):

(2.31)   Am   Ende hatte ich keine Frage   (Büring 1994: 86)
         at.the end had   I   no   question
         beantwortet.
         answered
         Am Ende hatte ich NEG [$_{VP}$ t$_{ich}$ eine Frage beanwortet].
         'At the end I had answered none of the questions.'

Büring (1994) also shows that directional prepositional objects, which cannot scramble and remain in the VP, occur to the right of the negative marker:

(2.32) a. Morgen   kann Peter nicht in die Stadt   (Büring 1994: 86)
            tomorrow can   Peter not   to the town
            fahren.
            go

        b. *Morgen   kann Peter in die Stadt nicht fahren.
            tomorrow can   Peter to the town   not   go
            'Tomorrow, Peter can't go into town.'

Thus, the evidence that clausal negation in German is situated to the left of
VP and that other surface word orders are produced by scrambling is fairly
convincing. Most recent literature on German clausal negation agrees on the
position of German negation above the VP, see Bayer (1990), Büring (1994),
Haftka (1994), Hinterhölzl (2006), Webelhuth (1992), Weiß (2002).

Nevertheless, there are a couple of suggestions that consider this view inadequate, for example Haider (1993) and Frey (2001). The evidence comes from
wh-indefinites. Haider (1993: 202) argues that *wh*-indefinites are unable to
scramble:[19]

(2.33) a. dass Max wem   was   zugesteckt hat
            that Max somebody.DAT something.ACC   slipped   has
        b. * dass Max was   wem   zugesteckt hat
            'that Max slipped something to somebody'
        c. dass Max es   ihm   zugesteckt hat
            that Max it.ACC him.DAT   slipped   has
            'that Max slipped it to him'

Now, if such sentences contain a negative marker that marker occurs right
before the verb:

(2.34) a. dass der Max [$_{VP}$ wem was nicht zugesteckt hat]
        b. ??dass der Max nicht [$_{VP}$ wem was zugesteckt hat]

Consequently, Haider (1993) argues, the negation cannot be situated to the left
of VP.

However, as the following data show, the negation can occur before the
subject if that is a non-*wh* weak indefinite (*einer*) merged with the negation

---

[19] This does not hold for 'more contentful' *wh*-indefinites (Haida 2007), e.g.

(i) A: Why are you selling only FRESH stuff?
     B: Weil   [was   verGAMmeltes]   keiner   kauft.
         because something gone.mouldy.ACC   nobody.NOM   buys
         'Because nobody buys things gone mouldy.'

(= *keiner* 'nobody'), and if in addition there is a *wh*-indefinite in the clause. Also note that the negation scopes over the subject here: *not > somebody*.

(2.35) a. dass keiner   was   kauft   (*not>somebody*)
            that nobody something.ACC buys

        b. dass NEG [$_{VP}$ einer   was   kauft]
            that neg   somebody.NOM something.ACC buys
            'that nobody buys anything'

If the subject scopes over the negation, we find the negation in front of the verb again:

(2.36) a. dass einer   was   nicht   (*somebody>not*)
            that somebody.NOM something.ACC not
            kauft
            buys

        b. ??dass einer nicht was kauft
            'that somebody does not buy something'

Importantly, *was* ('something') also escapes the scope of the negation here. In order to express the scope *not>something* we must use the word *nichts* ('nothing'). Thus, we have the normal fusion of the negation with the adjacent *wh*-indefinite *not+was* ('not something'):

(2.37) a. dass einer   nichts   kauft   (*somebody>not>something*)
            that somebody nothing buys

        b. dass einer   NEG [$_{VP}$ t$_{einer}$ etwas   kauft]
            that somebody   something buys
            'that somebody doesn't buy anything'

Going back to example (2.34) from above, repeated below in (2.38), we find just the same for the scope between the *wh*-indefinites and the negation. The *wh*-indefinites escape the scope of the negation if they are not c-commanded by it, see (2.38a). If the negation is to scope over the *wh*-indefinites, the highest indefinite must fuse with it, producing *keinem* ('nobody'), see (2.38b) versus (2.38c).

(2.38) a. dass der Max wem   was   (*sbd >sth >not*)
            that the Max somebody.DAT something.ACC
            nicht zugesteckt hat
            not   slipped   has

        b. ??dass der Max nicht wem was zugesteckt hat
            'that Max didn't slip something to somebody'

    c. dass der Max keinem   was   *(not>sbd>sth)*
        that the Max nobody.DAT something.ACC
        zugesteckt hat
        slipped   has

    c′. dass der Max NEG [$_{VP}$ wem was zugesteckt hat]
        'that Max didn't slip anything to anybody'

These data are clear evidence against the idea that the negation in German might be situated within the VP. The same conclusion, based on similar arguments, is reached by Hinterhölzl (2006).

Let me return to the NegP analysis for German. As opposed to English, the occurrence of the negative marker in German does not interfere with the movement of the finite verb to T and then to C. This holds both for auxiliaries (*haben* ('have') in (2.39a)) and for main verbs ((2.39b)):

(2.39) a. Hans hat nicht geweint t$_{hat}$.
          Hans has not   cried
          'Hans did not cry.'

      b. Hans grüßt seine Nachbarn   nicht t$_{grüßt}$.
          Hans greets his   neighbours not
          'Hans does not greet his neighbours.'

Thus, *nicht* is not expected to be a head.

I discussed above several potential reasons for the lack of head movement constraints. The head position of NegP can be empty and the negative marker can be situated in Spec,NegP, or the negation might be a modifier that adjoins to the VP (the traditional adverb analysis). Grewendorf (1990) suggests that *nicht* in German is the specifier of a NegP. One piece of evidence he considers are earlier stages of German (also see Büring 1994). As I mentioned in the previous section, German used to have the preverbal negative marker *en*, which later on was strengthened by the postverbal marker *niet*, similarly to contemporary French *ne pas*. Then the preverbal marker *en* got lost, just as preverbal *ne* in modern spoken French is often left out. French *pas* is usually analysed as a specifier of NegP. Grewendorf (1990) assumes the same for German *nicht*.

What else can be said for a specifier analysis of German *nicht*? Grewendorf (1990) investigates the following examples with neg-raising. Neg-raising is a phenomenon where a negation that occurs in the matrix clause is construed semantically with the embedded clause. Thus, (2.40) means that the speaker believes that Koreans cannot harvest olives:

(2.40)   Ich glaube nicht, dass Koreaner Oliven   (Grewendorf 1990: 88)
         I   believe not   that   Koreans   olives
         ernten   können.
         harvest   can
         'I don't think that Koreans can harvest olives.'
         = 'I think that Koreans cannot harvest olives.'

Now, with some verbs of saying and believing, embedded sentences in German can also occur as verb-second constructions, with the verb in C and not the complementizer *dass* ('that'). This is illustrated in (2.41a). Example (2.41b) shows that such a V2 construction does not allow a negative marker to occur in the matrix clause. Neg-raising is not possible: the negation has to be expressed in the embedded clause, see (2.41c).

(2.41)   a.   Ich glaube, Koreaner können Oliven ernten.
           I   believe Koreans   can   olives   harvest
                                         (Grewendorf 1990: 88)

       b.   *Ich glaube nicht, Koreaner können Oliven ernten.

       c.   Ich glaube, Koreaner können keine Oliven ernten.
           I   believe Koreans   can   no   olives   harvest

Grewendorf (1990) suggests that the reason for this is that the negation—being a phrase—moves through Spec,CP of the embedded clause and leaves a trace there. Therefore, the subject of the embedded clause, *Koreans*, cannot occupy that Spec,CP. In the verb-final version (2.40), this problem does not arise because the subject does not raise to Spec,CP but stays in Spec,IP.

Now, the problem with this account is that the environments where neg-raising can occur are severely restricted to particular verbs (Lerner and Sternefeld 1984). In addition, for *that*-deletion, there are important semantic and pragmatic restrictions on the semantics of the matrix verb (also see Chapter 5 on this). This makes a syntactic account of the above kind unlikely. Furthermore, note that in certain environments, it is actually possible to have a V2 structure under a negative matrix clause, where the negation is construed semantically with the embedded clause:

(2.42)   a.   Glauben Sie nicht, ich fürchtete mich   (Butulussi 1989: 136)
           believe   you not   I   fear.SUBJ REFL
           vor der süßen Last!
           of   this sweet   burden
           'Don't think that I would fear this sweet burden!'

b. Sie dürfen nicht glauben, das Gericht hätte
   You may   not   believe the court   had. SUBJ
   leichtfertig   entschieden.
   thoughtlessly decided
   'You mustn't think that the court took the decision thoughtlessly.'

(Butulussi 1989: 135)

Although these sentences display special characteristics—the group of verbs that allow this is restricted, the embedded verb appears in the subjunctive form, the matrix clause is not an 'ordinary' assertion (see Meinunger 2004)—they cast doubt on the generalization that a negation in the matrix clause blocks a V2 embedded clause. This, in turn, means that the negative marker should not be situated in Spec,NegP.

The final piece of evidence Grewendorf (1990) considers for a specifier analysis of *nicht* comes from sentences similar to those considered above for English (see (2.14) for an instance of adjunct extraction):

(2.43) a. Wen   glaubst du, dass dieses Beispiel
            Who.ACC believe you that this   example
            überzeugen kann?
            convince   can
            'Who do you think that this example can convince?'

        b. * Wen glaubst du nicht, dass dieses Beispiel überzeugen kann?
            'Who don't you think that this example can convince?'

For (2.43b), Grewendorf's idea is that *wen* has to move cyclically through the specifier NegP, and since this is filled with *nicht*, the movement is blocked. As in the English examples, we are dealing with a weak island effect and again I would like to argue that the effects are not merely due to syntactic restrictions[20] (see Section 2.1.1 above for details). In other words, we do not need to assume on the basis of these examples, that *nicht* should be a specifier.

Haftka (1994) is quite against a specifier analysis for *nicht* mainly because she assumes that *nicht* cannot occur in the forefield, an argument which I refuted at the beginning of this section. Haftka assumes that there is a PosP in German, whose head can be positive (zero) or negative (*nicht*). The specifier of PosP can be occupied by XPs. In the case of negative features on the head Pos, negative argument phrases move to Spec,Pos in fulfilment of the

---

[20] Note that sentences like (2.43b) are actually marked grammatical in Reis (2000) and Fanselow and Mahajan (2000)—as opposed to their embedded V2 counterparts. They seem clearly worse, though, than the versions without a negation.

NEG-criterion (Haegemann and Zanuttini 1991). If negative phrases move to Spec,PosP the head must be lexically empty:

(2.44)   dass sie [$_{PosP}$ keinen Reis [$_{Pos'}$ [$_{Pos\ (+Neg)}$ 0] [$_{VP}$ je t$_{sie}$ mit
         that they   no   rice   ever   with
         Stäbchen   aßen]]]
         chop.sticks   ate
         'that they never ate any rice with chop sticks'

This kind of analysis, according to Haftka, is supported by clauses such as the following, where a frequency adverb like *je* ('ever'), which she assumes to be adjoined to the VP, has to occur to the right of negative DPs:

(2.45)   a.   dass er   sicher   niemandem [$_{VP}$ je [$_{VP}$ t$_{er}$ t$_{niemandem}$
             that he presumably nobody   ever
             getraut hat]]
             trusted has

         b.   * dass er sicher [$_{VP}$ je [$_{VP}$ t$_{er}$ niemandem getraut hat]]
             'that he presumably didn't ever trust anybody'   (Haftka 1994: 141)

Haftka does not note, however, that *je*, which is the only adverb she uses to make her point, is a negative polarity item, which must be c-commanded by the negation no matter what (or must occur in some other licensing environment, which is not given in (2.45)). Indeed, if a different frequency adverb, for example *oft* ('often') is used, the sentence is fully grammatical:

(2.46)   dass er sicher oft niemandem getraut hat
         'that he presumably often did not trust anybody'

Clearly, we have to be careful with frequency adverbs. It has been suggested that they are not a homogenous adverb class restricted to one position only (Frey 2003). Rather, due to their semantics, frequency adverbs can have a distribution like frame adverbs, like event-internal adverbs, or like process-related adverbs. Indeed, there can be several frequency adverbs in one clause (Frey 2003: 193):

(2.47)   weil   häufig wer   mehrmals   diese Schraube zu
         because often somebody several.times this   screw   too
         oft   anzog
         frequently tightened
         'because often somebody tightened this screw too frequently, several times'

For temporal adverbs, Frey observes that they are situated above the highest argument of the VP, that is the subject. Adapting (2.46) accordingly, we find that the negative phrase can occur below it, which suggests that the negation can adjoin to the VP below that adverb:

(2.48)   dass er sicher morgen niemandem trauen wird
          'that he presumably will not trust anybody tomorrow'

Thus, it is not necessary to assume movement of the negative phrase into the specifier of PosP.

To sum up, I have found no evidence that there should be a NegP headed by *nicht* in German. Neither have I found conclusive evidence for a Neg,P with *nicht* in its specifier. It seems then that an analysis of the marker as an adverb, which is adjoined to the VP—or, as I will assume with an updated syntax, to *v*P—, is the most appropriate.

2.1.3 *Other languages*

The difference between English and German calls for more typological comparison of the gapping construction with respect to negation. It turns out that languages where the negative marker is tightly linked with the verb and has been suggested to be a head, behave like English. This is borne out, for instance, in languages with a preverbal negation marker, which typically has the characteristics of a head (see Section 2.1.1). In Polish, the negative marker *nie* cliticizes onto the verb in a preverbal position. Błaszczak (2001) argues extensively for a NegP analysis of Polish clausal negation with *nie* being the head of that NegP. In gapping, Polish allows a negative interpretation of the second conjunct if the verb plus cliticized negative head is gapped in the second conjunct:

(2.49)   POLISH
          Jan nie czytal ksiazek,   a[21] Maria gazet.
          Jan neg read   books.GEN and Maria newspapers.GEN.
          'Jan didn't read any books and Mary any papers.'

Sentences like this are slightly better without gapping but they are certainly possible. It is not possible to repeat only the negative marker in the elliptic conjunct. Furthermore, note that the object in the gapping conjunct just like its correlate in the antecedent conjunct must occur in the genitive case, which occurs (inter alia) on objects of sentences with clausal negation.

---

[21] The ordinary equivalent to English *and, i* must be replaced by *a* ('and', 'whereas') in gapping and other highly parallel coordinations.

In Slovak, as in Polish, the negation also attaches to the left of the finite verb. Again we find that a distributed reading of the negation is easily obtained:

(2.50)   SLOVAK

       Ján ne-čítal knihy   a   Mária noviny.
       Jan neg-read books.ACC and Mary papers.ACC
       'Jan didn't read any books and Mary any papers.'

In the discussion of English *n't* (Section 2.1.1), it was said that for the purposes of gapping it does not matter whether a negative marker is a head or whether it is part of the verbal head in the form of verbal inflection (also recall Zeijlstra's (2004) position that all of these must be heads anyhow). Now, if we look at languages where the negation is part of the verbal morphology, we observe that the second conjunct of a negative gapping sentence is straightforwardly interpreted as negative. Consider Turkish. The Turkish negative marker *me* follows reflexive, causative, or passive affixes and precedes tense, mood, and person affixes on the verb. In gapping with a negative first conjunct, the second conjunct is easily interpreted as negative:[22]

(2.51)   TURKISH

       Hasan karides-i   ye-me-di,   Mehmet de   istiridyey-i.
       Hasan shrimp-ACC eat-neg-PAST Mehmet and oyster-ACC
       'Hasan didn't eat the shrimp, and Mehmet the oyster.'

Similarly, in Japanese, where the negation also appears as an affix, it is easily interpreted when elided with the verb in gapping:

(2.52)   JAPANESE

       John-wa   ookami-wo, sosite Mary-wa   usagi-wo   utta-nakatta.
       John-TOP wolf-ACC,   and   Mary-TOP rabbit-ACC shot-neg
       'John didn't shoot the wolf and Mary the rabbit.'

Languages which use adverbial markers for clausal negation, behave very much like German. This is, for instance, the case in Dutch and in Danish:

(2.53)   DUTCH

       Jan heeft Maartje niet gebeld en   Piet Heidi *(niet).
       Jan has   Maartje not called and Piet Heidi   not
       'Jan didn't call Maartje en Piet Heidi.'

---

[22] Pressed for choice, speakers prefer to have the gap in the first conjunct. This, however, can be considered a right node raising construction (cf. Kornfilt 2000 contra Bozsahin 2000, who analyses it as an instance of gapping).

(2.54) DANISH

> Hans har ikke læst bøger   og Peter ikke tidsskrifter.
> Hans has not read the.books and Peter not the.magazines
> 'Hans didn't read the books and Peter the magazines.'

Obviously, we need more typological comparison here, and even more so for languages that realize clausal negation in a completely different way. I will have to leave this open.

To sum up, Section 2.1 has shown that English and German clausal negation differ in that English has a NegP with the negative marker as the head whereas in German the clausal negation is an adverb. For English gapping, I observed that finite verb plus clausal negation gaps can be interpreted with relative ease. In German, this is more problematic. Usually, the negative marker is repeated in the second conjunct. Exceptions are sentences in which the verbal head is a negative polarity item.

It is worth noting in this connection that it is not possible to let the English sentential negation marker appear on its own, that is without an auxiliary, in the second conjunct of a gapping sentence:

(2.55) * John has not called Rosie and Paul not Mary.

It is possible, however—at least in some (unambiguous) structures—to repeat non-clausal *not* in English, which generally is believed to be an adverb:

(2.56) Arthur might have been not crying and Leo *(not) laughing.

In (2.56), the negative marker only scopes over the predicate. Repeating the marker poses no problems. There are various potential reasons why it should not be possible to elide clausal *not* in (2.55). The first that comes to mind is that *not* obviously needs *do*-support. On the other hand, recall that in VP ellipsis involving subjunctives no *do*-support is required (see (example 2.20)). Why should gapping not be another exception? Wilder's (1995, 1996) head condition, which I discussed in Chapter 1, is an answer to this: in forward deletion, under which Wilder also subsumes gapping, an ellipsis site may not be c-commanded by a non-deleted head in its conjunct. Thus, if the verb is elided, which in English is below clausal negation, the negation must go, too.

2.2 Adjuncts in gapping

In this section I investigate two questions. First, in what ways are adjuncts different from heads or arguments in general in grammar? The answer will be that the most important feature of adjuncts is that they are not obligatory in the same sense as heads or arguments are. Second, do adjuncts other than the negation show a specific behaviour in gapping? The answer to this question will be yes.

2.2.1 *Adjuncts, heads, and arguments*

To start, let us examine what a head is. According to Zwicky (1985) and Hudson (1987, 1996) heads can be identified by the following criteria:[23] (a) the head is a semantic functor; (b) it does not determine agreement; (c) it is the morpho-syntactic locus of the phrase; (d) it is a subcategorizer; (e) it can be the distributional equivalent of its phrase (as in VP ellipsis); (f) it is obligatory. Svenonius further suggests that (g) a head is unique (in contrast to adverbs); (h) it is an X° element, that is a single word; (i) it determines word order (e.g. OV versus VO). Not all of these criteria are relevant in the present context. I investigated criterion (e) to some extent in Section 2.1, where we saw that *not* in English licenses VP ellipsis (Potsdam 1997). Another important criterion is that (f) heads are obligatory. At first sight, this does not seem to matter much in a comparison between English and German. A German negative clause is interpreted as negative just as its English equivalent is, and a German negative marker is interpreted as negative just as its English counterpart is. Nevertheless, I suggest that in gapping, the obligatoriness of heads contrasts with the optionality of adjuncts in the sense that heads— as well as arguments—are copied to the second conjunct whereas adjuncts are not.

Apart from the aspect of obligatoriness, adjuncts have been assumed to be different from heads, and arguments in other ways as well. It has been argued by many that adjuncts enter the derivation later than arguments, that is post-cyclically, for example Boškovič (1997), Boškovič and Lasnik (1999), Chomsky (1993), Fox (1999, 2000), Fox and Nissenbaum (1999), Freidin (1986), Lebeaux (1988, 1991, 2000), Nissenbaum (1998, 2000), Ochi (1999), Sauerland (2000), Stepanov (2001), van Riemsdijk (1981), and Winkler (1997*a*). Post-cyclic adjunction has been made responsible, for instance, for the apparently universal ban on extraction from adjuncts (Stepanov 2001), the different behaviour of arguments versus adjuncts with respect to stress and focus projection (Winkler 1997*a*), and certain asymmetries in simple matrix clauses with *wh*-phrases versus long-distance matrix questions (Boškovič 1997). The 'classical' piece of evidence for the late merger of adjuncts are anti-reconstruction

---

[23] Hudson (1987) is a re-examination of Zwicky (1985). The list above is based on Hudson (1987).

effects involving condition C, discussed by Lebeaux (1988) and Freidin (1986).[24]

Evidence for substantial differences between arguments and adjuncts can also be found in the field of language comprehension. For instance, the *construal hypothesis* of Frazier and Clifton (1996) says that an input x preferentially should be analyzed as a so-called primary phrase (subject, predicate, complement, and 'obligatory' elements) so that a fully determinate analysis can be carried out. If a phrase cannot be analyzed as a primary phrase, the input x will only be *associated* into the current thematic processing domain (the extended projection of the last actual theta-assigner). An exact analysis can be postponed. Let us look at an example:

(2.57)   a.   the daughter of the colonel that ...

b.   the daughter with the colonel that ...

The relative clause that is introduced by *that* in both (2.57a) and (2.57b) can be attached either to the NP *the daughter* or to the NP *the colonel*. In the analysis of primary phrases—which is the analysis the parser will try first—principles from the Garden-Path Theory (Frazier 1978) like *Late Closure* (more or less: branch right as long as you can) and *Minimal Attachment* (Do not produce unnecessary structure) are at work and determine the outcome of the analysis. Accordingly, the relative clauses in (2.57a) and (2.57b) should be preferentially attached to the NP *the colonel*. That is not, however, what happens reliably during comprehension. In a written questionnaire study in English and in Spanish, Gilboy *et al.* (1995) found that although participants tend to assign the relative clause more often to the second NP (*the colonel*) in the (b)-cases, they do not do so in the (a)-cases. The difference between the (a)-cases and the (b)-cases is that the (b)-cases contain an additional theta-assigner, namely the preposition *with*. Thus, as the construal hypothesis predicts, it is the most recent thematic processing domain into which the adjunct is associated. The crucial point is that adjuncts seem to be processed according to different principles from arguments.

The evidence we have seen so far both from the theoretical literature and from the processing literature should have made it clear that there are important differences between heads and arguments, on the one hand, and adjuncts, on the other hand. Heads and arguments are clausal core elements whereas adjuncts are not. There is a natural divide between these categories, which, as we shall see in the next chapter carries over to gapping constructions.

---

[24] These have actually been called into question by Lasnik (1998) and others. There is a whole debate about the alleviation of Principle C effects. For a discussion of relevant data and analyses, see for instance Bianchi (1995), Culicover (1997), Heycock (1995), Kuno (1997), Postal (1997), Safir (1999), Sauerland (2000).

2.2.2 *Non-negative adjuncts in gapping*

We have just seen that adjuncts are different from heads and arguments. We also saw that the English negative marker is a head whereas the German negative marker is an adverb, and that the two languages differ with respect to the reliability with which the negation is interpreted in the second conjunct of a gapping construction if the negative marker is left out of there. What about other adjuncts in gapping? Are they reliably interpreted in the second conjunct? This section will show that they are not.

Coppen *et al.* (1993: 39), who investigate gapping in Dutch, suggest that elements without equivalent in the ellipsis clause are 'almost always' filled in during interpretation, yet they show that there are exceptions to this. Maybe unsurprisingly, these exceptions involve adjuncts. Thus, whereas in (2.58a) the interpretation of the locative adverbial is more or less obligatory, this is less mandatory in (2.58b):

(2.58) a. In Amsterdam heeft Jan een taxi genomen en Marie
            in Amsterdam has Jan a   taxi taken   and Marie
            de bus.
            the bus
            'Jan took a taxi in Amsterdam and Mary the bus.'

        b. Wim had in Amsterdam in korte tijd meer vrienden
            Wim had in Amsterdam in short time more friends
            gemaakt dan ik ooit vijanden.[25]
            made   than I ever enemies
            'Wim had made more friends in Amsterdam in a short time than
            I ever made enemies {there | anywhere}.'   (*Dutch*)

In (2.58b), it is unclear whether the speaker wishes to express that s/he made fewer enemies only in Amsterdam or in general, other places included.

Van den Wyngærd (1998: 20) also suggests that the second conjunct in such cases 'just happens to be vague in this respect'. He uses an example from Evers (1975) to illustrate his point:

(2.59) weil   Johann auf der Terrasse eine Sarabande tanzen will
        because Johann on the terrace a   saraband   dance want
        und Cecilia eine Pavane
        and Cecilia a   pavane
        'because Johann wants to dance a saraband on the terrace and Cecilia
        a pavane'

---

[25] This is a comparative. This is irrelevant for the argument-adjunct asymmetry.

In this example, it is unclear where Cecilia wants to dance. Van den Wyngærd argues that Cecilia's wish to dance the pavane on the terrace is subsumed under the wish to dance the pavane in a particular place, or with a particular partner, at a particular time. He suggests that the locative adjunct is readily available in this example because of pragmatic factors such as the general preference for (but non-exclusive constraint on) parallelism between the conjuncts (e.g. Lang 1977; Schachter 1977; Zwicky and Sadock 1975).

Van den Wyngærd (1998) furthermore cites an example from Hudson (1976: 536) which shows that the effect is more widespread and that subordinations can behave quite similarly in this respect:

(2.60)   He turned off the fire in his study because it was too warm.

The subordinate clause is interpreted as referring to the temperature in the agent's study. Van den Wyngærd suggests that the same effect arises in the non-gapped variant of sentence (2.59):

(2.61)   weil Johann auf der Terasse eine Sarabande tanzen will
         und (weil) Cecilia eine Pavane tanzen will[26]
         'because Johann wants to dance a saraband on the terrace and Cecilia
         wants to dance a pavane.'

Now, these last two cases clearly are different from the gapping cases because no ellipsis is involved. They demonstrate that temporal or local variables can be filled in pragmatically. The fact that gapping is not more stringent in this respect, however, is what is really surprising because in ellipsis the parallelism requirements are usually stricter than in non-elliptic coordinations. Also note that ellipsis types like sluicing ((2.62)) or right node raising ((2.63)) do not display the 'adjunct ambiguity' we find in gapping. Both examples are interpreted with *auf der Terasse* in the ellipsis site.

(2.62)   Johann will   auf der Terasse eine Sarabande tanzen, aber ich
         Johann wants   on the terrace a   saraband dance   but I
         weiß nicht welche.
         know not   which
         'Johann wants to dance a saraband on the terrace but I don't know
         which sarabande.'

---

[26] Van den Wyngærd presents the sentence without the repeated *weil* ('because') but I think that makes the sentence marginal. The effect concerning the adjunct is the same.

(2.63) Johann will   eine Sarabande und Maria will   eine Pavane
       Johann wants a   saraband   and Maria wants a   pavane
       auf der Terasse tanzen.
       on   the   terrace   dance
       'Johann wants to dance a saraband on the terrace and Maria wants to
       dance a pavane on the terrace.'

To summarize, the interpretation of adjuncts in gapping constructions is not as reliable as one would expect. Obviously, one would think that adjunction of a negative marker should not be quite as flexible since it changes the meaning of a sentence to an extent where it means the opposite. Nevertheless, it seems that the elided negative marker in the distributed scope cases in German behaves just like other adjuncts in gapping, that is its presence can be somewhat undecided. This generally renders the outcome unacceptable. In the next section, I will propose a syntactic analysis of gapping which builds on the observations I made about adjuncts and the negation.

2.3 The syntax of gapping: Proposal

2.3.1 *Gapping is copying*

Let us start with the following assumption made by Nunes (2004: 23): 'PF should reflect the number of occurrences of each lexical item specified in the initial numeration'. Nunes makes this, in his view 'natural' assumption outside an ellipsis context. Obviously, ellipsis is a special case when it comes to PF. Nevertheless, I suggest adopting this assumption for gapping. Furthermore, I follow Chomsky (2000) in the assumption that there are sub-arrays for numerations.[27] I assume that the first conjunct has a separate numeration from the second. Applied to a gapping sentence like (2.64a), this means that the second[28] conjunct has the numeration in (2.64b). Only elements that are realized at PF actually occur in the numeration. Furthermore, there are no functional elements like T or v present.

---

[27] One of the reasons for this assumptions are minimal pairs like (i) and (ii), which arguably are built from the same numeration. If there were a global numeration for the entire sentence, economy considerations would always prefer *there* to be inserted as a next step when the derivation has reached the stage given in (iii). Thus, the grammatical sentence in (ii) could not be derived.

(i)   The fact is that there is someone in the room.

(ii)   There is the fact that someone is in the room.

(iii)   [is someone in the room]

[28] In head-final languages like Korean or Japanese this holds for the first conjunct.

(2.64) a. John got the food and Pete the drinks.

b. $N_{conjunct\ 2}$ = {and, Pete, the, drinks}

Chomsky (2000) proposes that each numeration contains either a complementizer (C) or a light verb (v).[29] This is obviously not given in (2.64b) because there is no C or v. But then, (2.64b) is the numeration of an elliptic conjunct. I shall assume here that the presence of the conjunction *and*, which is a coordination head, also qualifies to make a numeration formally complete.[30]

The two conjuncts of a gapping coordination are derived separately (each with its own numeration). Separate assembly is unproblematic for the first conjunct but not for the second. The numeration in (2.64) is not sufficient to feed the derivation of a structure that converges at LF, let alone produce an interpretable structure: it is impossible to build a syntactically sentential object which could denote a semantic object of propositional type. This situation can be remedied if sideward movement (Nunes 1995, 2004) is applied. I introduced the concept of sideward movement when I discussed Winkler's (2005) account of gapping in Chapter 1. I will repeat the crucial ideas here for ease of exposition.

Within minimalism, movement has been recast in terms of copy-and-merge (Chomsky 1995). An element in a structure is copied and the new copy is merged higher up in the same structure. Nunes (1995, 2004) points out that this latter assumption is by no means necessary. Once copied, a copy can also be merged with a phrase marker that is assembled in parallel with the 'source' phrase marker. This is what Nunes has termed sideward movement. In gapping—as we saw in the discussion of Winkler (2005) in Section 1.3.2— sideward movement can target an element in one conjunct, copy it, and merge it in the other conjunct.

Now, recall that Winkler applies another ingredient of Nunes' theory— chain reduction—to derive the ellipsis site in gapping, illustrated in (2.65) as strikethrough. Nunes assumes that all copies are equally available for realization at PF.[31] The fact that it is usually the head rather than the tail of a chain that is realized follows from independent considerations (Kayne's 1994 linear correspondence axiom in conjunction with economy). Crucially, chain reduction depends on c-command, that is for a lower copy to be chain-reduced,

---

[29] Phases which are the parts of the derivation that have access to a given subarray are assumed to be propositional, i.e. correspond to vP or CP. For reasons of identifiability of a subarray, Chomsky proposes that it should contain one lexical item that will label the resulting phase.

[30] Also see te Velde (2006) for the assumption that conjuncts are phases.

[31] Also see e.g. Landau (2006), von Stechow (1992), Groat & O'Neill (1996), Pesetsky (1998), Sabel (1998), and Fanselow and Ćavar (2001, 2002) for discussion.

it must be c-commanded by a higher copy. This is given in (2.65) because the highest vP_3, which is situated outside the coordination, c-commands both lower copies.

(2.65)   Manny loves Anna and Leo Hanna.

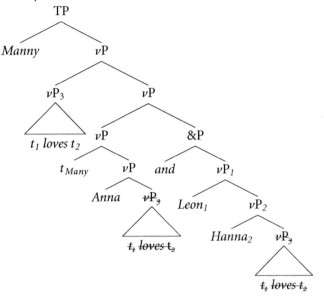

Now, I have argued that a small conjunct analysis of the sort in (2.65) faces some problems I think should be overcome (see Chapter 1, Section 1.3) and that for the distributed scope readings a large conjunct analysis is more appropriate. This leaves us with the problem that there is no copy above the coordination that could license chain reduction—and thus gapping—of the lower copies. I will maintain my stance that the distributed scope readings in gapping are the coordination of large conjuncts. To derive the gap(s), I suggest that in gapping sideward movement occurs after the phonology of the first conjunct has been shipped off to PF. This means that material to be copied from the first conjunct comes without phonology.[32]

I said above that from the numeration of a second conjunct in gapping no interpretable structure can be built because no propositional object can

---

[32] Note in this connection that it is sometimes assumed that once a phrase has been spelt out it behaves like a lexical item and the elements contained in it are not available any more for the syntactic computation (e.g. Uriagereka 1999). I do not follow this assumption, which by the way, is also problematic for deletion accounts that require syntactic isomorphy at LF. Such a position precludes the possibility of non-simultaneous spellout at LF and PF, which has been argued for on independent grounds by e.g. Felser (2004) and Marušič and Žaucer (2006), also see Sauerland and Elbourne (2002) for related architectural concerns.

be formed. So sideward movement is motivated by the need to build such a structure. The elements that are required to build such a structure are the sentential functional categories v, T, (C), and the category V. Apart from that, the elements in the numeration of the second conjunct also have unchecked features that need to be checked. This motivates copying of potential case-checkers from conjunct 1. Let us consider (2.64) from above in more detail. The DPs in the numeration for conjunct 2 come with the case features shown in (2.66b) (I abstract away from the internal structure of the DPs and treat them as a word):

(2.66) a. John got the food and Pete the drinks.

b. $N_{conjunct\ 2}$ = {and, Pete-CASE, [the drinks]-CASE}

These case features need to be checked. Let us assume that the first conjunct of (2.66) has the structure in (2.67). Checked features are marked with small caps and are subscripted, unchecked features just have small caps. The lower copy of *John* has an unchecked case feature whereas the higher copy has this feature checked because it agrees with the ϕ-feature of T (and moves into Spec,TP because of the EPP-feature of T).

(2.67) [$_{TP}$ John-N-ϕ-$_{CASE}$ T-$_{D-\phi}$ [$_{vP}$ John-N-ϕ-CASE [$_{v'}$got[$_{VP}$ got
[$_{DP}$ the food-N-ϕ-$_{CASE}$]]]]]

Of course, unchecked features cause a derivation to crash at the interfaces so the lower copy of *John* should cause such a crash. To take care of this, Nunes (1995, 2004) suggests the following. On the PF side, chain reduction eliminates the offending features.[33] On the LF side, there is a chain uniformity condition, which adapts lower copies with unchecked features so that they take over the checked status from their higher chain members.

For gapping, I assume that copying takes place after phonological spell-out of the first conjunct (see above) but before the chain uniformity condition is applied and the chain(s) are uniformized. Since chain reduction is an operation in the phonological component, all the copies that are given in (2.67) are available for potential copying. I assume that the derivation of the second conjunct proceeds in normal fashion, that is bottom to top. The verb is copied from the first conjunct to merge with the object of the second conjunct, which fits the verb's theta specifications. Then v is copied. It checks the case of the object. Next, the subject of the second conjunct can be merged in the specifier position of vP. It still has unchecked case. Since T is required to build an interpretable structure, T will be copied next.

[33] If chain reduction does not delete all the elements with formal features, an additional operation of formal feature deletion takes place.

Let me use the copying of T to take a closer look at the question of feature checking. T has its EPP and case features checked in the first conjunct. What happens to the subject of the second conjunct? There are two options here, one gapping-specific but in my view very plausible and therefore worth exploring, one gapping-unspecific, argued for in different contexts by Nunes (2000, 2004). I will start with the latter. According to Chomsky (1995) interpretable features remain available to the computation once checked, uninterpretable features do not. For the derivation of the second gapping conjunct both interpretable as well as uninterpretable features (e.g. case) need to be checked. Nunes (2000, 2004), investigating the evidence Chomsky (1995) brought forward for the erasure (i.e. non-availability after checking) of uninterpretable features, for example certain expletive constructions, raising constructions and covert movement, arrives at the conclusion that checked uninterpretable features should be available to the computation as well. We could assume that this also applies in gapping. To be sure, the issue usually arises with respect to lower copies (traces) but if the features of the goal are 'only' made invisible and not erased the same should hold for the probe. This means that the case features of the remnants in gapping should pose no problem even if the case features of their correlates have been checked by the same elements.

The other option to deal with the problem of feature visibility and feature availability, which is more specific to the gapping construction (and needs more scrutiny in other contexts of sideward movement), is the following. When T is copied from the first conjunct and merged with the second, it is no longer in a configuration where it is in a specifier–head relation with an element that matches the EPP feature. This, I would like to argue, makes the EPP feature visible at LF in the second conjunct because it is the structural relation which is required for feature matching.[34] Therefore, the EPP needs to be checked 'again' by an appropriate matching feature—in this case coming from the subject of the second conjunct. Let me illustrate this for the example in (2.66), repeated below as (2.68). Example (2.68a) is the first conjunct. T has its D-(EPP-)feature checked (and it has checked the case of *John*). Example (2.68b) is the stage of the derivation of the second conjunct before T gets copied. When T gets copied and moves sideward, it is bereft of its structural environment so that the features on the copied T are visible again. Thus, the copy arriving in the second conjunct is the one in (2.68c). I represent

---

[34] To alter a metaphor attributed to Bob Frank by Nunes (2004)—which says that features are painted blue when checked and the interfaces cannot see blue because it wears blue glasses—features are not painted blue but the configuration which enables feature checking is like a blue filter. Once a feature is not in that configuration anymore, it has lost its blue filter.

sideward-moved material, which comes without the phonology, in shaded font rather than by strikethrough to ease readability.

(2.68)   John got the food and Pete the drinks.

    a.   [$_{TP}$ John-N-ϕ-CASE [$_{T'}$ T-$_{D-\phi}$ [$_{vP}$ John-N-ϕ-CASE [$_{v'}$ got [$_{VP}$ got [$_{DP}$ the food-N-ϕ-CASE]]]]]

    b.   [$_{vP}$ Pete-N-ϕ-CASE [$_{v'}$ got [$_{VP}$ got [$_{DP}$ the drinks-N-ϕ-CASE]]]]

    c.   **T-D-$_\phi$**

Now, higher copies in a mono-clausal structure are obviously neither in the same feature matching configuration as their lower copies but features checked on lower copies should clearly not become visible again on the higher copies. I propose that chain formation of non-distinct copies ensures that they do not. Since in the structure I propose for gapping there is no c-command between the 'source' copies and the copies in the second conjunct, no chains can be formed and the features are visible in the new structural relation.

Similar observations as those for the EPP-feature of T hold for its ϕ-features. The copy of T which is to be merged in the second conjunct is not in a configuration anymore where its ϕ-features are checked. Therefore the ϕ-features are visible again. Like the EPP-feature, they will be checked by the subject of the second conjunct. This might result in different ϕ-features from those of the first conjunct: recall that the agreement on the gapped verb, onto which the affix(es) are eventually lowered, can be different from that of its antecedent, see (2.69), where the finite verb in the first conjunct agrees with a singular subject, and the gapped finite verb in the second conjunct, with a plural subject:

(2.69)   John is getting the food and the girls ~~are getting~~ the drinks.

The different ϕ-features on T are not realized phonologically because the phonology of the gapped verb has already been spelt out. So there is no identity of agreement features necessary in gapping. Interpretable features, on the other hand, such as tense or aspect are identical in the first and in the second conjunct because T (or Asp or the like) is copied with these interpretable features and therefore has the same contents in both conjuncts.

Let us next consider the case of gapped arguments such as *some grass* in (2.70):

(2.70)   John got some grass for his rabbits, and Mary ~~got some grass~~ for her guinea pigs.

Sideward movement of arguments of sentential heads is motivated by the subcategorization requirements of their heads. So a gapped direct object like *some grass* is copied because the verb *got*, which is copied for independent reasons (to build a convergent structure) has certain theta-specifications that need to be met.[35] In addition, case and agreement features need to be checked. Note that the verb, like the functional head T discussed above, leaves its structural configuration in the first conjunct when it is copied and merged with the second conjunct. The same holds for copied arguments. Therefore, the features on V as well as the argument(s) become visible and need to be checked 'again' in the second conjunct.

Once a convergent derivation for the second conjunct has been built, it can be spelt out. I assume that the normal operations necessary for this (e.g. chain reduction, chain uniformization) are carried out. The only difference with non-gapping sentences is that some material in the second conjunct has no phonology because that was spelt out before. Therefore, only the material that came in the numeration for the second conjunct will be realized at PF. Finally, first and second conjunct can be merged. The result is a structure like the one given in (2.71) for example (2.68) discussed above—neglecting movement to topic and focus positions for the moment. Again, sideward-moved material, which comes without phonology, is in shaded font. Chain reduced material is represented with strikethrough. Note that sideward-moved material does not need to be chain-reduced as it has no phonology. In this sense, it is immaterial for linearization. On the other hand, if we want to remain true to the spirit of Nunes' (1995, 2004) account of sideward movement and chain reduction, according to which all copies have the same status, we can assume that the sideward-moved copies are also subject to the linear correspondence axiom (Kayne 1994), which determines linearization and therefore chain reduction. The result will be the same because, again, the sideward-moved copies that are not chain-reduced have no phonology.

(2.71)   John got the food and Pete the drinks.
  [&P [TP John-N-ϕ-CASE [T' T-D–ϕ [νP ~~John-N-ϕ-CASE~~ [ν' got [VP ~~got~~
  [DP the food-N-ϕ-CASE]]]]]]
  [&' and [TP Pete-N-ϕ-CASE [T' T-D-ϕ [νP Pete-N-ϕ-CASE [ν' got [VP got
  [DP the drinks-N-ϕ-CASE]]]]]]]]]

Next I turn to the question of the negation in the distributed readings as well as adjuncts in gapping in general, which will deliver the main arguments for adopting a copying account rather than a deletion account for gapping.

---

[35] See Hornstein (1999) and Nunes (2004) for other contexts where movement into a theta-position is considered a trigger for sideward movement.

2.3.2 *Copying the negation (not!)*

Recall that English is more permissive when it comes to the interpretation of
an elided negation in the second conjunct than German. To account for this
I propose the following. If the negation is the head of a NegP (PolP) as in
English, it is copied because NegP (PolP) belongs to the sentential functional
projections. Its presence is categorially determined by T. If, however, the negation is an adjunct on *v*P, as in German, it is not copied—there is nothing that
requires this operation and economy forbids unnecessary copying. This proposal essentially makes use of the fact that sideward movement—like any other
operation in syntax—needs to serve a purpose, such as feature checking or
building a convergent derivation. As should have become clear in the previous
section, all that is needed to build a convergent structure from the numeration
of the second conjunct in gapping are the heads of the sentential (functional)
projections and their arguments. Adjuncts are not needed. Therefore, they are
not copied. This proposal is obviously only compatible with the assumption
that adverb(ial)s come in the form of adjuncts (e.g. Ernst 2002; Haider 2004)
and not in functional projections (e.g. Cinque 1999).

Now, as already mentioned in the introduction to this chapter, there are
cases where the negation, even in languages such as German, is interpreted
with perfect ease as being present in the second conjunct, see the examples in
(2.5), one of which is repeated here as (2.72):

(2.72)   Paul kann den russischen Film nicht ausstehen und Maria
          Paul can   the Russian   film not   stand   and Maria
          den französischen.
          the French
          'Paul can't stand the Russian film and Maria the French one.'

The verbal complex *ausstehen können* ('can stand') is a negative polarity item.
In the derivation of this gapping sentence, *ausstehen können*[36] will be copied
because it is required to produce an interpretable structure and because it will
check the case of the object. Since it is a negative polarity item, however, the
verbal complex needs to be licensed by the negation. Syntax is one of many
factors in the licensing of negative polarity items, which overall has received
great attention in the literature.[37] It is not quite clear how deeply syntax is

---

[36] Modals like *können* ('can') are also copied as they are one of the sentential functional projections
(see Chapter 4 for some references).

[37] See for instance Acquaviva (1997), Błaszczak (2001), Dowty (1994), Giannakidou (1998), Haege-
man (1995), Haspelmath (1997), Hoeksema (1983), Horn (1989, 1997), Kadmon and Landman (1993),
Krifka (1995), Ladusaw (1980, 1996), Lahiri (1998); Laka (1990), Linebarger (1987, 1991), Mahajan (1990),
Progovac (1994), Rowlett (1998), Tovena (1998), van der Wouden (1997), and many others.

involved in the relation between licenser and licensee but it seems clear that it plays a role. Negative polarity items must usually be c-commanded by their licenser, in our case, the negation. The relevant level is LF (e.g. Błaszczak 2001; Giannakidou 1998; Lahiri 1998; Linebarger 1987; Mahajan 1990; Progovac 1994). I therefore assume that the negation in (2.72) must be copied. Otherwise the derivation would crash.

I said that adjunct negation in normal, that is in non-NPI gapping, is not copied because this is not motivated. If this is indeed the case, one might expect the second conjunct to receive an interpretation with positive polarity, that is a narrow scope reading should arise. This, however, is not the case. Instead, the resulting gapping sentence is unacceptable, or marginal at best, the basic intuition being that the second conjunct dangles between a positive and negative interpretation. One might argue that this is because there is no positive morpheme, which realizes the polarity in the second conjunct, yet whether such a morpheme has to be present in every clause if there is no corresponding functional projection like a PolP, is far from clear.[38] If a polarity morpheme really is required in every clause, then even adjunct negation should be copied from the first conjunct—it would be required to form a convergent structure and the second conjunct should be negative. This is not what we find. Thus, since polarity morphemes are not required in a structure if they are not in a functional projection, a positive reading of the second conjunct should be available, contrary to fact.

In Chapter 3, I shall introduce the principle of balanced contrast in gapping (with 'and'). This principle says that the two conjuncts of a gapping coordination must make the same contribution to an overarching discourse topic. This is not given when one of the conjuncts is positive and the other negative and the contrasts evoked by the lexical material are balanced, for example:

(2.73)   #John didn't get the food and Pete got the drinks.

In a context where it is not expected that John and Pete would behave differently, for example in helping with the preparations for a party—which out-of-the-blue is a default situation—the coordination in (2.73) is distinctly odd. We shall see in Chapter 3 that the use of the conjunction *but* is what is required here. What we end up with then in the case of German gapping is a situation

---

[38] In Chapter 3, I shall argue that such a silent positive morpheme (for English the head of a PolP) is present in the second conjunct of the narrow scope readings. It contrasts with the negative morpheme of the first conjunct (directly or as part of a predicate), and comes with the numeration of the second conjunct.

where a positive reading is excluded for semantic-pragmatic reasons and a negative reading cannot be derived syntactically.

For adjuncts other than the negation, the failure to copy them does not have such drastic consequences. As we saw earlier (Section 2.2.2), even in non-elliptic contexts, it is possible to accommodate, for example local specifications, from the left context. I repeat the relevant example:

(2.74)   He turned off the fire in his study because it was too warm.

(Hudson 1976: 536)

The cause clause in (2.74) is underspecified. It can mean that is was too warm outside or in the study, or that the fire itself was too warm. The most likely interpretation is that it was too warm in the study. I shall assume here that similar accommodation processes are available in gapping. The parallelism required in gapping will aid such accommodation. Accommodation is *not* available for the negation:[39] accommodation of the negation from the context is very implausible as the accommodated structure would have the opposite meaning to the non-accommodated structure. The general availability of such accommodation would create chaos in conversation.

It is important to note that the reluctance to interpret the negation in the second conjunct of a gapping sentence is a problem specific to the gapping construction. I pointed this out above where I showed that, for instance, sluicing and right node raising, which like VP ellipsis are often assumed to be derived via deletion, do not display this behaviour.[40] Also, the problem obviously does not arise in non-elliptic contexts. Since the numeration in non-elliptic clauses contains all those elements that are visible at PF, it also contains the negative marker (as well as 'invisible' functional elements). Importantly, before a derivation can converge, the numeration has to be emptied. So, if the negation (or anything else) remains in the numeration, the derivation cannot converge because the numeration is not empty.

Similarly, if sluicing and right node raising are derived by deletion (e.g. Merchant 2001 for sluicing, Hartmann 2000 for right node raising) we do not expect adjuncts, including the negation, to behave in any special way. The conjuncts are derived in the same way as their non-elliptic counterparts— they have the same numerations as their non-elliptic counterparts (save,

---

[39] There might be some exceptions to this. See note 3 in this chapter for a context that clearly aids a negative interpretation, which makes the sentence in note 3 acceptable for some speakers.

[40] VP ellipsis itself is irrelevant here because a negation in the elliptic conjunct always is expressed overtly:

(i)   John read the book but Pete did *(not).

perhaps for an E(llipsis)-feature on one of the heads). The ellipsis is a PF-phenomenon.

Obviously, it has also been argued that sluicing might be the result of LF copying (e.g. Chung *et al.* 1995; Fortin 2007). The difference with copying in gapping, I would like to argue, is that if sluicing is indeed derived by copying, the elements that are copied are different from those that are copied in gapping. The copying accounts of sluicing assume that the *wh*-phrase in the second conjunct is merged in Spec,CP and then an entire TP is copied from the first conjunct, with everything that is in it. This includes the negation. The second conjunct in gapping, in contrast, I argued would be built from bottom to top, where material which needs to be copied from the second conjunct is copied in individual steps. Since adjunct negation is not needed to build a convergent derivation it is not copied.

My analysis of gapping also sets gapping apart from sluicing and right node raising when it comes to island-sensitivity.[41] I mentioned in Chapter 1 that sluicing is insensitive to many islands. The same holds for right node raising (Hartmann 2000). Gapping is much more restricted.[42] In his deletion account of sluicing, Merchant (2001) proposes that islands are a feature of PF and that through the PF deletion process island violations are erased, which is why sluicing can violate islands. Similarly, Hartmann (2000) assumes that right node raising is a process of phonological deletion so that islands should not play a role. If gapping is not deletion as I argue, it is not expected to behave like sluicing or right node raising with respect to islands.

The copying accounts of sluicing (e.g. Chung *et al.* 1995; Fortin 2007) can also explain the islands facts: since the *wh*-phrase in Spec,CP does not arrive there by movement, sluicing is not expected to violate islands. The copying process in gapping is different. The derivation is built like any ordinary derivation from bottom to top. If the contrastive phrases are moved to a higher topic and focus position gapping should violate islands and so it does. Thus, no matter whether sluicing is derived by deletion or by copying, there are good reasons to assume that the different behaviour of gapping versus sluicing and right node raising with respect to the negation and islands falls out from the differential analyses.

To conclude, I have argued that gapping is a copying process where the second conjunct is derived from the first by sideward movement of material whose phonology has already been spelt out. The copying process is licensed

---

[41] VP ellipsis is subject to islands, see Chapter 1, note 9.

[42] I am glossing over the many additional issues of embedding in gapping here.

by the requirement to build a convergent structure from a numeration that only contains those elements that are visible on the surface in the gapping conjunct. Elements which are required for the derivation of a convergent structure but are not part of the numeration are copied. Since adjuncts are not required in this sense they are not copied.[43]

---

[43] This account is different from the one I proposed in Repp (2005), which faces some problems that are not shared by the account I developed above. Nevertheless, it has some attractive features that are worth exploring. Starting from the idea of post-cyclic adjunction (see Section 2.2.1, I proposed in Repp (2005) that adjuncts are copied post-cyclically in gapping. The fact that they are copied at all I ascribed to the parallelism requirement in gapping. I assumed that as soon as LF can produce an interpretable structure the semantic component will try an interpretation. This happens after the cyclic operations have been completed. The result is a narrow scope reading. There is a second time round, though, for the semantic component. A second interpretation can be carried out after post-cyclic merger. This results in a distributed reading, i.e. the second conjunct would be interpreted as negative. Since the result of the first interpretation and that of the second interpretation are contradictory for the second conjunct, the resulting sentence is ungrammatical. There is a fatal ambiguity if you will. For adjuncts other than the negation, the late merger has not such drastic consequences: as in the present account, I assumed that accommodation was available. The problem with this view is that ambiguity is an ordinary phenomenon (although ellipsis avoids *some* ambiguity, cf. Fox (2000) and the literature cited therein). It should not lead to unacceptability. Also, it is not quite clear why the second interpretation should not simply overwrite the first.

3

The right kind of contrast: Narrow scope readings

There are various contexts that produce narrow scope readings. The topic of this chapter is the narrow scope readings that arise in contexts other than corrections (see Chapter 4 for the latter). The narrow scope readings investigated here—as different as the details in their analysis may be—arise for one main reason: the contrast between the conjuncts must be right. What this means, depends on the conjunction used.[1] With the conjunction *and*, gapping wants its conjuncts to be as parallel as possible, which for the contrastive relationship between the conjuncts means that the contrast must be balanced. Balanced contrast is contrast where both conjuncts, although different, make the same kind of contribution to a discourse topic. What this means precisely will be made explicit in Section 3.2, where I argue for the following principle:

(3.1) PRINCIPLE OF BALANCED CONTRAST (PBC), CONJUNCTION 'AND'
In gapping, both conjuncts must make the same kind of contribution to a common discourse topic.

The PBC accounts for the occurrence of narrow scope readings in auxiliary gapping (Section 3.3) and in gapping with focus particles (Section 3.4). I also

---

[1] I am only considering contrastive *but*, corrective *but* (Chapter 4), and *and* in this book. There is of course the conjunction *or*, which brings along its own felicity conditions when it comes to negation as we might already expect from its logical underpinnings. Furthermore, there are conjunctions such as Dutch *laat staan* or German *geschweige denn*, both similar to English *let alone*, which also elicit narrow scope readings in gapping, see (i) for a Dutch example. These conjunctions are also interesting for the fact that they select for a subordinated clause that in its underlying form is introduced by a complementizer, which is a challenge for the otherwise observed parallelism in gapping.

(i) Johan heeft Karin niet meer opgebeld, laat staan ~~dat~~ Karin Johan ~~heeft opgebeld~~.
Johan has Karin not more called   let stand that Karin Johan has   called
'Johan hasn't called Karin anymore, let alone Karin Johan.'   (Van der Heijden 1999: 127)

I shall also pass over complex conjunctions like *both–and, either–or, neither–nor*.

appealed to it in Chapter 2 when I discussed differences between English and German in the distributed scope readings.

For contrastive *but* (German *aber*), the right kind of contrast also plays an important role. Here, we find that the two conjuncts make opposing contributions to a discourse topic. Importantly, *but* interacts with the information structure of the coordinations it occurs in (e.g. Umbach 2001, 2005; Sæbø 2003), which I take to be the reason for the occurrence of the narrow scope readings in gapping. I begin my discussion with contrastive *but* in Section 3.1 (for more details, see Repp to appear).

3.1 Contrastive *but*

In the introduction to this study, I showed that the presence of *but* in a gapping structure can result in a positive interpretation of the second conjunct, that is to say it can produce a narrow scope reading. I repeat the relevant example:

(3.2)   Pete wasn't called by Vanessa but John by Jessie.
        = Pete wasn't called by Vanessa but John was called by Jessie.
        $(\neg A) \wedge B$

It has been suggested that contrastive *but*, German *aber*, marks a scope boundary for negation and other propositional operators (Lang 1991).[2] The aim of the present section is to find out why it should do that. Since *but* is problematic in most environments in English (See Section 1.1), I restrict my discussion to German *aber*.

3.1.1 *The meaning of contrastive* but

The meaning of *but* has been of interest in the philosophical and linguistic literature at least since Frege (1879), see Merin (1996) for an overview. Defining its semantics has proven difficult because it is very flexible in its use. The common intuition about *but* is that it signals a contrast between two

---

[2] It is indeed only propositional negation which is affected here and not e.g. constituent negation. In the gapping example below, the *als*-phrase, which can be considered a small clause, marks the scope boundary for the negation contained in it. The conjunction *but* does not interact with this negation:

(i)   Peter erwies   sich   erst   Gestern   als   nicht   freundlich   aber   Maria   schon   vor
      Peter turned.out REFL   only   yesterday as   not   friendly   but   Mary   already before
      einigen   Tagen.
      a.few   days
      'Peter turned out to be not friendly only yesterday but Mary already (turned out to be not friendly) a few days ago.'

states-of-affairs, and that the state-of-affairs denoted by the second conjunct denies or negates conclusions that (might) have been drawn from the meaning of the first conjunct. There have been several attempts to distinguish various uses of *but*. Lakoff (1971) distinguishes semantic opposition, illustrated in (3.3a), and denial of expectation, illustrated in (3.3b).

(3.3)   a.   The girl is short but the boy is tall.

b.   The girl is tall but no good at basketball.

In semantic opposition, the order of the conjuncts is irrelevant. There is no logical relation between them. The predicate of one conjunct is negated in the other. In denial of expectation, the order of the conjuncts does matter. A presupposition of the first conjunct is not met in the second conjunct, or the first conjunct produces an expectation, which is claimed to be unjustified by the second conjunct. Thus, in (3.3b), the first conjunct suggests that the girl should be good at basketball—considering that she is tall—and the second conjunct says that this expectation is not borne out: the girl is no good at basketball. Schematically, this can be expressed as follows:

(3.4)   *p but q* corresponds to *p and therefore* $\neg$ *q, but actually q.*

This formula has become somewhat of a standard formula for the semantics of the conjunction. Nevertheless, it can been seen as a special case of a more general formula which expresses the relation between the two conjuncts in a more indirect way in the sense that there is a third proposition in the background which serves as a point of reference: whereas the first conjunct supports this proposition, the second conjunct does not (e.g. Anscombre and Ducrot 1977; Dik 1968; Ducrot 1973; Fogelin 1967; Lang 1991; Merin 1996). Thus, in a sentence such as (3.5) the proposition in the background could be that the child can be trusted with some urgent and delicate job. The first conjunct supports this proposition, the second does not.

(3.5)   The child is quick enough but he's too clumsy.

It has been a matter of dispute how the third proposition in the background is actually arrived at if it is not given as a more or less explicit discourse topic. World knowledge has been made responsible (Lang 1991) but also the (information structure of the) conjuncts themselves (Umbach 2005). I shall not go into this matter here.

There have been several proposals to unify the different 'uses' of *but* in a minimal semantic or pragmatic formula. Most take one of the two aspects just highlighted—semantic opposition (or contrast), denial of expectation—or also concession, as a basis. Since gapping requires at least two contrasts between its two conjuncts (see Chapter 1), an exploration of the semantics of *but* in terms of contrast seems the most promising. Such theories have been proposed by Lang (1991), Sæbø (2003) and Umbach (2001, 2005). The latter two accounts additionally argue that *but* interacts with the information structure of the coordination, which will be the key to my analysis of the gapping sentences.[3] For more discussion of alternative accounts, the interested reader is referred to the literature, see for instance Adamíkova (2004), Asher (1993), Bach (1999), Blakemore (1987, 2000), Gaerdenfors (1994), Koenig and Benndorf (1998), Lang (1984, 1991, 2001, 2002, 2003, 2004), Lang and Adamíkova (2007), Lang and Umbach (2002), Malchukov (2004), Mann and Thompson (1988), Merin (1996), Oversteegen (1997), Rieber (1997), Winter and Rimon (1994); for an overview of the literature up to the late 1980s see Rudolph (1996).

To get started on the notion of contrast in coordinations with contrastive *but* consider Lang's (1991) general instruction for these structures:

(3.6)   SIMUL X, Y: [CONTRAST X, Y]

SIMUL is a meaning component that combines conjoined states-of-affairs, individuals, or predicates as compatible instances of a common integrator—roughly, a common theme. SIMUL is part of the meaning of many conjunctions. Besides *but*, *and* is also among them (see Section 3.2). Since in (3.7) the conjuncts are incompatible, the coordination—with *and* or *but*—is ungrammatical (also e.g. Anscombre and Ducrot 1977):

(3.7)   *Max$_i$ is tall but/and he$_i$ is short.

The second part of the formula in (3.6) requires the two conjuncts to contrast. Lang (1991) follows here the 'indirect' approach via a third proposition in the background discussed above.[4] In addition, he points out that coordinations with *but* are often structured along the following schema:

(3.8)   A-B but A′-C
        B is predicated of A; C is predicated of A′; A′ is a minimally different variant of A.

This is illustrated in (3.9), where the subjects of the two conjuncts correspond to A and A′ respectively, and the predicates to B and C:

---

[3] Lang (2002, 2004), Adamíkova (2004) and Lang and Adamíkova (2007) also investigate the information structure of coordinations with *aber* but do not go as far as to assume that the conjunction 'associates' with (contrastive) topics, which is the route I will follow here.

[4] His term is a meaning 'dimension' in the background.

(3.9)   Max is tall but Mike is short.

The schema in (3.8) suggests that *but* involves at least two minimal semantic differences (the observation is originally due to Bellert 1972; also see Oversteegen 1997). This is why (3.10), where only the subjects contrast, is bad:[5]

(3.10)   *Max is tall but Mike is tall.

The schema in (3.8) covers this. It recurs in an information structural guise in the accounts of Umbach (2001, 2005) and Sæbø (2003). It is also quite similar to the shape of coordinations with contrastive topics coming with contrastive foci (e.g. Büring 1997a, 2003). Still, the schema cannot account in itself for the fact that the negation in the second conjunct of a gapping sentence 'disappears'. Consider the following example:

(3.11)   *Carl and Harry collect insects but they are not much interested in the winged varieties. When I had them over to show them my bug collection I offered Carl a tortoise shell butterfly and Harry a stick insect in exchange for some bugs they had brought for me:*
         Carl (obviously) didn't take the tortoise shell butterfly but, (curiously), Harry didn't take the stick insect (either).

Example (3.11) shows that both conjuncts can be negative if there is a suitable context, a suitable proposition in the background. There are two individuals, Carl and Harry, about whom different things are predicated. Furthermore, what is said about the first individual supports the background proposition, which is that Carl and Harry collect insects but are not much interested in the winged varieties, and what is said about the second individual does not support the background proposition. All requirements for the use of *but* are met. Nevertheless, both conjuncts happily accommodate a negation. In addition, since gapping typically involves two contrasts (where one usually involves the subjects and the other the objects), we do not expect a contrast between the polarities of the two conjuncts to be necessary in any way by the above account.[6]

---

[5] There are well-known exceptions to the two-contrast generalization:

(i)   Max is short but strong.

(ii) Max is tall but Mike is tall, too.

Lang gives an account for these (also see Merin (1996) for a proposal). They are not directly pertinent for my problem.

[6] There is an interesting case with differing polarities in the two conjuncts, which I shall not investigate in this study but which is worth drawing attention to: the example below, where *nicht aber*

3.1.2 Contrastive but is sensitive to information structure

I indicated that accounts which consider *but* to be sensitive to the information structure of the clause (Sæbø 2003; Umbach 2001, 2005) open up a way to motivate the behaviour of the negation in gapping. What does it mean for *but* to be sensitive to the information structure? Consider the following example from Umbach (2005: 208):

(3.12) Adam: What did the small children do today?   (Umbach 2005: 208)
Ben:

   a. The BIgger children stayed at home
       {but/ ??and} the smAller children went to the zoo.

   b. The smAller children stayed at home
       {but/ ??and} the BIgger children went to the zoo.

According to Umbach (2001, 2005), (3.12) shows that contrastive *but* can introduce a new topic—*the bigger children*—where *topic* is meant in the aboutness sense (Reinhart 1981) with the additional assumption that the topic be contrastive, that is that it elicit alternatives like a focus. Example (3.12) also shows that *and* cannot add such a topic in the given context.

Sæbø (2003) puts forward the following argument for the relevance of information structure to the analysis of *but*. In German, *aber* can take various positions in the clause. Sæbø suggests that *aber*, if placed after the constituent in the forefield (Spec,CP), demarcates this constituent as a contrastive topic, that is, like Umbach, he acknowledges the special role of a topic that comes with alternatives. The idea is that the context provides an alternative for the topic and contradicts the result of substituting the topic with its alternative. Consider the following example (Sæbø 2003: 262):

(3.13) Die Frauen machen 66% der   Beschäftigten im
        the women   make   66% the.GEN workforce   in.the
        öffentlichen Sektor aus—
        public   sector out
        'Women constitute 66% of the workforce in the public sector—'

occurs clause-initially in the first conjunct, is only good as an elliptical structure and in small conjunct coordination. These data, to my knowledge, have not received any attention yet.

(i) Warum vertauscht ein Spiegel rechts und links, nicht aber unten und oben?
     why   reverses   a   mirror right and left, not   but bottom and top
   / *warum vertauscht er nicht aber oben und unten?
      why   reverses   he not   but top and bottom
   'Why does a mirror reverse right and left, but not top and bottom?'

a. die Chefstellungen aber haben die Männer für sich
    the top.positions   but have the men   for themselves
    reserviert.
    reserved
    'but the top positions are occupied by men.'

b. ?die Männer aber haben die Chefstellungen für sich
    the men   but have the top.positions for themselves
    reserviert.
    reserved
    'but men occupy the top positions.'

In (3.13a), the first clause provides an alternative to the topic constituent *die Chefstellungen* ('the top positions'), which is *66% der Beschäftigten* ('66% of the workforce'). Replacing the topic by its alternative results in the claim that 66% of the workforce are men. This is contradicted by the first clause, which states that 66% of the workforce are women. The conditions for placing *but* after the element in Spec,CP are met, (3.13a) is good. In (3.13b), the topic is *die Männer* ('men'). If this is replaced by its alternative, which is *die Frauen* ('women'), the second clause says that women occupy the top positions. This is not contradicted by the first clause: the first clause does not have anything to say about top positions in relation to women. The use of *but* after Spec,CP is not warranted.

Additional evidence for the idea that the Spec,CP position before *aber* is reserved for contrastive aboutness topics comes from left dislocation data. There are two types of left dislocation in German. One is the hanging topic construction, illustrated in (3.14a). According to Frey (2004), 'hanging topic' really is a misnomer because this construction does not involve an aboutness topic. The other type is weak pronoun left dislocation, illustrated in (3.14b), which is an aboutness topic. In weak pronoun left dislocation, a resumptive weak d-pronoun (*die*) occurs before the finite verb. In a hanging topic left dislocation, a resumptive pronoun (or some other resuming expression) can occur lower down in the structure.

(3.14) a. ??Meine Schwester aber, laut   Max wird sie erst
            my   sister   but according.to Max will she only
            morgen   kommen.
            tomorrow   come
            'But my sister, according to Max, she will only come tomorrow.'

b. Meine Schwester aber, die hat mit dem Nachbarsjungen
   my   sister   but she has with the   neighbour's.boy
   gespielt.
   played
   'But my sister—she played with the boy from next door.'

The hanging topic construction in (3.14a) is considerably worse than the weak pronoun left dislocation in (3.14b), which indicates that *meine Schwester*, if placed before *aber*, must be a topic. Furthermore, according to Shaer and Frey (2004), the left-peripheral element in weak pronoun left dislocation must serve as a 'link' to previous discourse in terms of a partially ordered set relation to an entity evoked in previous discourse. This latter aspect agrees well with Sæbø's (2003) observations for the element in Spec,CP, before *aber*. Hanging topics do not necessarily serve as links and, as (3.14a) shows, *aber* is bad after hanging topics.

There are data that seem problematic for the topic analysis. As Hans-Martin Gärtner (p.c.) points out, *wh*-interrogatives can occur in Spec,CP before the conjunction *aber* even though they are generally considered bad topics:[7]

(3.15) Wer aber ist gekommen?
        who but is come
        'But who came?'

However, as is argued by Hinterwimmer and Repp (2008), *wh*-phrases do share some features with topics, more specifically with topical indefinites. Topical indefinites first establish a discourse address and then some information is stored under this address. It has been suggested that this can be captured via presuppositions: topical indefinites presuppose their existence and these presuppositions update the common ground first (Reinhart 1981; Cresti 1995; Yeom 1998; Portner and Yabushita 2001). As for *wh*-interrogatives, many analyses assume that an interrogative with a *wh*-phrase introduces a referent by presupposition (e.g. Comorovski 1996; Dayal 1996; Hagstrom 1998; Hintikka 1978; Karttunen 1977):[8]

(3.16) Who called John? *presupposes* Someone called John.

---

[7] For some remarks on the prosody of these constructions, see Repp (to appear).

[8] The matter is not undebated, largely because of the possibility of answering a question like (3.16) with (i). This, however, as has been argued by many, can be viewed as presupposition protest. Furthermore, as has been observed by Haida (2003), it is not possible to answer (3.16) with (ii) unless one wants to appear secretive or be impolite (also see the literature cited above).

(i) Nobody called John.

(ii) Somebody called John.

In addition, the interrogative requires that more information be provided about the presupposed referent: ideally, the answer reveals the identity of the caller. There is a clear parallel with topics here. An address is created by the *wh*-question under which the information supplied by the answer is to be stored. Against this background, it is not surprising that a *wh*-phrase can occur before *aber* in Spec,CP.

Finally, consider that elements which cannot bear focus and cannot be accented, such as weak *es*, are not allowed before *aber* in Spec,CP:

(3.17) a.   Das Mädchen aber hat auf dem Hof gespielt.
             the girl   but has on the   yard played

        b.   *Es aber hat auf dem Hof gespielt.
             it but has on the   yard played
             '{The girl/ *It}, however, played in the courtyard.'

To sum up, there are many reason to assume that the element in Spec,CP, if followed by *aber*, is a contrastive topic. Taken together with Umbach's (2001) findings this clearly indicates that *aber* associates with contrastive topics and is sensitive to the information structure of the clause (for more details and other positions in the clause *aber* can take, see Repp to appear).

Having argued that *aber* is sensitive to information structure, that it associates with contrastive topics, let us turn to the exact role this plays in the information-structural accounts of *aber* proposed by Umbach (2001, 2005) and Sæbø (2003).[9] I laid out the basics of Sæbø's (2003) account above, when I discussed example (3.13). Here is his semantics of the conjunction:[10]

(3.18) σ ⟦but φ ⟧ τ iff σ ⟦φ⟧ τ and σ |⊨ ¬φ [T(φ) / α] for some
        alternative α

Thus, a sentence φ containing *but* changes the information status σ to τ, iff the same sentence φ without *but* does so and iff σ presupposes that there is an alternative to the topic of that sentence, for which φ does not hold. Sæbø remarks that 'what is denied is not a context clause or an inference thereof, but some part of context clause combined with some part of the contrast clause' (2003: 270). Thus he explicitly departs from the more traditional assumption of a third proposition in the background.

Umbach's approach (2001, 2005) is very similar. She also proposes that *but* associates with a contrastive topic (or a focus) in the second conjunct of

---

[9] All-focus constructions are problematic for the idea that a topic is always the central component in the semantics of *but*. Sæbø (2003) can deal with such cases by some general accommodation mechanisms.

[10] This is not Sæbø's (2003) final version, which is not important for the present purposes.

a coordination. This provides the so-called expected alternative, which has a sister alternative in the first conjunct.[11] There is then a denial condition which says that the proposition which results from substituting the expected alternative for the sister alternative is false. So far Umbach's (2001, 2005) and Sæbø's (2003) accounts are more or less the same. The point where Umbach differs from Sæbø is that she subscribes to a version of the assumption that there is a third proposition in the background. Instead of a proposition, though, she works with a question, the so-called quaestio—roughly, a backward-looking question under discussion, which is reconstructed from the information structure of the actual utterance. Umbach (2005: 211) considers the quaestio 'a diagnostic tool displaying the contextual conditions for the utterance to be felicitious'. In the case of *but*-coordinations, the quaestio is assumed to be a two-part question, see (3.19). The first conjunct is supposed to answer the quaestio in the positive whereas the second conjunct answers it in the negative:

(3.19)   [John $_{\text{topic/sister alternative}}$] [cleared the room $_{\text{Foc}}$] but
         [Bill $_{\text{topic/expected alternative}}$][did the dishes $_{\text{Foc}}$].
         Quaestio: Did John clear up the room and did he wash the dishes?

The quaestio can be compared to a discourse topic if that is formulated as a question.[12] To ensure coherence of the conjuncts within the coordination and of the coordination with the context, Umbach furthermore suggests that the quaestio interacts with an additional, forward-looking question. I shall not go into the details of this here.

Umbach (2001) looks at two-contrast coordinations such as the one in (3.19) in quite some detail.[13] She points out that (3.19) meets her confirm+denial condition without involving an explicit negation. The denial is implicit: (3.19)

---

[11] The two alternatives contain each other in their respective alternative sets. This is basically what Rooth (1992) and Hartmann (2000) state for contrastive coordinations (see subsection 3.4.1.5 for details).

[12] The formulation of the quaestio can get rather complicated. Also, it is not always clear, why a two-part question is necessary: in the above example a single polarity question such as *Did John do the housework?* can do the job, too. The first conjunct answers this question in the positive and the second in the negative.

[13] Sæbø (2003) has problems with two-contrast coordinations because he relies on the notion of presupposition. Consider (i) and assume that the subjects are the topics:

(i)   [Tom$_{\text{alternative}}$] is tall but [Pete $_{\text{topic}}$] is strong.
      $\sigma \Vdash \neg$ (Pete is strong) [Pete $_{\text{topic}}$ /Tom $_{\text{alternative}}$] iff
      $\sigma \Vdash \neg$ (Tom is strong) $= false$

Contrary to what is indicated by the formula, the context does not presuppose (or assert) that it is not the case that Tom is strong. It only says that Tom is tall. With the predicates as topics (a possibility Sæbø generally allows) the result is also not as desired. As *strong-tall* are not a priori alternatives, the alternativeness has to be accommodated: Sæbø (2003: 10) suggests that the complement of the entails that John did not do the dishes and that Bill did not clear the room. These entailments are typical of *but* yet they can occur as implicatures with *and*. As implicatures, they can be cancelled:[14]

(3.20)   John cleared the room $^{??}but/$ *and* Bill did the dishes, actually though, {Bill cleared the room too / John did the dishes too}.

Umbach (2005) suggests that the entailments arise due to a distinctiveness condition (Krifka 1999), which requires contrastive topics to have different focus predications. Also see Büring (2003) on this. I will demonstrate in the next section that this distinctiveness in combination with *but*'s (or *aber*'s) association with a contrastive topic can account for the narrow scope readings in gapping with negation.

3.1.3 *Contrastive* but *and negation in gapping: contrastive topics and foci*

The next step in the exploration of *aber* and the information structure of the coordinations it occurs in is to investigate the exact information structure of the narrow scope readings in gapping. In order to do this, I shall have a close look at the intonation of these constructions. I use the example in (3.21) in this section, which can be intoned in various ways, two of which are given in (3.21a, 3.21b). The fully grammatical version is the one in (3.21a), where the subject and object of the first conjunct carry a rising accent, and the negation carries a falling accent. The second conjunct has a rising accent on the subject and a falling accent on the object. The two conjuncts form individual intonational phrases (with a rising or falling boundary tone). The difference between (3.21a) versus (3.21b) is that the latter does not have an accent on the negation and a high boundary tone in the first conjunct:[15]

---

predicate serves as the topic. What is substituted, however, is the predicate without the negation, so that the formula makes the wrong predictions:

(ii) $\sigma \Vdash \neg\,(\neg[\text{Pete is strong}])\ [\text{strong}_{\text{topic}}/\text{tall}_{\text{alternative}}]$ iff
        $\sigma \Vdash \neg\,(\neg(\text{Pete is tall}))$ iff
        $\sigma \Vdash (\text{Pete is tall}). = \textit{false}$

The third possibility, that the second conjunct is all focus, does not match the contrastive structure of (i).

[14] See Repp (to appear) for an argument that in the case of *but* we are actually dealing with cancellable implicatures, too.

[15] The data have been tested with native speakers in a non-laboratory situation. The actual phonetic parameters obviously need to be determined in an experimental set-up. The accent on the object *meine Katze* in the first conjunct is in principle optional because the cat is given in the context. With an accent, however, the construction sounds more natural and is preferred by speakers: the intonation is more in line with the contrast marking within the coordination, more on this below. The same holds for the subject.

(3.21)   *Carl and Harry hate ordinary pets. Last Christmas, I asked Carl to look after my cat for a week, and Harry to look after my hamster.*

    a.   Carl hat meine Katze nicht genommen, aber
        L* H   L* H   H* L   L- L%
        Harry meinen Hamster.
        L* H   H* L L%

    b.   ?Carl hat meine Katze nicht genommen, aber Harry meinen
        L* H   L* H   H-H%   L* H
        Hamster.
        H* L L%
        'Carl did not take my cat but Harry took my hamster.'

In the following discussion I use a forward slash to mark the L*H accent and a backward slash to mark the H*L accent. Note that (3.21a) can also be expressed by a construction that has an affirmative particle such as *schon* ('still') in the second conjunct. This makes the contrast relations between the two conjuncts explicit, and the intonation in the two conjuncts absolutely parallel, in the sense that the second conjunct like the first has rising accents on the subject and object, and a falling accent on a polarity element.

(3.22)   /Carl hat meine /Katze \nicht genommen, aber /Harry meinen /Hamster \schon.

Importantly, the accent pattern given in (3.21a) and (3.22) is typical of the conjunction *but*. If *but* is replaced by *and*, with the falling accent on the negation retained, the coordination becomes ungrammatical:

(3.23)   */Carl hat meine /Katze \nicht genommen, und /Harry meinen \Hamster.

I argued above that *but* associates with contrastive topics and assumed that contrastive topics come with their respective foci. I propose that the foci in question are the negative and the positive polarity. Contrastive topics in German are usually assumed to be marked by a rising accent L*H (e.g. Büring 1994, 1997a, 2003; Féry 1993; Frascarelli & Hinterhölzl 2007; Höhle 1992; Jacobs 1982, 1996;[16] Krifka 1998). A focus is assumed to be marked by a fall H* L, at least when in nuclear position (prenuclear foci can be indicated by L*H,

---

[16] Jacobs (1996) actually argues that a fall–rise accent HL* H is the appropriate accent. Evidence from corpora (Frascarelli and Hinterhölzl 2007) and experiments (Féry 1993), however, suggest that L* H is sufficient.

Féry 1993). The two accents together, that is a sequence of a contrastive topic and a focus is known by the name of *bridge* or *hat contour*. This suggests that the falling accent on the negation (3.21a) and (3.22) signals a focus, whereas the other accents might be contrastive topics (although they might also be prenuclear foci).

Turning to context, observe that a typical discourse question that the sentence in (3.21a) would answer is a polarity question like (3.24a), or, abstracting over the conjuncts, like (3.24b) (also recall Umbach's 2001, 2005 observations on this).

(3.24)   a.   Did Carl and Harry take the pets?

         b.   Did x take y?

Thus, the discourse clearly indicates that the focus of the answer is the polarity. Since foci are typically accented in German we expect an accent on the negation (for the missing accent on the positive polarity in the second conjunct of felicitous (3.21a), see below).

Büring's (1997*a*, 2003) theory of contrastive topics and foci in a well-formed discourse, as it is developed in Büring (2003) is well-suited to make the above claims more explicit. Büring (2003), similarly to van Kuppevelt (1995, 1996) represents discourses in discourse trees (also see Roberts 1996). Each node in such a tree represents a syntactic phrase marker which corresponds to a declarative or interrogative sentence. Büring proposes that a contrastive topic *indicates a strategy* in a discourse, where a *strategy* is a subtree in the discourse tree that is rooted in a node representing an interrogative sentence, and where *to indicate a strategy* means:

(3.25)   To INDICATE a STRATEGY (Büring 2003: 520):
         There is a non-singleton set Q' of questions such that for each $Q \in Q'$

         (i)   Q is identical to or a sister of the question that immediately dominates the utterance U containing the contrastive topic accent, and

         (ii) $[\![Q]\!]^\circ \in [\![U]\!]^{ct}$

The notation $[\![\ ]\!]^{ct}$ indicates a function that yields CT-values, which is an extension of the function that produces focus semantic values (Rooth 1992; also see Section 3.4.1). Informally, it is formed in two steps. First the focus is replaced by a *wh*-word, which is then fronted; or, if the finite verb or the negation are focused, the finite verb is fronted instead. Second, a set of questions is formed from the result of step 1 by replacing the contrastive topic by some alternative to it. To illustrate, consider a simplified variant of the first conjunct in (3.21a)—one with only two accents: a rising accent on the subject and a falling accent on the negation. (I come back to the version with three accents below):

(3.26)   /CARL hat meine Katze\NICHT genommen.
          step 1: Did Carl$_{CT}$ not stroke my cat?—*fronting of finite verb*
          step 2: Did Harry$_{alternative}$ not stroke my cat?—*substitution by alternative*

The formal CT-value, which is an abstraction over the question set,[17] looks as follows:

(3.27)   ⟦Carl$_{CT}$ did not take my cat$_F$⟧^{ct}= {{(x took my cat); ¬(x took my cat)} | x ∈ D$_e$} ≈ Did x not take my cat?

When inferring a strategy from a contrastive topic, hearers also infer a more complex discourse structure. The utterance /CARL *did* \NOT *take my cat* constitutes only the left branch of the strategy it indicates. Hearers infer that in addition there is a right branch. This right branch, like the left branch, must answer the question *Did x not take my cat?* It is prompted by a(n implicit) sub-question such as *Did Harry not take my cat?* The assumption that there must be a right branch of a strategy is a conventional implicature triggered by the contrastive accent. Furthermore, as already mentioned above, speakers infer that for a different x from Carl, the answer to the question *Did x not take my cat?* will be different than for Carl.[18] This means that in the sentences under investigation, a focus accent on the negation in the first conjunct makes the hearer expect a difference in polarity in the second conjunct.

Let us turn to (3.21a) in its original version, that is with three accents in the first conjunct instead of only two. The question that immediately comes to mind is whether the third accent on the object is a topic accent or a focus accent. I suggest that it is a topic accent and that the object—and the subject—are contrastive topics 'of sorts'. 'Of sorts' because there cannot be two contrastive topics that come with only one focus. There are two routes one can take from here. One is to argue that we have what I shall call a *complex topic*, the other is to assume that there are *stacked topics*. Both options have been

---

[17] The alternative set of the topics and foci must be contextually restricted, also see subsection 3.4.1.5 on this.

[18] The option to continue potential left branches with *but I don't know about the others* or the like makes clear that the implicature about the contrastiveness of the focus can be cancelled. For more on the exact implicatures, see for instance Hara (2006) or Hara and Van Rooy (2007).

suggested in different contexts before: the complex topic by Büring (2003), the stacked topics by Krifka (1999). In the case of stacked topics, there are several topics where one takes scope over the other. The idea Krifka (1999) sketches is that the speaker selects a discourse entity as the main topic where a piece of information is to be stored and divides this piece of information further into a secondary topic and a comment. A complex topic allows for the occurrence of 'equally ranked sub-alternatives' in one clause, as in (3.28) below. In (3.28), the contrastive topic in A1 is the entire subject, the CT-value being a question set of the form *Where will x sit?* Observe that the contrastive topic contains two accented elements as well as deaccented material. The deaccented material, *of the couple*, is also part of the CT, as is evidenced by the second answer A2. For this second answer to be felicitous, the CT-value could not be a question set like *Where will x of the couple sit?* Now, according to Büring, a contrastive topic is in reality a combination of a CT-mark and an F-mark (also see Krifka 1998). Whereas CTs mark strategies, F-marks are assumed to mark elements that are not given (principle Avoid F!, Schwarzschild 1999). The CT-mark dominates the F-mark. Thus, the CT in (3.28) contains two F-marks and the deaccented material:

(3.28) *Where will the guests at Ivan and Theona's wedding be seated?*
    A1: [Friends$_F$ and Relatives$_F$ of the couple]$_{CT}$ will sit [at the Table]$_F$
    A2: [Reporters]$_{CT}$ have to sit [in the back]$_F$.

Note that it would not make sense to speak of *friends* and *relatives* as stacked topics, they are not hierarchically structured with respect to each other.

For the gapping example above, it is not so clear what the preferred option would be—stacked topics or complex topic. The latter would look roughly as follows:

(3.29) [/Carl$_F$ hat meine /Katze$_F$]$_{CT}$\nicht$_F$ genommen
    aber [/Harry$_F$ meinen \ Hamster$_F$]$_{CT}$.
    CT-value:
    [Carl$_{CT}$ did not$_{CF}$ take my cat$_{CT}$]^{ct}= {{¬(x took y); (x took y)}| x ∈ D$_e$ ∧ y ∈ D$_e$} ≈ Did x take y?

This corresponds to the discourse topic I identified earlier as appropriate for this sentence, see (3.24) above. What the exact status of such a complex topic is must remain unexplored here. Topics are usually assumed to correspond to referents and not to predicates or the like. What a stacked topic structure would look like also needs more research. Roughly, we could say that *Carl* is the topic with widest scope and the comment coming with it is something like $[\lambda x. \neg \; took(x)(my \; cat)]$. *Cat* could then be a subordinated topic, the comment coming with it could be $[\lambda y. \neg \; took(x)(y)]$. There is some evidence that this is indeed a form of information packaging we find in gapping (see Hinterwimmer and Repp 2008) but since this issue would lead me too far away from the theme of this book I cannot discuss it here. So for the present purposes, I will assume that we have something like a complex contrastive topic in the gapping sentence in (3.29), which comes with a focus on the polarity.

Before I turn to the degraded example in (3.21b), I need to say some more on the intonation of the sentence in (3.21a) (= (3.29) directly above). The last contrastive topic accent on *Hamster* in the second conjunct is a falling accent producing a hat pattern for the whole conjunct. This seems to clash with the observation that topics are typically realized with rising accents. I assume that the realization as a falling accent is due to the fact that the underlying rising accent combines with the low boundary tone typical for the end of a declarative sentence. The result is a contrastive topic accent that looks like a focus accent.[19] The other thing that needs to be commented on is that the focus—the positive polarity—is elided in the second conjunct.[20,21] I assume that this is possible because positive polarity generally does not receive a great deal of attention in natural language in terms of being marked by morpho-syntactic means. This is part of a general asymmetry between negative and positive polarity. Whereas a negative assertion has to be especially marked with linguistic material, this is not the case for positive assertions (Horn 1989). In Section 3.3, I will show that this phenomenon also occurs in auxiliary gapping with slightly different information-structural underpinnings.

There obviously are means to stress positive polarity in a sentence, such as VERUM focus marking (Höhle 1988, 1991) or the addition of affirmative elements like *schon*, which, as I demonstrated above, is possible in gapping

[19] Féry (1993) shows that in multiple focus sequences there is a similar phenomenon. Two simple pitch accents can be linked completely, so that the familiar hat pattern emerges.

[20] This carries over to stripping where the focused polarity can be elided too (contra Winkler (2005), who considers polarity adverbs obligatory in stripping):

(i) /Das MÄDchen hat die Katze \NICHT gestreichelt, aber \der JUNGe.
     the girl   has die cat   not   stroked   but the boy
     'The girl did not stroke the cat but the boy did.'

[21] It seems generally possible to deaccent the focus in the full clause counterparts of the gapping sentences, see (i), which is the full version of (3.21a).

(i) /CARL hat meine /KAtze \NICHT genommen, aber /HARry hat meinen \HAMster genommen.

(ex. (3.22)). In other languages, for instance in Dutch, gapping with *but* HAS to come with an affirmative particle, here *wel*:

(3.30) /KArel heft mijn /KAT \NIET genomen maar /HArry mijn
        Karel has my   cat not taken   but Harry my
        /HAMster \WEL.
        hamster PART
        'Karl did not take my cat but Harry did take my hamster.'

Similarly, the use of pseudogapping in English allows the speaker to highlight the polarity of the second conjunct. Why the particle should be obligatory in Dutch but not in German I do not know. It seems that German contrastive *but* in general is more lenient when in comes to the marking of contrast: recall the general restrictions on the use of English contrastive *but* in gapping sentences. It might also have to do with the fact that both Dutch and English lack the lexical *aber–sondern* distinction.

It should be easy to see now why the alternative intonation pattern of our original example in (3.21b) is not good for a narrow scope reading: if the negation is not accented it cannot serve as a contrastive focus that in the second conjunct has the positive polarity as its alternative. The CT value in Büring's algorithm yields the following for the first conjunct of (3.21b):

(3.31) /CARL hat meine /KAtze nicht genommen.
        'Carl did not take my cat.'
        $[\![CARL_{CT} \text{ did not take my } CAT_F]\!]^{ct} = \{\{\neg(x \text{ took } y) \mid y \in D_e\} \, x \in D_e\}$
        $\approx$ Who did not take whom?

The CT-value is no longer a set of polarity questions. Instead, it corresponds to a set of multiple *wh*-questions, where one of the *wh*-phrases will be answered by the contrastive topics and the other, by the foci. This means that this pattern should be good in a coordination where the second conjunct also contains a negation. This is indeed the case as (3.32) illustrates. The discourse is coherent (in (3.11) above I gave an example for a context where coordinations with two negative conjuncts are plausible):

(3.32) /CARL hat meine /KAtze nicht genommen, aber / HArry hat meinen
        \HAMster nicht genommen.
        'Carl did not take my cat but Harry did not take my hamster.'

This interpretation, however, is not available in a gapping sentence because the negation is not copied in German.

To conclude the discussion and highlight the contribution of contrastive *but* in all this, let me briefly return to the fact that the intonation pattern and the information structure which I have identified as typical for gapping sentences with *but* is not available for corresponding gapping sentences with *and*. I illustrated this with example (3.23) above, repeated below as (3.33):

(3.33)   */Carl hat meine /Katze \nicht genommen, und /Harry meinen \Hamster.
'Carl didn't take my cat and Harry took my hamster.'

An account of contrastive topics alone cannot explain this. Büring's (1997a, 2003) proposal does not differentiate between *and* and *but*. We do need the semantics of *but* with its confirm–denial characteristic, as well as the principle of balanced contrast mentioned in the introduction and to be elaborated upon in Section 3.2 to explain the way the data pattern. Whereas *but* requires the conjuncts of the coordination it occurs in to make opposing contributions to a discourse topic, *and* in gapping requires the conjuncts to make the same kind of contribution. While it might be possible to come up with a context where a focus on the negation and a focus on the positive polarity of a conjunct in relation to their respective topics both support or both do not support a background assumption, that is make the same contribution, this is not what would be expected in an ordinary context—after all, the use of a negation signals the opposite of its non-use. This is the realm of *but*. Although *and* can support such readings in general (see Section 3.2), the principle of balanced contrast prevents these from occurring in gapping.

To sum up, I have offered an account of contrastive *but*, German *aber*, that builds on the assumption that the conjunction is sensitive to information structure. It associates with contrastive topics and foci. The first conjunct of the coordination through its intonational make-up establishes a contrastive topic and focus. The second conjunct picks up on these and provides appropriate alternatives. In a narrow scope reading with *but*, the focus in the first conjunct is the negation, which has the positive polarity in the second conjunct as its alternative. It is this information-structural set-up which interacts with the semantics of *but*. Whereas the first conjunct with its topic and focus supports a given discourse topic, the second conjunct, with an alternative topic and different focus does not support this discourse topic.

3.1.4 *Structuring gapping with contrastive* but

The story I have told of gapping sentences with contrastive *but* rests on information-structural and semantic-pragmatic aspects. For the syntax of these constructions I propose that the second conjunct comes with a positive morpheme which is silent. We saw above that the polarity in gapping with *but* does not need to be expressed overtly, although this is possible, for example through the use of certain particles/adverbs like *schon* ('indeed'). Example (3.34) gives the LF for the example I used throughout this section. I assume a Split-C domain (Rizzi 1997) with topic and focus positions even though the question of focus movement in gapping has not been settled (Sections 1.2, 1.3, and 2.3). In contrast to most earlier approaches (except Hendriks 2004; Winkler 2005) I assume that gapping is a topic-focus structure rather than a multiple focus structure. This is a result of the discussion in the present section as well as of independent findings presented in Hinterwimmer and Repp (2008). I use two topic phrases for the elements of the 'complex topic' in the structure below. This needs more research. StrengthP will be motivated in Chapter 4. For the exact derivation of the second conjunct, see Section 2.3—recall that gapping is a copying process that copies material from the first conjunct after the phonology of that conjunct has been sent off (shaded material in the tree below is material without phonology). Phonological spell-out of the second conjunct (and the first) occurs before topic and focus movement take place.

(3.34) /CARL hat meine /KATZE \NICHT genommen, aber /HARRY meinen \HAMster.

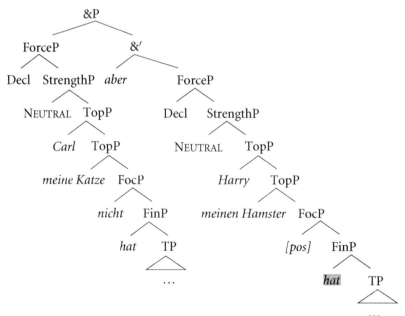

3.2 *And* and the principle of balanced contrast

And is the most general amongst the conjunctions. Lang (1991) points out that it is subject to the fewest syntactic and semantic restrictions, can be used in more contexts than any other conjunction, and has the least specific meaning as well as the highest degree of context dependence. He proposes as a minimal definition of *and* the meaning component SIMUL, which we encountered in Lang's definition of contrastive *but* and which holds that the two (or more) conjuncts of a coordination conjoined with *and* are compatible—they can be true at the same time. The operative meaning of *and*—the instruction as to how the coordination is to be processed—is to combine the denoted states-of-affairs, entities, or predicates as compatible instances of a common integrator (common discourse topic). An alternative view on *and* is that the conjunction signals 'add information', which is the simplest operator in dynamic semantics.

Amongst the many different uses *and* can be put to, one is particularly relevant for the present purposes because it is incompatible with gapping. The following examples illustrate:

(3.35)   a.   Paul is a LINGuist and he can't SPELL.

(Blakemore and Carston 2005, ex. 4)

　　　　 b.   Mein Vater ist ernsthaft KRANK   und meine   (Lang 2001)
　　　　　　　　　　　　　　　L* H H%
　　　　　　 My   father is seriously ill   and my
　　　　　　 MUTter geht ARbeiten!
　　　　　　 H*   ↑H* LL%
　　　　　　 mother goes work
　　　　　　 'My father is seriously ill and—imagine—my mother is working.'

The conjuncts in these examples are contrastive in the sense of contrastive *but*. However, they are not conjoined by *but*. Instead, *and* is used. To be sure, *but* could be used here as well, yet it seems that the contrastive relation between the two conjuncts does not have to be indicated explicitly by lexical means. The effect of using *and* here is that the coordinations communicate some kind of comment or surprise. Example (3.35a) says: isn't it surprising that Paul is a linguist and at the same time he can't spell. Example (3.35b) says: isn't it surprising that my mother should go to work even though my father is seriously ill.

Such cases are investigated in some detail by Lang (2001, 2004) and by Blakemore and Carston (2005) (see also Kitis 2000; König 1985). Blakemore and Carston (2005), who couch their analysis in the framework of Relevance Theory (Sperber and Wilson 1986), elaborate an account of Blakemore's (1987) and propose that conjuncts conjoined by *and* 'play the same role in the inferential processes leading to a particular cognitive effect'.[22] What happens in cases like (3.35), which Blakemore and Carston dub the 'attitudinal' use of *and*, is that the conjuncts elicit parallel but separate inferential processes each issuing in the same conclusion (in Lang's terms the common integrator). Whereas they consider the operative meaning of the conjunction *but* (roughly) to contradict and eliminate a mutually manifest assumption (Blakemore 1987, 2000),[23] attitudinal *and* is assumed to signal the truth of the coordination to be at odds with a mutually manifest assumption. Nevertheless, the hearer is not expected to eliminate it. Rather, the acceptance of the truth of the coordination in the face of its oddness leads to an attitudinal or commentary reading, where the hearer takes the speaker to be communicating some kind of implicit comment like surprise or outrage. Similarly, Kitis (2000) points out that *and* can function as an 'emotional device' to express the speaker's attitude, such as surprise or disapproval.

I am not sure that we need a different semantics for *and* in cases like (3.35). Rather, it seems to be the flouting of the default reading of the conjunction—according to which *and* conjoins two conjuncts that play the same role in the inferential processes leading to a particular cognitive effect—which produces the commentary reading: the two conjuncts do not play the same role. Rather, as the free substitutability with *but* suggests, one conjunct supports some background hypothesis (such as that linguists know much about language and therefore spell well), whereas the other does not. So what happens is that two states-of-affairs make contrasting contributions to a background hypothesis, which is considered odd and consequently, an attitudinal reading arises.

Lang (2001, 2004) investigates in detail the effects of particular accents and their information structural contribution in syntactically parallel coordinations such as (3.35b) above. According to Lang, (3.35b) does not receive a parallel (i.e. contrastive) interpretation because of the raised high peak (Ladd 1996) on the verb and the prosodic asymmetry this produces between the conjuncts.

---

[22] In Relevance Theory, human cognitive processes are geared towards the maximization of relevance where relevance is a property of the stimuli that are offered for processing. A relevant stimulus is a stimulus that achieves a cognitive effect. For economy reasons, it is assumed that the hearer pays most attention to stimuli that have the most cognitive effects for the least processing efforts.

[23] Blakemore (1987, 2000) defends a unified denial-of-expectation account for *but* in relevance-theoretic terms.

The coordination receives an implicative, concessive interpretation.[24] Lang (2003) argues that the implicative component of the interpretation is induced by the prosodic asymmetry (in combination with the phrasing—the whole coordination is assumed to be one intonation phrase). The conjuncts do not make equal contributions because they are not completely symmetric. The concessive meaning component is produced by the raised high peak. The idea is that this raised high peak signals a contrastive focus whose value needs to be reconstructed from the context (here the first conjunct). As a consequence, this accent induces the following presupposition:

(3.36) $\lambda p. \exists v \, [[[v \in \text{ALT} \, (\text{be\_at\_work}') \, \text{at} \, t_0 \, \& \, p = v(\text{mother}')] \, \&$
          $\exists q \, [q \in \text{ALT} \, (C_2): [C_1 \, \& \, q] >> [C_1 \, \& \, C_2]]]$

The second line in (3.36) says that the combination of the first conjunct with an alternative proposition q to conjunct 2 is preferred over the combination of the first conjunct with the second conjunct; the variable q is to be instantiated by the context. The effect of this presupposition is the introduction of the meaning component of adversity (typical of *but*).

Now, what is important for our purposes is that attitudinal or implicative readings cannot be conveyed by a gapping construction. I propose that gapping with *and* is subject to the principle of balanced contrast:

(3.37)   PRINCIPLE OF BALANCED CONTRAST (PBC), CONJUNCTION 'AND'
          In gapping, both conjuncts must make the same kind of contribution to a common discourse topic.

This is illustrated in the following examples:

(3.38)   a.   #Isn't that odd:

Max	ist	auf	Montage	und	seine	Frau	kaum	zu	Hause.
Max	is	on	construction	and	his	wife	hardly	at	home

                                        (I wonder where she is . . .)
          'Max is away on the job and his wife is hardly at home.'

          b.   There won't be anybody at home:
                Max ist auf Montage und seine Frau kaum zu Hause. (She always works long hours.)

Example (3.38a) is meant to give an implicative reading. The elision of the auxiliary is degraded if compared to the full version. Sentence (3.38b), on the other hand goes through easily because it only requires a contrastive reading.

---

[24] There are other non-symmetric accent patterns which produce slightly different interpretations, see Lang (2001, 2004).

Other kinds of 'asymmetric' readings are not good in gapping either. For instance, Levin and Prince (1986) argue that a causal relation between the two conjuncts in the following example is not possible if the verb is elided:[25]

(3.39)   *Susan's histrionics in public have always gotten on Nan's nerves, but it's getting worse. Yesterday, when she couldn't get her daily Egg McMuffin because they were all out,*
Sue became upset and Nan {became / #~~became~~ } downright angry.

Kehler (1996) says that the reason for this lies in the different ways coherence relations between clauses are established. Causal relations, for instance, are established by accessing the semantics at the clause-level. The establishment of resemblance relations, which include the relations *parallel* and *contrast*, on the other hand, requires access to the semantics of the constituents of the conjoined clauses. Kehler, whose main objective is to explain certain differences between VP ellipsis, which allows great syntactic flexibility between the conjuncts, and gapping, which does not, suggests that elided information in the syntax of the target is only recovered if the coherence relation requires access to the semantics of syntactic nodes within the elided material, that is in resemblance relations (also see Kehler 2000, 2002).

Hendriks (2004) criticizes this view. She points out, amongst other things, that (3.39) is also bad if not gapping but deaccentuation of the verb is involved. Furthermore, she is wary of the potential circularity of the argument: in order to establish a coherence relation, the semantics of the conjuncts must be accessed but Kehler proposes that the ellipsis resolution depends on the establishment of the coherence relation. Hendriks herself proposes that resemblance relations always contain contrastive topics whereas causal relations, for instance, do not. Thus, for (3.39) she suggests that the coordination in question is about Sue rather than Nan and Sue (on a par), that is no contrastive topics are involved. The idea then is that since gapping involves contrastive topics (an assumption that is supported by my analysis of gapping with contrastive *but*), the resemblance relation in a case like (3.39) is more prominent, which, however, is not compatible with the context. For an empirical study on and subsequent criticism of Kehler's coherence relations approach, also see Frazier and Clifton (2006).

---

[25] In German, such sentences can be saved by adding appropriate adverbs (e.g. *daraufhin* ('as a consequence')). This needs closer scrutiny.

(i)   Sue wurde   sauer und Nan daraufhin   regelrecht wütend.
        Sue became upset and Nan as.a.consequence downright angry
        'Sue became upset and Nan as a consequence downright angry.'

I conclude my discussion of *and* here. The on-going message from this section is that gapping does not support attitudinal or commentary readings of *and*. Gapping is subject to the PBC, which requires that the gapping conjuncts must make the same kind of contribution to a discourse topic (or background hypothesis). I corroborate this proposal with plenty of examples in the next sections. The PBC is at work in auxiliary gapping, in gapping with focus particles, and, as we saw in Section 2.3, in gapping with distributed scope readings.

3.3 Auxiliary gapping and contrasting *v*Ps

In contrast to main verb gapping, auxiliary gapping has been thought to be unable to accommodate distributed scope readings. Johnson (1996/2003) suggests that auxiliary gapping is only compatible with a wide scope reading of the negation. I will show here that this is not the case. Although auxiliary gapping indeed does not allow distributed scope readings it is not restricted to wide scope readings. It can also induce narrow scope readings. The reason for the unavailability of distributed scope of the negation, I argue, is that auxiliary gapping introduces a new *v*P in the second conjunct, which comes with its own quantificational layer hosting by default positive polarity. The resulting narrow scope reading is only felicitous—and the corresponding gapping sentence grammatical—if the principle of balanced contrast (PBC), introduced in the previous section, is obeyed. In the case of auxiliary gapping this requires particularly careful balancing of the conjuncts which is due to the presence of two different predicates.

3.3.1 *The data*

Recall the contrast in (3.40) from the introduction. The main verb gapping example in (3.40a) depending on the intonation, can have a distributed or a wide scope reading. The auxiliary gapping example in (3.40b) can only have a wide scope reading, which comes with the intonation typical of that reading, that is the whole coordination is uttered as one intonational phrase and the main accent lies on the auxiliary (plus negation).

(3.40)   a.   Kim didn't play bingo and Sandy golf.
                 = Kim didn't play bingo and Sandy didn't play golf. *(distributed scope)* or
                 = It is not the case that (Kim played bingo and Sandy played golf). *(wide scope)*

b. Kim didn't play bingo and Sandy sit at home all night.
    = It is not the case that (Kim played bingo and Sandy sat at home all night). *(wide scope)*

Similar observations can be made for German. Example (3.41a) is a case of combined auxiliary plus main verb gapping and *and* is bad for the reasons discussed in Chapter 2. Example (3.41b) is auxiliary gapping and seems even worse. A wide scope reading is not possible here either because the negative marker in the wide scope readings needs to take a different position (see Chapter 4):

(3.41) *Max and Paul haven't done everything they were supposed to do to help in the kitchen:*

a. ^{??}Max hat den Kuchenteller nicht abgewaschen und Paul
    Max has the cake.dish   not   washed   and Paul
    die Salatschüssel.
    the salad.bowl
    'Max didn't wash the cake dish and Paul the salad bowl.'

b. *Max hat den Kuchenteller nicht abgewaschen und Paul
    Max has the cake.dish   not   washed   and Paul
    die Salatschüssel abgetrocknet.
    the salad.bowl   dried
    'Max didn't wash the cake dish and Paul dried the salad bowl.'

The most striking difference between auxiliary and main verb gapping is that the structural parallelism between the two conjuncts in the former is 'more relaxed' than in the latter. This is illustrated in the following examples. In none of them are the conjuncts as parallel as we would normally expect them to be in run-of-the-mill gapping, where typically subjects are contrasted with subjects and objects with objects.

(3.42) *What are the plans for the afternoon?*
    Max will   Schuhe kaufen gehen und Martha etwas
    Max wants shoes   buy   go   and Martha a.little
    vor   dem Fernseher abhängen.
    in.front.of the TV   veg.out
    'Max wants to go and buy shoes and Martha wants to veg out in front of the television.'

(3.43)   *In the next two hours, nothing much happened:*
Max hat seine Mutter angerufen und Martha aus dem
Max has his   mother called   and Martha out the
Fenster geguckt.
window looked
'Max called his mother and Martha looked out of the window.'

(3.44)   Mary must relax her tired feet and Gary pick up the kids from school.

All these examples have subject contrast pairs but, as can be easily seen, the predicates are quite different in the two conjuncts: transitive structures can be contrasted with intransitive or ditransitive structures. Thus, what is contrasted in these constructions are the subjects and two complex predicates rather than individual participants, as would be common in main verb gapping.[26]

This assumption is further supported by the intonation of the above structures. Apart from the accent on the subjects—which are the contrastive topics—only the deepest embedded argument carries an accent, and not, for instance, the main verb, which, if not the whole *v*P is contrasted, might be considered contrasted as well. Thus, we essentially get a default intonation (one that allows focus projection). This is illustrated for the example in (3.45) below:

(3.45)   *In the next two hours, nothing much happened:*

a. /Max hat seine /Mutter angerufen und /Martha aus dem
   Max has his   mother called and Martha out the
   \Fenster geguckt.
   window   looked.

b. */Max hat   seine /Mutter /Angerufen
   und /Martha aus   dem   /Fenster ge\guckt
   'Max called his mother and Martha looked out of the window.'

---

[26] It is not necessary that one of the contrast pairs be subjects:

(i)   Den   Canetti habe ich von meiner Mutter geborgt, und den   Joyce meinem
      the.ACC Canetti have I   from my   mother borrowed and the.ACC Joyce my
      Vater aus dem Kreuz geleiert.
      father out the   back wound
      'The Canetti, I borrowed from my mother and the Joyce, I sponged from my father'.

In (i), two direct objects are juxtaposed, and two predicates with a indirect object. Note, however, that the subjects are elided, too. The sentence deteriorates if a contrastive subject is added in the second conjunct. I have not investigated the restrictions on this systematically. There are certainly limits to the non-parallelism although I suspect that they are mainly of a pragmatic (availability of good contexts), or/and of a processing nature.

Let us go back to auxiliary gapping with negation. Consider (3.46). This is an example where the second conjunct contains a verb with an inherently negative meaning:

(3.46) *Same context as in (3.41) above: Max and Paul haven't done everything*
        they were supposed to do to help in the kitchen:
        Max hat den Kuchenteller nicht abgewaschen und Paul die
        Max has the cake.dish   not   washed   and Paul the
        Salatschüssel vergessen.
        salad.bowl   forgot
        'Max didn't wash the cake dish and Paul forgot the salad bowl.'

Example (3.46) is fine. Importantly, the interpretation of the second conjunct proceeds without clausal negation. In other words, we have an instance of narrow scope here. What is going on in (3.46) is that *not washing the cake dish* is contrasted with *forgetting the salad bowl*. Thus, the negation in the first conjunct is part of the contrasted complex predicate. Similar examples can be found in English:

(3.47) *Context: Asking John and Pete to help in the kitchen is useless. They*
        always mess things up. Don't ask them tomorrow to help with the cake:
        John will not find any of the ingredients and Pete smash the cake
        bowl.

Again, the negative predicate of the first conjunct, *not find any ingredients*, is contrasted with the (grammatically) positive predicate of the second conjunct, *smash the cake bowl*.

Why is the positive reading of (3.46) not available in (3.41b), where instead of the verb *forget* we had *dry* in the second conjunct? The answer to these questions lies in the requirements the conjunction *and* imposes on the two conjuncts of a (gapping) coordination as formulated in the principle of balanced contrast from the previous section. *And* requires the conjuncts to make the same kind of contribution to a superordinated discourse topic, which in general, as well as in the present case, is restricted by the context. In (3.46), both conjuncts confirm that the two boys indeed have not done all the jobs they were asked to do: one didn't wash the cake dish and the other forgot (to wash, dry, etc.) the salad bowl. In (3.41b), in contrast, a positive second conjunct would not make the same kind of contribution to the discourse topic as the negative first conjunct. Whereas the first conjunct confirms that one of the boys, Max, has not done all of the assigned jobs—he did not wash the cake dish—the second conjunct says, or seems to say, that Paul has dried the salad bowl. No confirmation of the discourse topic is given. The sentence is ruled out.

It seems then that in auxiliary gapping a new predicate is introduced in the second conjunct and, for some reason, this invariably produces a reading with positive polarity, which, if compatible with the PBC, results in a grammatical sentence. Note that this holds both for German (example (3.46)) and for English (example (3.47)). For German, this might not be so surprising: I argued in Chapter 2 that adjunct negation is not copied anyway. Auxiliary gapping turns out to be a case where this produces an acceptable reading with respect to the PBC (in contrast to the distributed readings).[27] For English, however, the positive polarity in the second conjunct is unexpected: I argued in Chapter 2 that English negation is copied because it is the head of a sentential functional projection.

3.3.2 *Events, V-phases, and negation in auxiliary gapping*

To understand what is going on in auxiliary gapping with negation, it is worth taking a look at various ways to interpret clausal negation. There has been a long debate on whether clausal negation should be a propositional operator or a predicate operator, see Horn (1989) for an extensive discussion. The difference can be made explicit as follows:

(3.48)   *My hoover isn't working*

      a. $\neg$ [my hoover is working]

      b.   my hoover is [$\neg$ working]

Whereas (3.48a) shows the negation of a proposition, (3.48b) assigns a negated predicate to the subject. Thus, there is a scopal ambiguity in sentences with a clausal negative marker.[28] Predicate negation, it seems, is the reading that surfaces in auxiliary gapping. Recall that in (3.46) above, *not washing the cake dish* is contrasted with *forgetting the salad bowl*, and in (3.47), *not finding any ingredients*, is contrasted with *smashing the cake bowl*. Each time, a negative predicate is contrasted with a positive one.

Now, it seems plausible that a negated predicate can be contrasted with a predicate that in its lexical decomposition quite plausibly has an inherent negation, as is the case with *forget* above. As (3.47) above and the following

---

[27] Also recall from notes 3 and 39 in Chapter 2 that for some German speakers some contexts trigger accommodation of a negative reading of the second conjunct in main verb gapping. In auxiliary gapping such accommodation invariably fails.

[28] See Herburger (2000) for an account of this and related negation phenomena in Davidsonian event semantics where the interpretive differences are put down to scopal differences without giving up on the function of the negation as a propositional operator.

example show, however, an inherent lexical negation is not necessary for the felicitous interpretation of a predicate in the second conjunct:

(3.49) Maria will   das Buch nicht zurückgeben und Max die
        Maria wants the book not   give.back   and Max the
        DVD behalten.
        DVD keep
        'Maria doesn't want to give the book back and Max wants to keep the DVD.'

Although *keep* could be considered as being similar to something like NEG_*give_back* it is not at all clear that there should indeed be a negation in its lexical structure. Similarly, for *smash* in (3.47), it is very implausible to assume that it contains a negation in its lexical decomposition. Thus if context allows, the contrast between the predicates can be a contrast between a negative predicate and a positive one independently of the lexical make-up of the latter as long as the two predicates say the same about the two individuals referred to by the subjects, that is as long as the PBC is obeyed. In (3.49) both Maria and Max want to keep the things they received from someone. In (3.47), both boys are argued to be useless in the kitchen.

Now, this does still not tell us much about why the introduction of a new verbal predicate in the second conjunct of auxiliary gapping precludes copying the negation from the first conjunct even if that is not an adjunct. I suggest that we approach this question by examining more closely the relation between events and propositions. A negatively described event, that is an event where a negated predicate is assigned to a subject, is different from a negated proposition. Furthermore, as we shall see presently, events correspond to a different part of the clausal structure from propositions. This, I shall argue, gives us a handle on the auxiliary gapping data.

Both the CP and the *v*P have been proposed to correspond to syntactic phases on the assumption that they are propositional (Chomsky 2000, 2001)— in a certain sense, that is. A CP obviously corresponds to a full proposition. It comprises tense, event structure, and illocutionary force. As a proposition, it can be evaluated for truth. For a *v*P, in contrast, this does not hold. A *v*P has full argument structure but it lacks tense information and therefore it cannot be evaluated for truth. Consequently, it is not propositional in the true sense of the word.

Nevertheless, the *v*P is semantically complete in the sense that it has full argument structure. And, there is more: as Kratzer (1996) and others have proposed, it is the denotation of an event (states and actions included). Kratzer

(1995, 1996) assumes that verbs have a Davidsonian event argument[29] (similarly Barwise and Perry 1983; Chierchia 1995; Higginbotham 1987, and many others). The event argument specifies what kind of event the verb denotes, that is whether it is an event in the close sense of the word, or an action, a state, etc. The event argument is an implicit semantic variable and it is selected by a particular voice head, which subcategorizes for a particular kind of event. Voice is situated directly above VP and has the following semantics (Kratzer 1996):

(3.50)   Semantics of voice
         $\lambda x_e.\lambda e_s.$ [thematic role (x)(e)]

e is a variable over event types and x is a variable over individuals, that is voice predicates over an event and over an individual. The individual in the formula is the one denoted by the external argument of the verb. Kratzer (1996) follows Marantz (1984) in the assumption that the external argument is not really an argument of the verb and suggests that it is an argument of the functional voice head (also cf. Chomsky 1995; Hale and Keyser 1993).[30] It occupies the specifier of vP.

I assume that the vP is the syntactic representation of the event whereas the CP is the syntactic representation of the proposition. As we saw above, the negation can scope over either. It is not usually assumed, however, that two different markers are involved in this. Rather, both cases are covered by clausal negation. Interestingly, some languages do seem to distinguish the two scope positions with different negative markers. This is for instance the case in Benghali (Ramchand 2004). In Benghali, the negative marker *ni* expresses propositional negation whereas the marker *na* expresses the occurrence of a negatively described event. Evidence comes for instance from the use of these two markers in particular discourses (where they exclude each other). In the following example, the time span in which the relevant event did not occur is restricted. In such a context, only the marker for negatively described events *na* is good:

---

[29] Kratzer (1995) assumes that only non-individual level predicates have this event argument.

[30] The position that an external argument is not an argument of the verb is fuelled by the observation that internal arguments correlate with particular meanings of the verb, whereas external arguments do not (Marantz 1984: 25):

(i)   throw a baseball—throw support behind a candidate—throw a fit

(ii) The policeman threw NP—Aardvarks throw NP—Throw NP!

(3.51)   a.   jokhon Mary amTa   khel-o   na, tokhon John khub
When   Mary the.mango eat-past3rd neg then   John very
rege   gælo.
angry got

   b.   *jokhon Mary amTa   kha-y ni,   tokhon
When   Mary the.mango eat-3rd neg.perf.past^{31} then
John khub rege   gælo.
John very angry got
'When Mary didn't eat the mango (then) John got very angry.'
(Ramchand 2004)

In the following examples, the two markers produce different readings for the sentence under consideration:

(3.52)   a.   kalke   gaRi 'start' hoi   ni.   (Ramchand 2004)
yesterday car   start become.3rd neg.perf.past
'Yesterday, the car didn't start (at all).'

   b.   kalke   gaRi 'start' holo   na.
yesterday car   start become.past.3rd neg
'Yesterday, the car didn't start (but then the neighbour came and fixed it).'

Ramchand suggests that the time variable specifies the 'universe of discourse' for the proposition's time variable. If this time variable is quantified by negative *ni*, we get the reading glossed in (3.52a). In (3.52b), on the other hand, it is only the event variable that gets negatively quantified by *na*. As a result, the sentence says that there was a single event when the car did not start, or, an event of non-starting.

Butler (2004) takes this as evidence that there must be two different positions for the negation in the clause, one for propositional negation and one for negatively described events (which is the same as the more traditional 'predicate negation', also see Butler 2003). Butler (2004) proposes a theory of ph(r)ase structure which is worth looking at in some detail. There are three kinds of phases: the D-phase (DPs), the V-phase (*v*Ps), and the T-phase (the traditional CP). These phases all have a core, or a domain, which is where predication and selection, etc. take place. This domain is headed by a property-denoting head, such as V or T. Furthermore, each phase has an edge, which functions as a space for movement and which is where quantificational information (e.g. through modal operators) is encoded to bind the

---

^{31} Ramchand says that *ni* is itself specified for tense whereas *na* is not.

domain-internal variables. This latter feature actually is the kernel of Butler's definition of phases. For him, it is not the fact that phases are somehow propositional that is important, but that they are quantificational domains. So, the variables that are introduced in the domain of a phase are closed off in the edge. For the whole clause, we get the following structure:

(3.53)

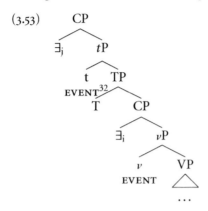

Butler assumes that the implicit event variable in the V-phase is subject to existential closure (exceptions are sentences with expletives). Existential closure is represented by the ∃-head of the V-phase's CP. This way, the vP is given referential status. The T-phase is organized in the same way. There also is an event variable, which is bound by a little head t. And again the phase is existentially closed off by an operator in the CP. This all interacts with the syntax of tense. I shall briefly come back to this in Chapter 5, when I discuss the notion of finiteness.

Now, Butler assumes that in the CP of each phase there is room for negation. He takes over the Split-CP from Rizzi (1997) and assumes that the negation sits in Foc.[33] He proposes that event (or predicate) negation is situated in the CP of the V-phase whereas propositional negation is situated in the CP of the T-phase.

The latter assumption is not really compatible with what we have seen so far for English or German negation. We saw that clausal negation in these languages is situated between VP and TP, which would correspond to the position of the V-phase-CP in Butler's system. A high position in the (traditional) CP, however, is not usually assumed (but see Klima 1964; Haegeman 1995). Butler points out that other languages, for instance Italian, have a similar high

---

[32] Butler calls events situations to include states and activities. I will use 'event' here, which, as in Kratzer (1996), includes states and activities.

[33] Note, however, that Rizzi (1997) only assumes that certain topicalized negative phrases that trigger negative inversion are moved to FocP.

position for the negation (cf. Zanuttini 1991) and says that it is certainly an available scope position for English clausal negation. I am not sure whether that is enough. Nonetheless, the idea that the *v*P comes with its own quantificational CP is undoubtedly very interesting and in what follows I shall try and see what it buys us for the gapping data.

Recall that in auxiliary gapping, the second conjunct introduces a new subject and a new (complex) predicate. In terms of phrase structure this corresponds to a *v*P. Here again is the relevant example:

(3.54) *Max and Paul haven't done everything they were supposed to do to help in the kitchen:*
        *Max hat den Kuchenteller nicht abgewaschen und Paul die
        Max has the cake.dish   not washed   and Paul the
        Salatschüssel abgetrocknet.
        salad.bowl   dried
        'Max didn't wash the cake dish and Paul dried the salad bowl.'

This new *v*P, as argued above, corresponds to an event and comes with its own quantificational structure. If the quantificational edge of the *v*P contains no negation, then the event by default is positive (in the literal sense). In order to produce a reading where the event is described negatively, that is an instance of predicate negation, the *v*P needs to contain a negative marker, as in the following example:

(3.55) Max hat den Kuchenteller nicht abgewaschen und Paul die
        Max has the cake.dish   not washed   and Paul the
        Salatschüssel nicht abgetrocknet.
        salad.bowl   not dried
        'Max didn't wash the cake dish and Paul didn't dry the salad bowl.'

Similarly in English, we find cases of auxiliary gapping where the second conjunct comes with its own negative marker, here an example repeated from Chapter 2, which contains adverbial negation:

(3.56) Arthur might have been not crying and Leo not laughing.

Unifying these assumptions with the syntax of main verb gapping I developed in Chapter 2, I assume that the narrow scope readings in auxiliary gapping arise in the following way—both in English and in German. The positive polarity of the second conjunct is part of the numeration for the second conjunct, as a positive morpheme, similarly to gapping with contrastive *but*. In contrast to the latter, however, the positive morpheme does not stand in a direct contrast relation with the negative marker of the first conjunct. It is part of a larger phrase, the *v*P, which represents the event expressed by the predicate and which is negative in the first conjunct and positive in the second conjunct. Thus, the result of contrasting two *v*Ps and not just a subject and an object in auxiliary gapping is that the *v*Ps bring along their own quantificational information, which, if not marked explicitly as in the first conjunct, is positive by default. If the resulting reading is incompatible with the PBC the sentence is ruled out. Below I give a structure for the German sentence in (3.46) above. It borrows from Butler (2004) but deviates from it. I am not assuming that the negation is in the FocP of the CP of *v*P but that it is an adjunct because this is the syntactic status of the negation in German. For better readability, I neglect the Split CP and topic and focus movement here, but will say a word about the information structure of that sentence in a moment. Strikethrough marks chain-reduced material. Shaded font marks copied lexical material from the first conjunct.

(3.57)   Max hat den Kuchenteller nicht abgewaschen und Paul die Salatschüssel vergessen.

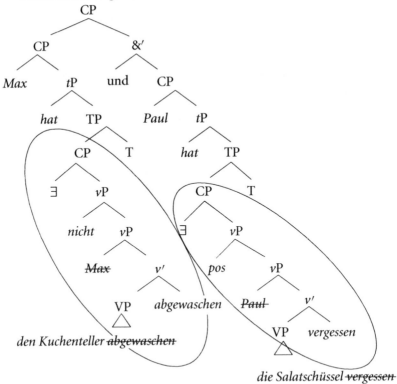

We see that the event in the vP is existentially closed off. In the first conjunct, this event is negative, in the second, positive. Note that the internal make-up of the CP(V-phase) is irrelevant for the copying process in the sense that the numeration for the second conjunct contains all the elements that are needed to build the vP. This is why in auxiliary gapping, the two conjuncts do not have to be as symmetric as in main verb gapping (recall examples (3.42)–(3.44) in the previous section).

As for the information structure of auxiliary gapping, I assume that auxiliary gapping like main verb gapping is a contrastive-topic–contrastive-focus structure (see Section 3.1 for motivation). The subjects are the contrastive topics, and the predicates, the contrastive foci. Thus, *Max* and *Paul* in the above structure will move to topic positions at LF. The (remnant) vPs (with their CP layer) will move to focus positions. This information-structural make-up is also reflected in the intonational make-up of auxiliary gapping, which patterns with main verb gapping in *and*-coordinations and not with contrastive-*but*-coordinations, that is the negative marker in the first conjunct is not accented—it is not a (narrow) contrastive focus.

There is much more to be said about events versus propositions, and especially about the precise syntax of predicate versus clausal negation. After all, they can be expressed by the same marker in English and German and there does not seem to be much of a difference. The auxiliary gapping data suggest that the difference in some environments is important. In auxiliary gapping only predicate negation, which I have described as marking a negatively described event, is available (note in this connection that the English example in (3.56) involves adverbial rather than clausal negation). There must be a reason for this and I have identified it as the introduction of a new event, which syntactically can be represented as a vP. Main verb gapping is not restricted to predicate negation as will become particularly clear in the next section where I show that the negation acts quite independently of the predicate.

3.4 Focus particles

The last environment where narrow scope readings arise which I will investigate here are coordinations with *and* where a focus particle occurs in the second conjunct. These environments do not obligatorily produce narrow scope readings. For *only* which I investigate in Section 3.4.1, I show that the semantic scope of the particle has a vital role to play. Only propositional scope is able to 'reverse the polarity' of the second conjunct. The effect arises because of the semantics of the particle—it excludes alternatives—and its context dependence in interaction with the principle of balanced contrast. Apart from *only*, this chapter also looks at *even* which also occurs in gapping sentences with a positive second conjunct but cannot 'produce' such a positive second conjunct in the same way as *only* does (Section 3.4.2).

3.4.1 *Only*

3.4.1.1 *The data*   The following examples illustrate that in gapping with *and*, the occurrence of the focus particle *only* (similarly *merely*) in the second conjunct can lead to a positive interpretation of that conjunct.[34] Compare examples (3.58a) and (3.58b), where a structure with *only* is juxtaposed with a structure without *only*:

(3.58)   a.   Mary wasn't greeted by John and Bill only by Sue.
              = 'Bill was only greeted by Sue.'

         b.   Mary wasn't greeted by John and Bill by Sue.
              = 'Bill wasn't greeted by Sue.'

The focus particle causes a reversal of polarity.

Before I start discussing this phenomenon, note that the intonation of the sentence in (3.58a) and all the sentences to be discussed in this chapter is that of 'ordinary' gapping, that is the two conjuncts are pronounced as individual intonational phrases, the finite verb is deaccented, and the contrast pairs must carry pitch accents. The only difference is that the focus particle itself may carry a rising pitch accent.[35]

(3.59)   MAry wasn't greeted by JOHN   and BILL {ONly/only} by
         L* H   L* H H-H%,   L* H (L* H)
         SUE.
         H* L L%

For German *nur* and similar focus particles like *bloß* or *lediglich* (both meaning *merely*), analogous observations obtain. A sentence which, without *only* would receive a distributed scope reading (which is ungrammatical in German for the reasons discussed in Chapter 2, see (3.60b)), has a narrow scope reading if *only* is added to the second conjunct, see (3.60a).

---

[34]   Chris Wilder first drew my attention to these data.

[35]   It is generally possible to have a wide scope reading intonation contour for sentences of the above type, i.e. the finite verb may carry a pitch accent and the conjuncts be uttered as one intonational phrase. This produces a wide scope interpretation of the negation, which is not of interest in the present context.

(3.60)   a.   Maria hat die Linde nicht erkannt   und Max nur
              Maria has the linden not   recognized and Max only
              die Buche.
              the beech
              'Mary didn't recognize the linden and Max only recognized the
              beech.'

         b.   ??Maria hat die Linde nicht erkannt   und Max
              Maria has the linden not   recognized and Max
              die Buche.
              the beech
              'Mary didn't recognize the linden and Max didn't recognize the
              beech.'

There is another set of data, where the presence of *only* in the second conjunct
does not actually reverse the polarity of the sentence but where it improves
a sentence that without *only* would be ungrammatical. The auxiliary gapping examples in (3.61) are a case in point. Here, the addition of German
nur improves sentences which even without *only* would receive a positive
interpretation of the second conjunct—see the discussion of auxiliary gapping in Section 3.3—but somehow do not quite make it without the focus
particle:

(3.61)   a.   ??Max hat die Tomaten nicht gepflanzt und Martha ein
              Max has the tomatoes not   planted   and Martha a
              bisschen Unkraut gezupft.
              little   weeds   plucked

         b.   Max hat die Tomaten nicht gepflanzt und Martha nur ein bisschen
              Unkraut gezupft.
              'Max did not plant the tomatoes and Mary (only) plucked at a few
              of the weeds.'

Similar examples can be found in main verb gapping in English. In the
(a)-cases in (3.62) and (3.63) below, a negative interpretation of the second
conjunct discourse-wise does not make much sense. The contrast which is
suggested in (3.62), for instance, not earning anything at all and not earning
10 dollars—cannot be interpreted at all without a very specific context. Comparing the fact that there is no x such that John earned it, with the fact that
there is a specific x (10$), which Bill did not earn, needs a very specific scenario
which I will refrain from suggesting here. A positive interpretation fares much
better but, by the looks of it, needs *only*.

(3.62)　a.　ʔJohn didn't earn anything at all and Bill, ten dollars.

　　　　b.　John didn't earn anything at all and Bill, only ten dollars.

(3.63)　a.　ʔTo Mary, John didn't say anything and to Sue, that he was hungry.

　　　　b.　To Mary, John didn't say anything and to Sue, only that he was hungry.

To sum up, there are two varieties of gapping sentences with *only*: those where the second conjunct would be understood as negative without *only* and those where that second conjunct would be interpreted as positive although the whole coordination does not seem to be fully grammatical. In the first case, *only* reverses the polarity of the second conjunct to positive; in the second, the addition of *only* produces a fully grammatical sentence.

I propose that both varieties arise as a consequence of the principle of balanced contrast (PBC). Consider first the instances of auxiliary gapping in (3.61), which receive a narrow scope reading even without *only*, albeit a degraded one. In (3.61a) it is hard to accommodate a plausible discourse topic[36] that could serve the PBC: not planting the tomatoes and plucking at a few weeds do not necessarily lend themselves to a parallel interpretation as undesired or desired deeds. Adding *only* to the second conjunct makes this much easier: only plucking at a few weeds means that more could have been done (see more on the semantics of *only* below) so both predicates express something negative in terms of expected, or desired, deeds.

In sentences where the second conjunct without *only* receives a straightforward, PBC-compatible negative reading as in (3.64a) (and its gapping counterpart in (3.58b) above), the addition of *only* disturbs the balance of the conjuncts, see (3.64b). Example (3.64b) seems to imply that not being greeted by Sue is a somewhat lesser evil than not being greeted by John, which out of the blue is not plausible and certainly does not obey the PBC: Mary got off much worse than Bill. If, however, the second conjunct containing *only* is interpreted as positive the balance between the conjuncts is retained, see (3.64c): Mary experienced something unpleasant as she was not greeted by John (say, at a party), and Bill also experienced something unpleasant because he was only greeted by one person—meaning everybody else ignored him.

---

[36] Most sentences I discuss in this chapter obviously need a more or less specific context, which I normally do not give for reasons of space. So I use 'out of the blue' utterances. What is important for my purposes is that the (implicit) context is unspecific enough for the reader to accommodate it easily, i.e. the reader can easily imagine a situation where the relevant sentence might have been uttered.

(3.64)   a.   Mary wasn't greeted by John and Bill wasn't greeted by Sue.

   b.   ?Mary wasn't greeted by John and Bill only wasn't greeted by Sue.

   c.   Mary wasn't greeted by John and Bill was only greeted by Sue.

What we find is that the reading that emerges in the gapped version of a coordination with *only*, such as (3.58a) above, repeated below as (3.65), quite straightforwardly corresponds to the interpretation that follows the PBC, that is (3.64c).[37]

(3.65)   Mary wasn't greeted by John and Bill only by Sue.

In what follows I will make explicit how exactly the addition of *only* disturbs the balance between the conjuncts and thus influences the interpretation of the negation in gapping. To do this, I first take a brief look at the syntax and semantics of the particle (subsections 3.4.1.2 and 3.4.1.3). We will see that *only* can receive different interpretations: scalar versus quantificational. These interpretations interact with the particle's semantic scope (propositional or not), which in turn is determined by its syntactic position in the clause. These observations will become crucial in subsection 3.4.1.4, where I will show that just propositional *only* has the effects in gapping that I presented above whereas *only* with non-propositional scope does not. In subsection 3.4.1.5, I will demonstrate that the context-sensitive interpretation of *only*—which takes into account both conjuncts—is responsible for the effects the focus particle has on the contrast relations in the coordination. Finally, I look at coordinations that contain both the focus particle *only* and the conjunction *but* (subsection 3.4.1.6). In general, the discussion will focus on those gapping sentences where the addition of *only* actually leads to a reversal of the polarity of the sentences. The other cases are quite similar to the examples involving *even* discussed in Section 3.4.2.

3.4.1.2 *Brief overview of the syntax and semantics of* only   Only has traditionally been assumed to associate with focus, that is it associates with an element that contains a prosodically marked pitch accent (in languages that have pitch accents). *Only* asserts that the proposition it occurs in is true for the focus that it associates with but not true for any alternative to that focus.[38] Formally, this can be captured as follows:

(3.66)   only: $\lambda P \lambda x [\forall Q [Q(x) \land Q \in C \rightarrow Q = P]]$

---

[37] I only consider the possibility where *only* scopes over *not* here. *Not only* is quite different and will be investigated in a separate section (see subsection 3.4.1.7 below).

[38] In this sense, the focus particle contains a negation itself.

In words, all properties Q that hold of x which are also in a set of properties C are identical to property P. The truth-conditional effects of *only* are demonstrated in the following examples:

(3.67)   a.   John only introduced B<small>ILL</small> to Sue,
              {√he didn't introduce Peter to Sue / *he didn't introduce Bill to Mary}.

         b.   John introduced only Bill to S<small>UE</small>,
              {*he didn't introduce Peter to Sue / √he didn't introduce Bill to Mary}.

This effect on truth conditions distinguishes *only* from its focus particle relatives such as *even*, or German *sogar* and *auch (too)*, as well as from the contrastive coordination *but*, for which, as we saw above, a semantics has been suggested that in its presuppositional part is more or less equal to the assertion part of *only*. The presupposition[39] carried by *only* is the following: the proposition stripped off the particle is true on its own. For more details on the semantics of *only*, see for instance Horn (1969), Karttunen and Peters (1979), Krifka (1992, 2006), Rooth (1985, 1992), von Stechow (1991b), and below.

    Apart from the focus, it is important to identify the semantic scope of the focus particle, which interacts with its syntactic position. As for the latter, it is usually assumed that in English the focus particle can attach to various maximal projections, including DPs and VPs (vPs):[40]

(3.68) $[_{\text{IP}}$ I $[_{\text{VP}}$ only $[_{\text{VP}}$ read $[_{\text{DP}}$ a Novel]]]].
         $[_{\text{IP}}$ I $[_{\text{VP}}$ read $[_{\text{DP}}$ only $[_{\text{DP}}$ a Novel]]]].

For German, there has been a lively debate over the ability of focus particles to attach to DPs. Whereas Büring and Hartmann (2001), who build on earlier work by Jacobs (1983, 1986), claim that adjunction to a DP is not possible, von Stechow (1991a) and (Bayer 1996, 1999) contend that focus particles in German can attach to any maximal projection. Büring and Hartmann (2001) propose that German focus particles attach only to non-argument XPs, where a principle of *Closeness* is used to explain the requirement of *only* to associate with a focus in its vicinity. The main data that have fuelled the discussion in German are as follows:

---

[39] The status of this meaning part as a presupposition, an entailment, or an implicature has been debated (see Horn 1996). For our purposes this distinction is not important. The original presuppositional account is due to Horn (1969).

[40] For a different position, see Kayne (1998).

(3.69) a. [$_{CP}$ Peter will [$_{PP}$ nur [$_{PP}$ mit [$_{DP}$ MaRIa]]] ausgehen]
Peter will   only   with   Mary   go.out

  b. *[$_{CP}$ Peter will [$_{PP}$ mit [$_{DP}$ nur [$_{DP}$ MaRIa]]] ausgehen]
'Peter wants to go out only with MARY.'

(3.70) a. [$_{CP}$ [$_{DP}$ Nur [$_{DP}$ der Vater [$_{DP}$ Marias]]] ist gekommen]
only   the father   Mary$_{GEN}$ is   come

  b. *[$_{CP}$ Der Vater [$_{DP}$ nur [$_{DP}$ Marias]] ist gekommen]
'Only MARY's father came.'

The examples in (3.69) and (3.70), which are labelled according to the analysis where adjunction to any XP should be possible, show that adjunction to a DP is not permitted if that DP is an argument of a preposition or if it is a genitive DP. Therefore, Jacobs (1983) argues that focus particles in general cannot adjoin to DPs, and Büring and Hartmann (2001) suggest that the focus particle always adjoins to the (non-argument) extended verbal projection (EVP) immediately dominating the DP in question (i.e. VP, IP, or CP), and not to the DP itself. 'Immediately' here is only relevant in comparison to other EVPs of the same verb. Thus, in (3.69a) the relevant EVP is the VP dominating the PP, and in (3.70a) it is the CP, both bold-faced in (3.71):

(3.71) a. [$_{CP}$ Peter will [$_{VP}$ nur [$_{VP}$ [$_{PP}$ mit [$_{DP}$ MaRIa]] ausgehen]]]

  b. [$_{CP}$Nur [$_{CP}$ [$_{DP}$ der Vater [$_{DP}$ Marias]] ist gekommen]]

The b-examples in (3.69) and (3.70) are ruled out under this analysis because the position of the focus particle is not adjoined to an EVP.

   The main argument by those allowing attachment to DP is the fact that structures like (3.71b) violate the quite robust verb-second constraint in German. To account for the ungrammaticality of (3.69b) and (3.70b), Bayer (1996) suggests that although syntactic adjunction to any XP is allowed, such structures are excluded on semantic grounds: they cannot be interpreted. He argues that the particle needs to take scope over a domain where it can be interpreted, that is a domain which can serve as a domain of quantification. In most cases, this would be the VP (vP), which semantically corresponds to the proposition (for other cases see below). A particle takes syntactic scope over an XP if the particle itself and its associated phrase are governed by a head whose projection can serve as a domain of quantification (Bayer 1996: 53). Thus, if the governor is a V, which projects to some EVP, the particle can be interpreted on a propositional level. According to these conditions, the (a)-cases in (3.69) and (3.70) are licit: the quantified phrase (particle + XP) is governed by V. In cases where these conditions are not met, the quantified phrase can be quantifier-raised to a higher position—provided constraints on movement are respected. Inside a PP (e.g. (3.69b)), the particle cannot take scope over the VP because it fails to be governed by V. Yet, neither can the quantified phrase be raised on LF because in German the PP is a barrier for movement, see Bayer (1996). As a consequence, the derivation will crash if the quantifier cannot be interpreted locally, that is within the PP. This leads us to question under what circumstances a quantifier like *only* MAY be interpreted locally, by which we arrive at the issue of scope.

3.4.1.3 *Propositional and narrow scope of* only   The clearest case in point for a local interpretation of *only* is the scalar use of the particle, which can be identified most easily in constructions where *only* associates with numerals or with degree adverbs (e.g. Altmann 1976; Horn 1969; Löbner 1990). The examples in (3.72) show how the scope of the focus particle in such a context can change with the particle's position:

(3.72)   a.   Max kann auf nur EINEM Arm laufen.
                 Max can   on only one   arm walk
                 'Max can walk on only one arm.'

          b.   Max kann nur auf EINEM Arm laufen.
                 'Max can only walk on one arm.'

Example (3.72b) asserts that the only thing Max can do is walk on one arm (= VP scope). Example (3.72a), on the other hand, asserts that Max can walk on one arm, and that 'one' is little compared to other elements in the set of numbers 'x' (as far as arms are concerned). The scope in (3.72a) is clearly not the VP but smaller, here the numeral. Similar effects are found with degree adverbs:

(3.73)   a.   Hans liebäugelt   mit nur WEnig gebrauchten
                 Hans has.set.his.eyes with only little used
                 Oldtimern.
                 vintage.cars
                 'Hans has set his eyes on only little-used vintage cars.'

          b.   Hans liebäugelt nur mit WEnig gebrauchten Oldtimern.
                 'Hans has only set his eyes on little-used vintage cars.'

Sentence (3.73b) says that the only thing Hans has set his eyes on are little-used vintage cars whereas (3.73a) says that Hans has set his eyes on little-used vintage cars and that 'little' is indeed little as compared to other degrees of having used a vintage car.

Numerals and degree adverbs are natural elements on a scale. *Only* picks an element which is on a low point on that scale. Whereas *only* in its purely quantificational use asserts that the proposition at hand only holds for one out of a set of several alternatives, the scalar use of *only* adds an evaluative meaning.[41] Importantly, the domain of quantification in the scalar cases does not have to be a proposition. The examples in (3.73) show that the scope can be a numeral, or a degree phrase alone, so that *little-used* is in a set with *much-used*, etc.

The English gloss in (3.73) indicates that the outcome in English is pretty much the same as in German even though English in general allows adjunction to DP which may result in VP-scope of the particle (cf. *John talked to only Mary*). Sometimes, speakers do not seem to be able to detect the difference between sentences like (3.73a) and (3.73b) easily. Bayer (1996) offers a way of bringing out the difference more cleary. His examples are given in (3.74). Whereas (3.74a), where the particle in the second conjunct takes scope over the degree phrase is felicitous with the first conjunct as context, (3.74b), where the particle scopes over the whole proposition is not. Excluding all alternatives to talking to weakly gifted students also excludes talking to brilliant students. This, however, is not what the first conjunct claims to be true of John. Therefore, the discourse is incoherent and contradictory.

(3.74)   a.   Today, John talked to some brilliant students and he talked to only WEAKly gifted students.   (Bayer 1996: 69)

     b.   #Today, John talked to some brilliant students and he talked only to WEAKly gifted students.

Bayer (1996) suggests that even though LF movement should be possible in (3.74a) and could create VP scope—in English PPs are not islands—this does not happen because of economy considerations. Bayer follows Reinhart (1998) in assuming that LF movement is a costly process and will only be carried out if it delivers distinguishable interpretations (also cf. Fox 2000 on this idea). For the case of the focus particles, Bayer argues that quantifier raising usually results in marked results. In the example above, an alternative in situ interpretation of *only*—that is with a scalar meaning—is available, so this is the reading which is chosen.

---

[41] The quantificational and scalar uses of *only* cannot always be clearly distinguished:

(i)   They bought only a bottle of red WINE.
     quantificational: They didn't buy anything else.
     scalar: They didn't buy champagne.

We see here that nouns or properties that are not scalar by themselves, can receive a scalar interpretation. In (i), red wine is considered lower on an evaluative scale than champagne.

Jacobs (1983), who, recall, only allows adjunction to certain kinds of XPs excluding DPs, proposes that the syntactic position taken by the particle in cases like (3.72) or (3.73) corresponds directly to its semantic scope. Thus in (3.72), where a numeral is the focus associate, *only* associates with the numeral (the determiner in Jacob's terms). In (3.73), the particle adjoins to the adjective. In the cases with VP-scope, the adjunction site is the VP (see above). This analysis is basically taken over by Büring and Hartmann (2001), who present new arguments supporting this view.

Scope smaller than the VP is not limited to scalar uses of *only*. The following example is modelled on Bayer (1996, ch. 5):

(3.75) a. Wir haben ein nur dem KRANKen bekömmliches Gericht
            we have a only the patient   digestible   dish
            ausgewählt.
            chosen
            'We chose a dish that was only digestible by the patient.'

        b. Wir haben nur ein dem KRANKen bekömmliches Gericht
            ausgewählt.
            'We only chose a dish that was digestible by the patient.'

In (3.75a), the scope of *only* is restricted to the adjectival phrase. In (3.75b), on the other hand, the focus particle takes clausal scope. Nevertheless, no scalar interpretation is invoked in the (a)-case. The meaning of that sentence is that nobody but the sick person could eat the dish, whereas the (b) sentence says that we did not choose any other dish than the one that could be eaten by the sick person. A predicate like $\lambda x(x\ be\ digestible)$ can serve as a (local) domain of quantification. Therefore, although extraction from the prenominal position in German is impossible (see (3.76)),[42] the sentence is grammatical (Bayer 1996).

(3.76) *Dem Kranken$_i$ haben wir ein t$_i$ bekömmliches Gericht
         the patient   have we a   digestible   dish
         ausgewählt.
         chosen
         Intended: 'We chose a dish that was digestible by the patient.'

3.4.1.4 *The scope of* only *and gapping*   Let me start the discussion with an example from above (= ex. (3.58a)), repeated as (3.77), where the presence of *only* in the second conjunct changes the polarity of that conjunct from negative to positive:

---

[42] Note that (3.76) is grammatical under the reading *We chose a digestible dish for the patient.*

(3.77)   Mary wasn't greeted by John and Bill only by SUE.

Example (3.78a) shows the corresponding full clause coordination. The ellipsis site is marked by strikethrough, the intended focus exponent by small capitals. The focus *only* associates with is marked by FOC:

(3.78)   Mary wasn't greeted by John and Bill ~~was~~ [$_{vP}$ only [$_{vP}$ ~~greeted~~ [$_{PP}$ by SUE]$_{Foc}$]].

We see that *only* takes propositional scope. It attaches to vP, which is a domain where the particle can be interpreted on a propositional level.

Next consider examples where the particle does not take propositional scope. We saw above that this is, for instance, the case if *only* associates with adjectives or numerals that can receive a scalar interpretation. Here is a minimal pair:

(3.79)   a.   John didn't meet up with brilliant students and Mary only with weakly gifted ones.

conjunct 2 = 'Mary only met up with weakly gifted students.'

    b.   John didn't meet up with brilliant students and Mary with only weakly gifted ones.

conjunct 2 = 'Mary didn't meet up with only weakly gifted students.'

Whereas in (3.79a) the negation disappears, in (3.79b), where *only* occurs within a PP and associates with the degree adverb *weakly*, the second conjunct can still be negated. The focus particle does not take propositional scope in (3.79b). It does not interfere with the interpretation of the negation because it can be interpreted locally. The structural difference in the second conjunct is shown in (3.80):

(3.80)   a.   Mary [$_{vP}$ only [$_{vP}$ ~~met~~ [$_{PP}$ with [$_{DP}$ WEAKly gifted ones]]]].

    b.   Mary [$_{vP}$ ~~met~~ [$_{PP}$ with [$_{DP}$ [$_{AP}$ [$_{DegP}$ only [$_{DegP}$ WEAKly] gifted] students]]]].

In German, the data are similar although the effects are slightly obscured by the fact that adjunct negation is not copied. Let us therefore consider an example with a negative polarity item in the gap that needs to be licensed by the negation so that it gets copied. The following example contains the NPI *sich nicht träumen lassen* ('to never think it possible'):

(3.81) a. *Paul hat sich die Reise   in die Pyrenäen nicht
            Paul has REFL the journey in the Pyrenees not
            träumen lassen und Maria nur die Reise   in den
            dream   let   and Mary only the journey in the
            wenig besuchten Jemen.
            little visited   Yemen
            'Paul never thought it possible that he could travel to the Pyrenees
            and Mary only thought it possible that she could travel to little-
            visited Yemen.'

        b. Paul hat sich die Reise in die Pyrenäen nicht träumen lassen
            und Maria die Reise in den nur wenig besuchten Jemen.
            'Paul never thought it possible that he could travel to the Pyrenees
            and Mary never thought it possible that she could travel to only
            little-visited Yemen.'

Again, we see that if *only* does not take propositional scope (3.81b), the negation is present in the second conjunct. If *only* does take propositional scope
(3.81a), it interferes with the interpretation of the negation, which in the
present case results in ungrammaticality because the NPI requires the presence
of the negation.

Next consider gapping coordinations that contain numerals. According to
the theory of scalar interpretation of *only*, a quantified phrase with a numeral
can be interpreted in situ. From what we saw so far, it should therefore not
interact with the negation. Nevertheless, the positive reading emerges quite
easily both in English and in German: the sentences are ambiguous between a
positive and a negative reading:

(3.82) CONTEXT: *A ball game where children are supposed to hit as many tins
        as possible:*

        a. ?Peter hat ZEHN Büchsen nicht getroffen und MARIA nur SIEben.

        b. ?PEter didn't hit TEN cans and MARY only SEVEN.
            = 'Mary only hit seven cans' *or* 'Mary only didn't hit seven cans.'

If we look at an example where *only* occurs outside versus inside a prepositional phrase, that is if we make use of the island constraints in German,
compare (3.83a) versus (3.83b), we find that the case where *only* sits outside the
PP (3.83a) clearly has a positive reading. Thus, even though the interpretation
is scalar, the domain of interpretation is propositional. If *only* sits inside the PP,
see (3.83b), the result is marginal due to the difficulty of copying the negation
in the second conjunct. Thus, it seems that a negative reading is attempted.

(3.83) a. PEter steht   nicht auf ZWEI Stelzen und MAX nur
            Peter stands not   on two   stilts   and Max only
            auf EINer.
            on one

        b. ??PEter steht nicht auf ZWEI Stelzen und MAX auf nur EINer.
            'Peter does not stand on two stilts and
            {a: Max stands only on one | b: Max stands on only one}'

In general, the cases with numerals are much less clear than other examples. They indicate that in the absence of syntactic restrictions such as island
restrictions, the possibility of interpreting the focus particle locally does not
prevent it from taking scope over the whole proposition. With Bayer (1996)
and Reinhart (1998), we can assume that the 'additional' LF movement is
possible because it delivers a reading which is both interpretable and distinguishable from the *in situ* interpretation. The examples also show, however,
that quantifier raising in this case does not produce marked results.

In the final set of examples, the focus particle associates with a DP sub-
categorized by a noun-modifying adjective (e.g. example (3.75) above). Here
the scope is narrower than the proposition but no scale is involved. Rather,
the embedded predicate can serve as a domain of quantification because it is
clausal itself. Example (3.84) shows that the scope *only* takes again has effects
on the interpretation of the polarity of the second conjunct:

(3.84) MARIa hat ihre berüchtigte KOHLsuppe   nicht gekocht...
        Maria has her infamous   cabbage.soup not   cooked
        'Mary did not cook her infamous cabbage soup...'

        a. ??... und MAX sein nur ihm SELBST bekömmliches
                and Max his only him REFL   digestible
            FISCHcurry.
            fish.curry
            '...and Max (didn't cook) his fish curry which is only digestible
            by himself.'

        b. ...und MAX nur sein JEdermann bekömmliches FISCHcurry.
               and Max only his everybody digestible   fish.curry
            '...and Max only (cooked) his fish curry, which is digestible by
            everybody *(he did not cook that terribly hot chilly curry)*.'

In Example (3.84a), the second conjunct is interpreted as negated. Here, the
focus particle just scopes over the argument of the adjective *bekömmlich*
('digestible'). The negation of the matrix clause and the embedded focus particle do not interact. In (3.84b), the focus particle scopes over the matrix clause

and the second conjunct is interpreted as positive. Note that I have adapted the contents of the second conjunct in a way that supports the negative versus positive reading in (3.84a) versus (3.84b). Exchanging *selbst* ('himself') for *jedermann* ('everybody') would result in incoherence. The glosses indicate that the English data, which have the focus particle either in the matrix clause or in the relative clause behave in the same way as the German data.

To sum up, the scope of the focus particle *only* and the interpretation of the negation in the second conjunct of a gapping coordination interact quite reliably with each other. When *only* takes scope over the entire proposition, the negation in the second conjunct disappears. When *only* takes narrow scope, for example over an embedded proposition or over scalar expressions in syntactic islands, the negation in the second conjunct is preserved.

3.4.1.5 *Contextual restrictions on interpretation*   Having established that *only* produces narrow scope readings of the negation in gapping only if it takes propositional scope, the next step is to find out why exactly that is. I start again from the principle of balanced contrast: when I presented the *only* data in subsection 3.4.1.1, I argued that the balance between the conjuncts is disturbed by the presence of *only* if the second conjunct is interpreted as negative. I suggest that this has to do with the context-sensitivity of *only*. *Only* is a focus-sensitive operator, which means that it works with the alternatives induced by the focus. Importantly, the set of alternatives that focus induces has to be restricted by the context. As von Stechow (1991*a*) points out (also see Rooth 1985, 1992), a sentence like (3.85) could never be true if it were not evaluated with respect to a specific context:

(3.85)   Bill only works.

Bill cannot only have one property like *working*: he also is the son of somebody, his eyes are a certain colour, etc. Consequently, von Stechow (1991*a*: 821) suggests the semantics given in (3.86) for (3.85).

(3.86)   for any P: P is in $||\text{working}||_{p,c}$ and Bill has P, then P = $||\text{working}||$,
         i.e. the only property relevant at context c which Bill has is working.

In other words, a focus particle must be interpreted within a particular *contextual* domain of quantification.[43]

There are various ways to deal with this context-sensitivity. One is to assume that there is a focus variable involved in focus interpretation and that this

---

[43] The use of *domain of quantification* here differs from the one used above, where a *v*P was a domain of quantification, i.e. a domain where the particle could be interpreted.

variable needs an antecedent which is fixed by the context. This is the approach taken within the framework of alternative semantics (Rooth 1992; von Fintel 1994) and I will basically follow this idea.[44] In alternative semantics (Rooth 1985, 1992), which I assume the reader is familiar with, the binary '$\sim$' operator takes as its first argument the expression containing the focus and as its second argument, the focus variable C, which is the same type as the focus expression α (or the type of a set of objects with the same type as α). The value of C is *constrained* by the focus-semantic value $[\![\alpha]\!]^f$: it must be a subset of the focus semantic value containing at least the ordinary semantic value and one alternative. C's value is *fixed* pragmatically—it is essentially anaphoric. Von Fintel (1994) investigates the anaphoricity of C more closely and suggests that the focus variable and the contextual quantifier domain are not linked with each other directly. Rather, they both are anaphoric to a common discourse topic. Consider the following example, which involves the adverbial quantifier *usually*:

(3.87) A: How does John get to School?   (von Fintel 1994: 50)

  B: He usually WALKS$_F$.

In B's answer, the focus variable C corresponds to a subset of the focus semantic value $[\![$he (WALKS)$_F]\!]^f$, that is, a subset of the situations where John does something. The question which forms the context here denotes the set of propositions that John gets to school in manner x. This is the contextual domain of quantification of the adverb in B's answer. It is also contained in the subset of the focus semantic value: John's getting to school in manner x is in the subset of John's doing something. Therefore, John's getting to school in manner x can serve as an antecedent for the focus variable. This is what von Fintel considers to be the discourse topic. As in my analysis, for von Fintel, a discourse topic corresponds to an explicit or an implicit question which is under discussion. It is the mediator between the focus variable and contextual domain of quantification: it can serve as an antecedent for all.

The above kind of anaphoric analysis of focus has been applied to gapping sentences without *only* by Rooth (1992) and also by Hartmann (2000). They suggest that the two conjuncts of a highly parallel coordination provide alternatives to each other for the purpose of focus interpretation. This means that we have two contextual variables C_1 and C_2, one in each conjunct, where C_1 has its antecedent in conjunct 1 and C_2 has its antecedent in conjunct 2. This is illustrated below for the focus on the object:

---

[44] For more discussion of context-sensitivity, see for instance Cohen (1999), Dryer (1994), Krifka (1997), Schwabe (2000), Schwarzschild (1997).

(3.88)   Mary recognized the linden and Max the beech.

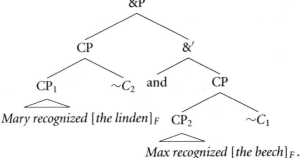

The ordinary and the focus semantic values of the first conjunct CP_1 are:

(3.89) $[\![$ Mary recognized $(\text{LINDEN}_F)]\!]^\circ$ = recognize (mary, linden)
         $[\![$ Mary recognized $(\text{LINDEN}_F)]\!]^f$ = recognize (mary, x) $\mid$ x $\in$ A (linden)

The antecedent of the variable C_2, which is adjoined to CP_1 must be a subset of this focus value and it must contain at least the ordinary semantic value of that CP and an alternative to it. An appropriate antecedent is the set:

(3.90)   Antecedent of C_2: {(recognize (mary, linden)), (recognize (mary, beech))}.

The second element in this set is provided by the ordinary semantic value of the second conjunct CP_2 and its focus *beech*. For the other conjunct, the derivation is reciprocal. The generalization for contrastive constructions is then (cf. Hartmann 2000; Rooth 1992):

(3.91)   Contrast: $[\![\alpha]\!]^\circ \in [\![\beta]\!]^f$ and $[\![\beta]\!]^\circ \in [\![\alpha]\!]^f$

I do not consider the subjects in this section for ease of exposition. Recall that I assume that gapping is a contrastive-topic–contrastive-focus structure and I assume that the antecedent of the respective variables is a set of sets of alternatives, along the lines of Büring (1997a; 2003, see Section 3.1); also see Hartmann (2000) for multiple focus.

How is the focus particle *only* interpreted in such a scenario with contrastive conjuncts? Not very differently from other environments. Recall that von Fintel (1994) suggests that a quantificational adverb and a focus are related via an anaphor and not directly. We can use this in the present context. The idea is that *only* simply associates with the same anaphor as the contrastive focus would do without the occurrence of *only*. In other words, the focus particle has in its contextual quantificational domain the appropriate alternative from the first conjunct as well as the ordinary semantic value of the proposition it occurs in. Technically, the focus particle is co-indexed with the variable C as shown in the subtree below (cf. Rooth 1992).

(3.92)

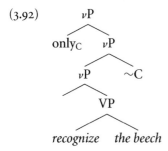

Let us look at the interpretation of the gapping example in (3.60), repeated as a coordination of full clauses in (3.93), in detail:

(3.93) a. $^?$ Mary didn't recognize [the LINden]$_F$ and Max only didn't recognize [the BEECH]$_F$.

       b. Mary didn't recognize [the LINden]$_F$ and Max only recognized [the BEECH]$_F$.

The derivation for (3.93a) is given in (3.94). Example (3.94a) is the focus semantic value of the VP of the second conjunct without the meaning of *only*. Example (3.94b) is the value of the variable $C_{(1)}$, which is determined by the context, that is it (also) contains an alternative to the focus provided by conjunct 1 (*the linden*). Example (3.94c) is the meaning of the VP of the second conjunct combined with the meaning of *only*.

(3.94) a. Conj2: $[\![$ not recognize (the BEECH$_F$)$]\!]^f = \lambda$x. $\neg$ recognize (x, y) | y $\in$ A(beech)

       b. C_2: $\{(\lambda$x.$\neg$ recognize (x, linden)), (λx. $\neg$ recognize (x, beech))$\}$

       c. λx. $\neg$ recognize (x, beech) $\wedge \forall$P$\in$C [P(x) $\rightarrow$ P = λx.$\neg$recognize (x, beech)]]

Since by the contribution of *only* to conjunct 2, all P in C must be λx.$\neg$*recognize (x, beech)*, alternatives to the focus provided by the context, which are contained in C, are excluded. This means that a predicate like λx.$\neg$ *recognize (x, linden)*, where the focus *beech* is replaced by a contextual alternative, *linden*, does not apply to Max. Thus, by entailment, Max recognized the linden—he did not not recognize it. This is the exact opposite of what is predicated of Mary in the first conjunct, viz. $\lambda x.\neg recognize\ (x,\ linden)$. We end up with a relation where the two conjuncts are not balanced for the requirements of the PBC. Note, by the way, that we should expect this example to be the better with *but*, which is prototypically used to conjoin clauses that make opposing contributions to a superordinate discourse topic (see Section 3.1). This is indeed the case, as (3.95) shows. Still, although (3.95) is clearly better than its counterpart with *and*, it seems that we need a rather specific context (such as the beech being more easily recognizable than the linden):

(3.95) Mary didn't recognize the linden but Max only didn't recognize the beech.

Such sentences are impeccable if natural scales are involved, as I demonstrate in subsection 3.4.1.6.

Now, turning to the sentence in (3.93b), where the second conjunct is interpreted as positive, we find that the contextual domain of the focus particle in contrast to (3.93a) does provide for a coherent discourse. Example (3.96a) gives the focus semantic value of conjunct 2 without *only*. Example (3.96b) is the value of C. Example (3.96c) gives the meaning of conjunct 2 with *only*:

(3.96) Mary didn't recognize [the LINden]$_F$ and Max only recognized [the BEECH]$_F$.

   a. Conj2: $[\![recognize\ (the\ BEECH_F)]\!]^f$: $\lambda x.\ recognize\ (x,\ y)\ |\ y \in A(beech)$

   b. $C_2 = \{(\lambda x.[recognize\ (x,\ linden)]),\ (\lambda x.\ recognize\ (x,\ beech))\}$

   c. $[[\lambda x.\ recognize\ (x,\ beech) \wedge \forall P \in C\ [P(x) \rightarrow P = \lambda x.\ recognize\ (x,\ beech)]$

Evaluating C, the last line entails that it is not the case that the alternative to the focus provided by the context, *the linden* could replace the focus *the beech*. Thus, it is not the case that Max recognized the linden. This is identical to what is predicated of Mary. The contrast is balanced, the principle of balanced contrast is obeyed.

Next consider an example with non-propositional *only*, (3.97). Sentence (3.97a) gives the focus semantic value of the second conjunct for the *only*-relevant focus (see below for more on this) without the focus particle *only*. Example (3.97b) gives the focus semantic value of the second conjunct with the semantics of *only*. This shows that *only* picks up just on the embedded focus, having non-propositional scope. The meaning of the matrix clause

[¬cook (x, z)] is not influenced by this and consequently there is no interaction with the negation of the first conjunct.

(3.97) Maria hat ihre berüchtigte Kohlsuppe nicht gekocht
und Max sein nur ihm SELBST$_F$ bekömmliches Fischcurry. = (3.84a)
'Mary did not cook her infamous cabbage soup and Max didn't cook his fish curry which is only digestible by himself.'

a. ⟦did not cook his fishcurrry which is digestible by HIMSELF$_F$⟧^{f}:
λx.$\exists$z [meal (z) $\wedge$ (digestible (z, y) | y $\in$ A(x)) $\wedge$ (¬cook (x, z)]

b. ⟦did not cook his fishcurrry which is only digestible by HIM-SELF$_F$⟧^{f}
λx.$\exists$z [meal (z) $\wedge$ digestible (z, y) $\wedge$ [$\forall$P$\in$\{digestible (z, y) | y $\in$ Alt (x)\} [P(z)(x) $\rightarrow$ P = (digestible (z, x))]] $\wedge$¬cook (x, z)]

As mentioned above, the formulas in (3.97) only look at the foci relevant for *only*. The example is quite interesting as the contrast pairs clearly are independent of these foci: the contrast pairs are the subjects *Maria* and *Max* on the one hand, and the objects *ihre berüchtigte Kohlsuppe* ('her infamous cabbage soup') and *sein nur ihm selbst bekömmliches Fischcurry* ('the fish curry that can only be digested by himself'). We end up having nested foci so that the focus semantic value would roughly look as follows (for reasons of readability again no subjects):

(3.98) ⟦did not cook [his fishcurrry which is only digestible [by HIM-SELF]$_F$]$_F$⟧^{f}:
λx.$\exists$z [meal (z) $\wedge$ digestible (z, y) $\wedge$
[$\forall$P$\in$\{digestible (z, y) | y $\in$ Alt (x)\}
[P(z)(x) $\rightarrow$ P = (digestible (z, x))]] $\wedge$
[¬cook (Max, z) | z $\in$ Alt (fish curry only digestible by himself)]]

For the cases with propositional *only*, the situation is slightly different. The contrast pairs here are the subjects and the predicates—and not just the objects: what is juxtaposed in (3.93b) is Mary's not recognizing something with Max's recognizing something. The focus particle, on the other hand, picks up on the objects for alternative sets.

3.4.1.6 *Coordinations with* but *and* only   I indicated above (example (3.95)) that the second conjunct of a gapping sentence which contains *only* and the conjunction *but*, can receive a negative interpretation. Let us consider the corresponding full clauses:

(3.99) Maria hat Peter, Klaus und Karl nicht geholfen, aber Max
        Maria has Peter Klaus and Karl not   helped   but   Max
        hat nur dem alten Mann nicht geholfen.
        has only the   old   man   not   helped
        'Mary did not help Peter, Klaus and Karl but Max only did not help
        the old man.'

(3.100) Maria hat vielen Leuten nicht geholfen, aber Max hat nur dem alten
        Mann nicht geholfen.
        'Mary did not help many people but Max only didn't help the old
        man.'

These examples are different from those considered in the previous section in
that they easily allow scalar readings of *only*. In (3.100), there is a scale whose
elements are the number of people that were helped by somebody. Whereas
Mary did not help many people, Max only didn't help one, namely the old
man. Using the quantificational semantics of *only*, this produces exactly the
same interpretation as in the above examples which did not involve scales. It
entails that Max helped everybody else in the relevant context set, including
the (many) people Mary did not help. Thus, what is predicated of Mary versus
Max is quite different which warrants the use of *but*. The difference between
(3.100) and the earlier (3.95) is that in (3.95) no scale was involved. I come
to that presently. The first conjunct of (3.99) refers to a set of people that
were not helped by Mary. The quantificational computation is the same as
above. I would like to argue that here too, a scalar interpretation is involved.
Not helping only the old man, that is only one person, is not as bad as not
helping three people. Again, the conjuncts make a different contribution to
the discourse topic.

As I said, the examples in (3.99) and (3.100) involve scales. But why is it that
only the evaluative scalar interpretation seems to be available in contrastive-
but coordinations like these? Jacobs (1983) suggests that the quantificational
and the evaluative scalar uses of *only* correspond to two meaning components
of the focus particle which—depending on the context (and on the syntactic
position of the focus particle)—can be neutralized or favoured. He argues
that the semantics of *only* is actually based on scales. These scales can be
structured in different ways. There are scales whose elements are ordered
in terms of probability or other evaluating functions. There are quantitative
scales. And there are also scales whose elements are not ordered. *Only* excludes
those alternatives that are higher on a scale or of equal value to the associated
element, which in the purely quantificational use of *only* results in the exclu-
sion of all other elements and not only those, for instance, that are above a

certain threshold, because they would all be of the same value as the focus associate.[45]

In which environments can one of the two readings be neutralized whereas the other is highlighted? Jacobs suggests that the exclusive use is neutralized if it is trivially true because it follows from the meaning of the rest of the sentence, which serves as a presupposition. Thus in (3.101), the exclusive reading is trivially true as a mediocre student cannot be a brilliant student or a bad student at the same time (Jacobs 1983: 172).

(3.101)   Peter is only a mediocre student.

Building on these considerations, I would like to offer the following speculation about what happens in the coordinations with *but*. In Section 3.1, I argued that *but* associates with contrastive topics, which come with their respective, that is different, foci. The focus coming with one contrastive topic cannot be applied to the other (recall Umbach's discussion of the distinctiveness condition). This is pretty similar to what *only* asserts of the proposition it occurs in: alternatives to the focus are excluded.[46] Therefore the entailments *but* introduces already carry the meaning that would be conveyed by the use of *only*. As a consequence, the use of exclusive *only* becomes tautological: there is no reason to say the same thing twice. This pushes the scalar meaning to the foreground. Yet this scalar reading is not felicitous in contexts were no scale is easily available. By the same token, the sentences with several antecedents or a plural antecedent are good: they provide a structured quantitative scale.

Let me summarize. In gapping sentences with a negative first conjunct and a second conjunct with the focus particle *only*, the second conjunct is interpreted in such a way that the principle of balanced contrast is obeyed. If positive polarity produces balanced contrast, it is positive polarity that surfaces in gapping: a narrow scope reading arises. If negative polarity produces balanced contrast it is negative polarity that surfaces in gapping: distributed scope arises. Whether the distributed reading is felicitous depends on the categorial status of the negation (adjunct or head). For the narrow scope reading, I assume that as in the other instances of narrow scope there is a positive morpheme in the numeration of the second conjunct. We saw that there are several factors that contribute to the interpretation of *only* in coordinations. The scope of *only* plays an important role as does the context-sensitivity of the focus particle since alternative sets are built from both conjuncts of the

---

[45] Against this background, Jacobs considers *only* vague in environments where both the quantificational and the scalar reading are available, see footnote 41 above.

[46] Umbach (2005) also notes the similarity between *only* and *but*.

coordination. For coordinations with *but* I had to make some additional assumptions.

In the next section I turn to *not only*, which is quite different from the interaction of negation and *only* I have considered so far.

3.4.1.7 *Not only*   *Not only* has a different semantics from what would be expected if it were the mere composition of propositional negation and *only*. As a matter of fact, I claim that the negation in *not only* does not operate on the level of the proposition at all. Rather it is a speech act operator. This analysis is supported by the environments *not only* occurs in, that is to say in denials and corrective structures (see Chapter 4 for the latter). For gapping this means that the presence of *not only* in the first conjunct produces narrow scope readings, as I will show below.

Horn (2000) observes that an important feature of *not only* is that a clause containing this element normally cannot stand on its own but needs some kind of continuation. In English, this is often the conjunction *but*.[47] The German equivalent involves corrective *but*, that is *sondern*:

(3.102)   a.   He is not only tall but he's also beautiful.[48]

        b.   Er ist nicht nur groß, sondern auch schön.

Horn argues that *not only A but B* is never concessive *(A but on the other hand B)*, which by many authors is considered an integral component of contrastive *but* (see Section 3.1). Rather, it is expansive *(A, but what's more B)*. For the latter concept, Horn builds on Dik's (1989: 284) treatment of these constructions as *expanding focus* constructions. Horn suggests that 'B represents a stronger predication than A, picking up where A leaves off' (Horn 2000: 153). In the above example, it is not the case that the person in question is only tall (on the exclusive reading). In addition, that person is also beautiful. Negating *only* and its focus associate asserts that there ARE other alternatives next to the one focused by *only*.

The focus particle *auch/too* in the second conjunct is more or less obligatory: it spells out what the negation of *only* asserts. At least, this holds for the non-scalar use of *not only*. Scalar *not only* translates into English as *not just*:

(3.103)   a.   *Er ist nicht nur groß, sondern schön.

       a'.   *He is not only tall but beautiful.

---

[47] Other continuations of *not only* apart from the one with *but* are possible as well:

(i)   John can't be trusted. He is not only a scaredy-cat. Worse: he talks.

[48] In contrast to 'ordinary' correction structures (see Chapter 4), the corrective-*but*-conjunct does not need to be elliptic here.

b. Er ist nicht nur groß, sondern sehr groß.

b′. He is not just tall but very tall.

Thus, *not only* occurs in corrections, where some (implicit) assumption picked up by *not only* is corrected in a second clause.

It is also possible to use *not only* to negate a previous utterance that contained *only*. This, then, is a straightforward denial. Relevant cases have been brought up in the literature for instance by Horn (1989; 2000), Reis (1977) and van der Auwera (1985), for example:

(3.104) A: Das war nur ein Blitz.
             that was only a   lightning.

         B: Das war nicht nur ein Blitz,   das war eine Explosion.
             that was not   only a   lightning that was a   explosion
         A′: That was only lightning. B′: It was not only lightning, it was an explosion.'

In gapping, *not only* behaves in a way that supports the analysis of the negation in it as a speech act operator (i.e. illocutionary negation, see Chapter 4). In (3.105a), the negation takes narrow scope over the first conjunct, even though the underlying version (3.105b) would actually allow a negative interpretation of the second conjunct. Both (3.105a) and (3.105b) can only be understood as a coordination of denials, with a heavy accent on the negation in the first conjunct. In the second conjunct of (3.105a), the focus particle carries an accent, and in (3.105b) the negation does.

(3.105) a. MaRIa hat NICHT nur der alten FRAU   geholfen und
             Mary has not   only the old   woman helped   and
             MAX NUR dem alten MANN.
             Max only the old   man
             'Mary didn't only help the old woman and Max (helped) only the old man.'

         b. MaRIa hat NICHT nur der alten FRAU geholfen und MAX hat
             NICHT nur dem alten MANN geholfen.
             'Mary didn't only help the old woman and Max didn't only help the old man.'

As I will argue in Chapter 4, denial negation is not copied into the second conjunct because it is situated outside the proposition, and the coordination. For the above example, this means that if the second conjunct is to receive a negative interpretation, this has to be made explicit, and if we find *nur* on its own, that is without an explicit negation, in the second conjunct of a gapping construction, it will never correspond to underlying *not only*.

3.4.2 *Even*

3.4.2.1 *The data* In the introductory part of Section 3.4.1, I demonstrated that *only* can improve gapping sentences whose second conjunct tends to be interpreted as positive but does not reach the level of grammaticality. This was, for instance, the case in auxiliary gapping. With *even*, we find similar effects:

(3.106) a. Max hat nicht geholfen und Maria _ $^?$(sogar) gelacht.
             Max has not   helped   and Mary has   even   laughed
             'Max did not help and Mary even laughed.'

         b. Max hat den Ball nicht vor   seinem Ende bewahren
             Max has the ball not   from its   end   prevent
             können und Maria _ $^?$(sogar) das ganze Spielzeughaus
             can   and Mary has   even   the whole toy.house
             zerstört.
             destroyed
             'Max could not prevent the ball's end and Mary even destroyed the toy house.'

The following is a control structure, which shows an analogous behaviour:

(3.107) Pete tried not to help and John $^{??}$(even) to hinder us.

(C. Wilder, p.c.)

In Examples (3.106) and (3.107), the positive reading of the second conjunct is already quite plausible without the focus particle. Nevertheless, gapping fails in these cases because the contrasts are not quite balanced—an attitudinal reading of *and* is evoked, which is not available for gapping because it is subject to the PBC. The addition of *even* seems to overcome the imbalance.

I show in the next section that *even* associates with a focus that has its alternatives on a scale of noteworthiness and picks out the most noteworthy one. This means that when considering examples with *even* it is important to take into account the 'direction' of the scale. For instance, in (3.108), not eating some old bread is no more noteworthy than not eating chocolate pudding ((3.108a)), whereas eating old bread can be considered more noteworthy than not eating chocolate pudding ((3.108b)). Hence, the unacceptability of a negative (3.108a) versus the acceptability of a positive second conjunct (3.108b) after the first conjunct in (3.108). In (3.109), in contrast, a negative conjunct is appropriate whereas a positive one is not. Not eating chocolate pudding is more noteworthy than not eating chicken drum sticks (in a world where chocolate pudding is a favourite food and chicken drum sticks are just ordinary), see (3.109a). Eating chocolate pudding, on the other hand, is not more noteworthy than not eating chicken drum sticks, see (3.109b). Note that in neither case—(3.108) nor (3.109)—is gapping available, see the (c)-examples.

(3.108)   John didn't eat the chocolate pudding—

    a.   * and Mary didn't even eat the old bread from last week.

    b.   and Mary even ate the old bread from last week.

    c.   * and Mary even the old bread from last week.

(3.109)   Mary didn't eat the chicken drum sticks—

    a.   and her brother didn't even eat the chocolate pudding.

    b.   * and her brother even ate the chocolate pudding.

    c.   * and her brother even the chocolate pudding.

The acceptable version with a positive second conjunct in (3.108b) involves an attitudinal reading of *and*. As I will show in subsection 3.4.2.3 below, juxtaposing a negative first conjunct with a positive second conjunct containing *even* in main verb gapping (as opposed to auxiliary gapping in (3.106) above) almost always[49] calls for an attitudinal reading of *and*, which is why gapping is not allowed—it is subject to the PBC. As for the unacceptability of gapping in the example with a plausible negative second conjunct, ((3.109c)), I argue that *not even* is different from a simple composition of *not* and *even*. This is supported by a parallel example in German, which uses a different lexical marker for *not even*, *nicht einmal* (literally 'not once'):

(3.110)   ?Maria hat die Hähnchenschenkel   nicht gegessen—
    Maria   has the chicken.drum.sticks not   eaten

    a.   und ihr Bruder hat sogar den Schokopudding   nicht
       and her brother has even   the chocolate.pudding not
       gegessen.
       eaten

    b.   und ihr Bruder hat nicht einmal den Schokopudding
       and her brother has not   once   the chocolate.pudding
       gegessen.
       eaten

Thus, *even* interacts in special ways with the negation which I argue to be behind the unacceptability of examples such as (3.109c).

---

[49]   The exception are constructions with numerals or other quantifiers.

Finally, note that unlike *only*, *even* cannot 'produce' a narrow scope reading in gapping where the same sentence without *even* would have received a distributed scope reading. Example (3.111a) is a balanced gapping sentence with a distributed scope reading. Example (3.111b) adds *even*, which results in ungrammaticality. Example (3.111c) is the corresponding full clause coordination with a positive second conjunct, and Example (3.111d) is the corresponding full clause coordination with a negative second conjunct. Out of context both are slightly marginal but can be accommodated.

(3.111)   a.   John didn't eat the chocolate pudding and Mary ~~didn't eat~~ the crème caramel.

           b.   *John didn't eat the chocolate pudding and Mary even the crème caramel.

          b′.   #John didn't eat the chocolate pudding and Mary even ate the crème caramel.

          b″.   #John didn't eat the chocolate pudding and Mary didn't even eat the crème caramel.

To sum up the data, *even* can improve a gapping sentence if that gapping sentence contains a second conjunct which most naturally would receive a positive interpretation but cannot do so without evoking an attitudinal reading of *and*. *Even* cannot occur with a negative second conjunct in gapping even if the corresponding full version is perfectly grammatical. *Even* does not 'change' the polarity of the second conjunct in gapping. It makes use of the contrasts of the coordination and changes them only slightly. To account for these effects, I proceed as with *only* although in an abbreviated form. I first look at the syntax and semantics of the focus particle and then investigate what this buys us for the interpretation and felicity of the gapping sentences.

3.4.2.2 *Brief overview over the syntax and semantics of* even   *Even* differs from *only* in a number of ways. It is generally[50] assumed to have no truth-conditional import (e.g. Horn 1969). The meaning contribution of *even* is usually taken to come in the form of a presupposition.[51] For the precise nature of that presupposition, varying suggestions have been made. The most widespread assumption is that some probability scale is involved: an element focused by the particle picks out an element that is less probable than one or more contextual relevant alternatives (Bennet 1982; Francescotti 1995; Krifka 1992) or it picks out an element that is the least probable (Fauconnier 1975; Jacobs 1983; Karttunen and Peters 1979). In other words, the use of *even* implies

---

[50] For different views, see for instance Lycan (1991) or Herburger (2000).
[51] For a discussion see for instance Kay (1990).

that if the element associated with *even* fulfils the proposition, (all the) other elements on the relevant probability scale do anyway. Apart from probability, notions like surprise, unexpectedness, or noteworthiness have also been invoked (e.g. Francescotti 1995; Jacobs 1983; Herburger 2000).[52] Kay (1990) suggests that *even* expresses a pragmatic relation along the lines of the Gricean maxim of quantity, more specifically 'a relation of greater informativeness' between the current clause and some explicit or implicit context, where p is more informative than q if p entails q. Consider the following example:

(3.112) A: It looks as if Mary is doing well at Consolidated Wiget. George [the second vice president] likes her work.

B: That's nothing. Even Bill [the president] likes her work.

(Kay 1990: 86)

B's sentence does not implicate that Bill was the least likely, or less likely than other individuals, to like Mary's work. Bill's liking Mary's work is more informative, however, because of Bill's high position in the company.[53] In the following, I assume that *even* comes with a presupposition which is of a scalar nature with the scale referring to informativeness or noteworthiness.

Even differs from *only* in that it does not convey a negative, exclusive meaning. Rather, it picks out an element from a set of elements that have the same property: in (3.112), both George and Bill like Mary's work. All *even* says is that Bill having that property is more noteworthy than George having it. Therefore, we would not expect *even* to be able to 'produce' a narrow scope reading of the negation in gapping in the same way as *only* does.

When it comes to negation as such, *even* displays quite an interesting behaviour (Horn 1969, 1989; Karttunen and Peters 1979; Kuroda 1977; Wilkinson 1996): it cannot occur in the scope of negation (at least in single clauses, see below for complex sentences):

(3.113) a. Even Muriel voted for Hubert.   (Horn 1969: 105)

b. Not even Muriel voted for Hubert.

Example (3.113b) does not mean that it is not the case that even Muriel voted for Hubert. Rather, it means that even Muriel did not vote for Hubert. Horn (1969) furthermore gives the following examples where in the (a)-case it is

---

[52] Also see Anscombre and Ducrot (1983), Ducrot (1973), Iten (2000) for more on this.

[53] Other examples where the semantics of *even* given above is not quite right are of the following sort:

(i) John even won the silver medal.

(i) does not imply that John also won the bronze medal or any other medal in the alternative set, which was more likely to be won. See e.g. Rullmann (1997), Schwarz (2005) for discussion.

only the proposition that is negated while the presupposition is maintained. The (b)-case is infelicitous as an answer.

(3.114)   Did even Muriel vote for Hubert?   (Horn 1969: 105)

    a.   No, she didn't.

    b.   #No, not even SHE did.

Importantly, although the negative sentences in (3.113b) and (3.114b), just as their positive counterparts, presuppose a scale, this scale picks out the most likely rather than the least likely element on that scale: if the proposition does not hold true for the focus associate of *even*, it will not hold true for any other element on the scale. So the presupposition, which is assumed to escape normal sentence negation, is not actually preserved. This observation has fuelled two kinds of theories. According to the theory of lexical ambiguity (Rooth 1985; Giannakidou 2007; Rullmann 1997; and others), in addition to ordinary *even*, which is a PPI, there is NPI-*even*, which has the *most-likely* presupposition just described. The scope theory (Guerzoni 2004; Karttunen and Peters 1979; Wilkinson 1996) assumes that *even* in the negative contexts needs to rise above the negation. Since a proposition p is more likely than a proposition q if the negation of p is less likely than the negation of q and vice versa, for example if Muriel is less likely to have voted for Hubert than Harry is, she is also more likely not to have voted for Hubert than Harry is, the outcome is as desired. There has been a lively debate around this issue (see the references above),with the lexical ambiguity position having been argued to be more successful because of overt lexical differences in other languages. One such language is German.

German *sogar*, which is the counterpart of positive *even*, feels particularly uneasy in the company of negation. For a start, the literal translation of *not even* is ungrammatical in German:

(3.115)   *Maria hat nicht sogar Max eingeladen.
            Maria has not   even Max invited
            Intended: 'Mary did not even invite Max.'

The construction *sogar nicht* is often considered clumsy or slightly marginal. It does exist, though and when I discuss *sogar* in German gapping I present a few examples where it is more or less acceptable. The preferred realizations for the meaning of English *not even* are *nicht einmal* (literally 'not once'), for example (3.116), (3.117), or *auch nur* (literally 'also only'; typically in combination with negative quantifiers), for example (3.118). Both items are often considered NPIs, for discussion see for example Guerzoni (2004), Rooth (1985), Rullmann (1997), Schwarz (2005), von Stechow (1991a):

(3.116) a. #Maria hat sogar MAX nicht eingeladen.
              Maria has even Max not   invited

         b. Maria hat nicht einmal MAX eingeladen.
             Mary has not   once Max invited
             'Mary did not even invite Max.'

(3.117) a. #Sogar MARIA hat Max nicht eingeladen.

         b. Nicht einmal MARIA hat Max eingeladen.
             'Not even Mary invited Max.'

(3.118) Niemand hat Maria auch nur geKÜSST.
         nobody has Mary also only kissed
         'Nobody even KISSED Mary.'

Since my focus in this section is on the meaning contribution of *sogar* and not so much on that of *nicht einmal* or *auch nur* I shall not discuss these elements here, see the references given above.

As for the syntax of *even*, most authors assume the same analysis as for *only* (see subsection 3.4.1.2), although there are some exceptions. The most relevant exception in the present context is the fact that *even* always has propositional scope and this seems to preclude certain syntactic positions. If the syntactic position forestalls propositional scope, *even* cannot be interpreted:

(3.119) a. * Peters Korb war mit   sogar SEHR großen Beeren gefüllt.
               Peter's basket was with even very big   berries filled

         b. Peters Korb war sogar mit SEHR großen Beeren gefüllt.

         c. Peters Korb war mit   nur sehr KLEINEN Beeren gefüllt.
             Peter's basket was with only very small   berries filled
             'Peters basket was filled (a) with even very big berries; (b) even with very big berries; (c) with only small berries.'

Examples where a proposition containing *even* is embedded in another proposition are fine:

(3.120) Peter kochte ein sogar dem Kranken bekömmliches Gericht.
         Peter cooked a   even the patient digestible   dish
         'Peter cooked a meal even digestible by the patient.'

I shall not discuss these cases here. For the purposes of gapping, they are parallel to those with *only*.

To sum up, the most important differences between *only* and *even* are as follows. In contrast to *only*, *even* does not convey a negative, exclusive meaning. Rather, it picks out an element from a set of elements with the same property and says that judging from the point of view of degrees of noteworthiness, the fact that the element in question is in the set is more noteworthy than the fact that other elements are in it. *Even* does not have truth-conditional effects whereas *only* does. *Even* can only take propositional scope whereas *only* can take both propositional and narrower scope. Similarly to *not only*, the semantics of *not even* is different from what might be expected in a simple composition of the two parts.

3.4.2.3 *Even in gapping*   For the analysis of gapping with *even* I assume the same contextual set-up as for *only* (subsection 3.4.1.5). As before, the context provided by the first conjunct is used to establish the value of the contextual variable C, which provides the alternative set against which the focus of *even* is evaluated. I begin with narrow scope auxiliary gapping. For (3.106a), repeated below as (3.121), I observed that the second conjunct on the most plausible interpretation has positive polarity:

(3.121)   Max hat nicht geholfen und Maria sogar gelacht. (= (3.106))
          'Max did not help and Mary even laughed.'

The scale used by *sogar* here is one that compares *not helping* with *laughing* where *laughing* is considered more noteworthy than *not helping*. It is fairly easy to accommodate a common discourse topic that follows the PBC in this case, for example one where both Max and Maria behaved very badly in a specific situation (e.g. where someone hurt him/herself). The elements on the scale used by *even* correspond to the negative and positive predicates of the two conjuncts. *Laughing* is a positive event, which is compared on the scale of noteworthiness with a negatively described event (*not helping*).

For main verb gapping, there are three types of examples. The first type is a gapping coordination with numerals or quantifiers calling for a positive interpretation of the second conjunct. As indicated in footnote 49 and demonstrated below, such cases are generally good:

(3.122)   a.   John doesn't earn as much as Sue and Bill, ?(even) less.

          b.   Max verdient nicht so viel wie Susanne, und Bill ?(sogar) weniger.

The examples involve scales of amounts of money. The two conjuncts make the same kind of contribution to a common discourse topic, that is that neither of the two subjects earns much. John does not earn as much as Sue, and Bill earns even less than John, which means that he does not earn as much as Sue either. The coordination is balanced. The elements on the scale relevant for *even* are *not as much as Sue*[54] and *less*.

---

[54]   The scales in this example actually deserve some closer scrutiny as *not as much as Sue* basically is a negative quantifier. I will not go into the details of this here.

For the other types of main verb gapping—those that do not contain numbers or the like—I found above that they are generally bad. The first example to be discussed here (=(3.108c) from above) is best if in a full clause coordination the second conjunct receives a positive interpretation. Gapping, however, is not available:

(3.123) * John didn't eat the chocolate pudding and Mary even the old bread from last week.

I mentioned above that in the corresponding full clause coordination the conjunction *and* receives an attitudinal rather than a balanced contrastive reading here. The second conjunct reads like a commentary on the first. Why this is can be seen if we take a close look at the contextual focus interpretation. Saying that Mary even ate the old bread from last week means that (all the) other things in the alternative set to *the old bread from last week* were eaten (by Mary or someone else), which, however, is less noteworthy. This, in turn, implies that *the chocolate pudding*, which, because it is in the appropriate contextual constellation (i.e. it is focused in the first conjunct) is in the same alternative set as *the old bread from last week*, was also eaten. Yet, the first conjunct tells us that John did not eat the chocolate pudding. So what is said about John differs from what is said about Mary to the extent that the two conjuncts make opposing contributions. Therefore, *and* receives an attitudinal reading.

Main verb gapping is different from auxiliary gapping here because the size of the focus is different. For auxiliary gapping, I identified the predicates (polarity included) as the focus. In main verb gapping, in contrast, the focus corresponds to just the DPs so the two predicates will always be the same. This means that it is difficult to arrive at a balanced contrast because the same predicate comes with negative polarity in one conjunct, and with positive polarity in the other. Such a constellation almost definitely will violate the PBC considering that the meaning contribution of even is rather 'weak' (as opposed to *only*).

Finally, consider an instance of main verb gapping where the second conjunct in a neutral context preferably receives a negative reading (= (3.109c) from above):

(3.124) * Mary didn't eat the chicken drum sticks and her brother even the chocolate pudding.

In this case, the negative reading cannot emerge in gapping because *not even* is a complex operator whose parts cannot be elided individually.

3.4.2.4 *Summary* In this section, I argued that the felicity of gapping and the interpretation of the second conjunct in the context of focus particles and negation depends on several factors. In general, the gapped sentence must correspond to a full clause version that can be interpreted in a way that is compatible with the principle of balanced contrast. For the formation of balanced contrast in gapping with focus particles I found that the context-sensitivity of the focus particle plays an important role: the two conjuncts of the coordination form the context for each other. Other factors that I identified as important are the scope of the particle *only*, and the formation of meaningful scales for scalar *only* and *even*.

3.5 Summary

The investigation of the narrow scope readings in gapping has shown that the formation of the right kind of contrast—balanced in gapping with *and*, inverse in gapping with *but*—is a very important licensing factor in gapping. That contrast is important in gapping has been known for a long time (e.g. Hankamer 1973; Kuno 1976; Hartmann 2000; Sag 1976). The study of gapping with negation has brought forward subtleties of this that were hitherto unknown. I showed that there is one principle—the principle of balanced contrast for gapping sentences with *and*—that can account for a variety of effects which at first sight might have seemed unrelated. Whether focus particles are added to the second conjunct, whether only an auxiliary or also predicates are gapped—the resulting gapping structure must always obey the PBC. Furthermore, I showed (and thereby confirmed earlier observations by e.g. Féry and Hartmann 2005; Hartmann 2000; Kim 1997; Lee 1998; Winkler 2005) that the information structure of a gapping sentence is crucial for its felicity and interpretation. The information structural-sensitivity of contrastive *but*, for instance, turned out to be crucial for a narrow scope reading of gapping with this conjunction. Similarly, in gapping with focus particles the contextual interpretation of the focus was paramount. The interpretation of gapping sentences with contrastive *but* has led me to an analysis of gapping as a contrastive-topic–contrastive-focus structure.

4

Negation and the speech act

The gapping sentences in this chapter share the characteristic that the negation involved is not ordinary negation on the propositional level but a negation that operates on the speech act level. In that sense the negation takes widest scope. This does not mean, however, that the negation necessarily scopes over the whole coordination. This negation, which I shall call *illocutionary negation*, occurs in narrow scope readings which are used as corrections, and it occurs in gapping with a wide scope reading. I shall argue that in both cases, the negation is situated outside the coordination. In the first section of this chapter (4.1), I discuss the narrow scope readings in corrections with corrective *but* (German *sondern*). That section also serves as a general introduction to the topic of illocutionary negation, and more specifically to the notion of denial. Corrections are essentially denials with a substitution part. In Section 4.2, I show that wide scope readings in declarative gapping sentences are denials, too. For interrogatives, which can also occur with wide scope of the negation in gapping, I show that they always involve what has been called *outer negation*, which I assume to be another case of illocutionary negation. The section on the wide scope readings is based on Repp (2006).

4.1 Corrections and corrective *but*: More narrow scope readings

In corrections, the negation, which is obligatory in the first conjunct, has narrow scope.[1] This holds both for stripping, which is the typical correction structure, see (4.1), and gapping, see (4.2):

(4.1)   Peter is not in Leipzig but in Berlin.

(4.2)   Peter bewundert nicht Luise sondern Luise Peter.
         Peter admires   not   Luise butCORR Luise Peter
         'Peter doesn't admire Luise: Luise admires Peter.'

---

[1] There can be an overt negation in the second conjunct if the first conjunct contains two negations. The lower one can occur in the second conjunct:

(i)   John cannot (not COOK) but he can(not BAKE).

Whereas English uses the same conjunction in corrections and in contrastive coordinations—*but*—other languages mark the difference lexically. German uses *aber* for contrastive coordinations and *sondern* for corrections. Spanish uses *pero/sino,* and Swedish *men/utan.* For English, it has been claimed that the difference is marked by the use of ellipsis, where correction is elliptic and contrast is not (Horn 1985). For stripping this seems to hold:

(4.3)   John isn't clever but lazy.—*correction*
         John isn't clever but he is lazy.—*contrast*

As far as gapping is concerned, however, the corrective reading does not seem to be obligatory. Example (4.4) can have a simple contrastive meaning (if we neglect the general difficulty to have *but* in an English gapping coordination, see Chapter 1).

(4.4)   John wasn't called by Jess but Mary by Benjamin.

It has been suggested that in corrections, we are actually dealing with a complex operator *not-but* (Lang 1984; Horn 1989; McCawley 1991). Its contribution is usually taken to signal to the addressee that some material is to be removed from the discourse record and must be replaced with some alternative provided by the speaker.[2] So corrections are denials that come with a substitution. For instance, (4.1) above means that rather than being in Leipzig (which is denied), Peter is in Berlin. In the gapping sentence in (4.2) the proposition that Peter admires Luise is rejected and corrected subsequently.

The negation in denials is often assumed to be different from ordinary negation. It does not seem to be part of the sentence meaning proper and has been considered as being outside the proposition. This is an assumption that in my view is correct. In this section, I will review evidence that has been brought forward to support this assumption: the negation in denials behaves differently from ordinary propositional negation with respect to non-propositional parts of an utterance and with respect to polarity items (Section 4.1.1). I also show that the negation in corrections takes a position it does not take in non-denials, which has been noted for stripping but also carries over to gapping. For gapping, the generalization is that the negation can take several positions in the clause but must c-command at least one of the correlates (Section 4.1.2). I shall not provide a detailed analysis of corrective-*but*-coordinations as such because taking the whole set of data into account, which concern not only gapping but also stripping, as well as full clause coordinations, is beyond the scope of this study.

---

[2] Because of this function, the negation in these structures has been called *replacive negation* by Jacobs (1991). Another term widely used is *contrastive negation* (e.g. McCawley 1991).

4.1.1 *Denials, metalinguistic negation, and corrective* but

A denial is a speech act that objects to a previous utterance.[3] According to van der Sandt (1991), it removes (part of) previously introduced material from the common ground and performs a correction operation on contextual information. Removing material from the common ground typically, though not necessarily, involves negation. A means to express a 'positive' denial is for instance VERUM FOCUS, for example a focus on the finite verb of the sentence, which highlights the positive polarity of the sentence (Höhle 1988, 1992; also see Chapter 5).

With Stenius (1967), the relation between a speech act and a proposition can be characterized as one between *mood* (an illocutionary operator) and *sentence radical* (the proposition). In a denial in contrast to an assertion, the negation is not part of the sentence radical:

(4.5)   MOOD (sentence radical)

(4.6)   a.   Max isn't tall.
             ASSERT ($\neg$ Max is tall)

        b.   Max ISN'T tall.
             DENIAL (Max is tall)

As a speech act, a denial can target all sorts of aspects of a previous utterance, including presuppositions, implicatures, or formal aspects such as pronunciation. The negation of these non-propositional parts of an utterance has been called metalinguistic negation by Horn (1985, 1989) and others (e.g. Burton-Roberts 1989, 1999; Carston 1996, 1998, 1999). It is important to remember, however, that denials are not restricted to metalinguistic aspects of the utterance. The following are examples of metalinguistic negation (from Geurts 1998: 287; accents added). In (4.7), the presupposition that Fred smoked, which is triggered by the embedding verb *to stop*, is rejected. In (4.8), the scalar implicature that not more than six beers were consumed (otherwise the speaker would have said so) is rejected. And in (4.9), the pronunciation of the word *tomato* is corrected.

(4.7)   A: Fred has stopped smoking.
        B: Fred HASn't stopped smoking: he never DID smoke.

(4.8)   A: Julius had six beers.
        B: Julius DIDn't have SIX beers: he had at least SEVEN.

---

[3] Note that the concept of denial as defined in the context of metalinguistic negation is quite different from the concept of denial-of-expectation used in some of the definitions of contrastive *but* (see Chapter 3).

(4.9)   A: Kurt swallowed a whole to[mɑː]to.
        B: Kurt DIDn't swallow a whole to[mɑː]to but a to[meɪ]to.
             (additional accents on [mɑː] and [meɪ])

Metalinguistic negation does not refer to the truth value of an utterance. It is only in the case of presupposition denials that the negation has an influence on the truth value—the utterance cannot be judged true or false because one of its presuppositions is not fulfilled.

Most modern theories of metalinguistic negation consider it a reflex of the negation taking wide scope over the entire utterance.[4] Van der Sandt (1991), for instance, suggests that an echo operator takes the sum of all information of a previous utterance ϕ_{-1}—presuppositions, implicatures, etc. included—as the propositional content of the utterance ϕ_0, which then removes ϕ_{-1} from the context. Consider an example:

(4.10)   a.   It is possible that the church is right.   (van der Sandt 1991: 333)

         b.   It is not possible, it is necessary that the church is right.

The informative content, that is the sum of all the information of (4.10a) consists of the proposition itself and, amongst other things, the implicature that it is not necessary that the church is right. The sum of proposition and implicature is picked up by (4.10b) and rejected. Example (4.10b) is semantically equivalent to (4.11):

(4.11)   It is not true that [it is possible and not necessary that the church is right],
         it is necessary that the church is right.   (van der Sandt 1991: 335)

For other proposals using wide scope of the negation see e.g. Jacobs (1982, 1991), Carston (1996), or Herburger (2000). Since the negation in denials can target both the proposition as well as utterance aspects that are outside the proposition, I shall call it illocutionary negation: it operates on the level of the speech act.

In the following I discuss a number of tests that have been suggested for denials, some of which I shall use in the analysis of the wide scope readings in Section 4.2 to argue that those are denials (e.g. the polarity item test). The tests demonstrate that the negation in denials—illocutionary negation—has

[4] Hypotheses favouring a semantic ambiguity of the negative marker (e.g. Blau 1977; Keenan 1972; Ladusaw 1980) are often held to be inadequate (Atlas 1977; Gazdar 1979; Horn 1989; Jacobs 1982; Reis 1977; Seuren 1988; van der Sandt 1988; Wilson 1975). Semantic ambiguity can be reflected in the existence of two different operators, where one operator leaves presuppositions and implicatures intact whereas the other is able to target such non-propositional aspects of the utterance. These operators are sometimes referred to as strong versus weak negation (see Jacobs 1991 for a discussion).

different characteristics from propositional negation, which will be the key to the analysis of the wide scope readings as small conjuncts rather than large conjuncts like the distributed or narrow scope readings. Similarly, corrections with *but* differ from contrastive coordinations with *but* in the type of negation involved—illocutionary and propositional, respectively.[5, 6] The latter are the constructions I focus on in this section. The tests I discuss have been suggested by Horn (1989) for metalinguistic negation, that is a type of negation that can only occur in denials.

The first test explicitly mentions corrective versus contrastive *but*. Horn (1985, 1989) proposes that corrective *but* is typically used for the expression of metalinguistic negation, that is in denials, while contrastive *but* is not. One of the arguments he gives is that implicature denials in English can only be expressed by an elliptic *but*-coordination, and that it is elliptic *but*-coordinations which are used to express corrections in that language. Full-clause *but*-coordinations are used to mark an utterance as contrastive (see above):

(4.12) a. We don't have three children but four.

   b. #We don't have three children but we have four children.

                                                   (Horn 1989: 404)

The data are parallel in German, where, as indicated earlier, correction and contrast are distinguished by lexical means: *aber* marks contrast and *sondern* marks correction:

(4.13) a. Wir haben nicht drei Kinder, sondern (#wir haben) vier.

   b. #Wir haben nicht drei Kindern, aber (wir haben) vier.

[5] (i) is a case that looks as if contrastive *but* can be used to deny non-propositional aspects. This, however, is only possible if *but* occurs utterance-initially after a turn-take. In (ii), the first conjunct presupposes something that is rejected by the second conjunct. This conflicts with the compatibility restriction on the two conjuncts of a contrastive-*but*-coordination (see Section 3.1). Also, (ii) is a self-denial, which would be a rather odd kind of speech-act.

(i)   A: John stopped smoking. B: But he never did smoke!

(ii) *John stopped smoking but he never did smoke.

In (i) utterance-initial *but* seems to clear the common ground of everything that was said before. *But* as part of a coordination cannot do this. (iii) looks like an exception to this:

(iii) Mary wants to marry the king of France but there is no king of France.

(iii) shows that the distinction of *de re—de dicto* readings also plays a role. In (iii) the *de re* reading is rejected. A presupposition relevant to the *de dicto* reading such as the existential presupposition elicited by the matrix clause subject *Mary*, cannot be rejected in the *but*-conjunct.

[6] For more on the difference between contrastive and corrective *but*, see e.g. Anscombre and Ducrot (1977, 1983), Asbach-Schnittker (1979), Drubig (1994, 2003), Horn (1989), Koenig & Benndorf (1998), Lang (1977, 1984, 1991), McCawley (1991), Pusch (1976).

McCawley (1991) refutes a perfect match between correction and metalinguistic negation and says there is nothing 'inherently' metalinguistic about it. Note, however, that the view advocated by van der Sandt (1991)—that the negation in denials takes scope over an entire utterance including its non-propositional aspects but obviously including the proposition itself too—is compatible with these data. Metalinguistic negation as such can only be used in denials. Examples (4.12) and (4.13) above show that contrastive *but/aber* cannot occur with metalinguistic negation.

Geurts (1998) also argues against Horn's generalization. He remarks that whereas implicature and form denials indeed typically occur with corrective *but* (see (4.9), and (4.12)/(4.13) above), presupposition denials do not. Example (4.14) is the type of example Geurts (1998) has in mind:

(4.14)   *Fred hat nicht den König von Frankreich getroffen, sondern
         Fred has not the king of France   met   butCORR
         es gibt gar keinen König von Frankreich.
         it gives PART no   king of France
         'Fred hasn't met the king of France but there is no king of France.'

However, (4.15) indicates that the matter is not quite so straightforward. The correction that is offered for the element in focus (the predicate) here includes the presupposition. Example (4.15) is fine:

(4.15)   Fred hat nicht AUFgehört zu rauchen, sondern er HAT
         Fred has not stopped to smoke   butCORR he has
         niemals geraucht.
         never   smoked
         'Fred didn't STOP smoking but he never DID smoke.'

The next test Horn (1985, 1989) proposes for metalinguistic negation is that it cannot be expressed by bound morphemes like *un-* or *non-* (also Blau 1977; Seuren 1988):

(4.16)   The king of France is {*unhappy / not happy}—there isn't any king of France

The reason Horn gives for this effect is that metalinguistic negation operates on a different grammatical level from propositional negation and therefore cannot interact with elements on the propositional level. Similarly, Jacobs (1982, 1991) argues that the levels of the two kinds of negation involved are distinct and points out that the negation in *unhappy* is morphological:[7] it

---

[7] Jacobs (1991) also calls attention to the fact that, for instance, *unhappy* and *not happy* are not synonymous. *Unhappy*, if you will, is a stronger negation than *not happy*.

only operates on the meaning of the stem *happy* so that the presupposition regarding the existence of the king of France can never be in the scope of the negation.[8] Jacobs (1991) shows that the scope of the negation always has to be taken into account when considering (presupposition) denials. The negation in an embedded (small) clause—be it morphological or syntactic—cannot take scope over a presupposition in the matrix clause:

(4.17)   *The king of France turned out to be {not / un-} friendly, because there is no king of France   (modelled on Jacobs 1991: 583)

The scope of the negation also matters in gapping with contrastive *but*, see (4.18), where the negation does not 'disappear' in the second conjunct as would be the case if the negation had propositional scope. The role of the scope of the negation in corrections is illustrated in (4.19). Example (4.19a) is ungrammatical because the negative marker occurs in an embedded (small) clause, compare the grammatical (4.19b).

(4.18)   Max erwies sich   erst GESTERN als nicht freundlich
         Max proved himself only yesterday as   not   friendly
         aber   Maria schon vor   einigen Tagen.
         butcontr Maria already before a.few   days
         'Max turned out to be not friendly only yesterday but Mary turned out to be not friendly already a few days ago.'

(4.19)   a. *Max erwies sich   als nicht FREUNDlich sondern als
            Max proved himself as   not   friendly   butcorr as
            überaus   nett.
            extremely nice

         'Max turned out to be not friendly but extremely nice.'

---

[8] Geurts (1998) adduces some cases where the presupposition apparently can be attacked by morphological negation, and consequently rejects this test:

(i)   It is impossible that you have met the king of France, because there is no such person.
                                                              (Geurts 1998: 280)

If we substitute *impossible* by another adverb, however, the result again is ungrammatical:

(ii) *It is unfortunate that you have met the king of France, because there is no such person.

Impossible just like other epistemic operators (*improbable, unlikely, doubtful*) calls the truth of the embedded clause into question, which *unfortunate* does not—it is factive. Therefore it is not surprising that a presupposition in an embedded clause might be attacked in the context of such an epistemic operator. This point is further supported by examples such as the following:

(iii) *It is impossible for you to leave now—it is necessary.   (Horn 1989: 392)

The morphological negative marker *im-* here is supposed to negate an implicature triggered by its own complement. This is not possible because of the narrow scope of the negation.

b. Max erwies sich   nicht als FREUNDlich sondern als
    Max proved himself not as friendly   butCORR as
    überaus   NETT.
    extremely nice
    'Max didn't turn out to be friendly but extremely nice.'

I shall come back to the particular position the negation can take in corrective-
but-coordinations in the next section.

The last aspect Horn (1985, 1989) discusses in connection with metalinguistic negation and denials is the behaviour of negative and positive polarity
items (NPIs and PPIs). Negative denials differ from negative assertions in two
crucial aspects: they do not license NPIs, see (4.20), and they do not interfere with the occurrence of PPIs, see (4.21) (e.g. Bolinger 1972, 1977; Carston
1996; Horn 1989; Jacobs 1982; Kruisinga 1931 (cited in Horn 1989); van der
Sandt 1991). This holds both for proposition denials (the (a)-cases) as well as
metalinguistic negation such as in presupposition denials (the (b)-cases) and
implicature denials (the (c)-cases).

(4.20) a. ??John DIDN'T drink a drop—he's a heavy DRINKer.

        b. ??The king of France did NOT lift a finger: there IS no king of
            France.

        c. ??He DIDN'T sleep a wink, he was COMATOSE.

(4.21) a. John does NOT still live in Paris—he DID live there but NOW he's
            moved to his girlfriend's in Lyon.
                                        (van der Sandt and Maier 2003, ex. 19)

        b. John does NOT still live in Paris—he has never set FOOT in France.
                                                            (ibid. ex. 20)

        c. Chris DIDN'T manage to solve {SOME/*ANY } of the problems—he
            managed to solve ALL of them.   (Horn 1989: 401)

The intuitive idea for the inability of a denial to accommodate an NPI is
that the utterance which is denied would have had to contain some sort
of positive counterpart to the NPI, which usually is impossible: except in
straightforward alternations such as *some* versus *any*, the literal meaning of
the NPI will often produce some jocular effect. Thus, an NPI would simply
not have been licensed in the denied utterance.[9] PPIs, on the other hand, are

---

[9] As an anonymous reviewer of Repp (2006) pointed out, NPIs can occur in denials if the NPI was
licensed by another item in the utterance to be denied, such as *doubt*:

(i) A: I doubt that I saw anyone. B: You DON'T doubt that you saw anyone.'

accepted in denials because the previous utterance might have contained some PPI. The idea here is that the negative marker of the denial clause will not affect the PPI because it takes the previous utterance as it is as an object to be denied.

Note that the examples in (4.20) and (4.21) come with an accent on the negative marker. The reason for this, Horn (1989) suggests, is that due to the flouting of the polarity sensitivity of some of the items involved, these examples can never be read as instances of ordinary propositional negation. Therefore, the option to read them as instances of metalinguistic negation must be indicated early on, that is in the clause containing the negative marker.[10]

From what we have seen so far, the prediction for coordinations with contrastive versus corrective *but* is that NPIs should be able to occur in the first conjunct of the former but not of the latter. The gapping example with contrastive *but* in (4.22a) and the stripping example with corrective *but* in (4.22b) show that this is indeed the case. The polarity item is *keine müde Mark* ('not a penny'):

(4.22) a. Max hat dem Kellner keine müde Mark Trinkgeld gegeben,
            Max has the waiter   no   tired Mark tip   given
            aber   Maria dem Türsteher ihr halbes Portemonnaie.
            but$_\text{CONTR}$ Maria the bouncer her half   purse
            'Max didn't give the waiter a penny in tips, but Mary gave the
            bouncer half her purse.'

---

[10] Geurts (1998) argues that in some presupposition denials, the test for polarity sensitivity cannot be used and concludes that the test in general is a bad test for metalinguistic denial:

(i)   Walter didn't give his ukulele to {?SOMEBODY / ANYBODY}. He never owned a ukulele.

Similar examples can be found in German. *Keiner Menschenseele* ('not to a single soul') in felicitious (ii) is an NPI.

(ii) Max hat sein neues Manuskript keiner Menschenseele gezeigt— es gibt   nämlich
      Max has his   new   manuscript no   human.soul   shown   it gives namely
      kein neues Manuskript.
      no   new   manuscript
      'Max didn't show his new manuscript to a single soul: there is no new manuscript.'

What distinguishes these examples from those in (4.20) and (4.21), is that the negative marker is not accented. This suggests that the denial reading of the first clause is not prominent: for the first-time hearer there is no denial involved. In point of fact, (i) with *anybody* and (ii) become ungrammatical if the negative markers (*didn't* and *keiner*) are accented. The intonation given in (i) and (ii), i.e. a neutral sentence accent, produces a garden-path for the hearer: s/he will accommodate all the presuppositions connected with the first clause. The second clause then requires a reanalysis due to the inconsistency between the presupposition and the assertion of the second clause. Thus, there is no reason to reject the polarity diagnostic as a test for the identification of denials.

b. *Max hat dem Kellner keine müde Mark Trinkgeld gegeben,
    sondern sein halbes Portemonnaie.
    butCORR his   half   purse
    'Max didn't give the waiter a penny in tips, but half his purse.'

PPIs, in contrast, should be allowed to occur freely with corrective *but* but not with contrastive *but*. This is confirmed by the next few examples, where *ziemlich* ('fairly') is a PPI. Example (4.23a) is (an attempt at) an implicature denial, (4.23b) is an attempt at a proposition denial. The correction version of (4.23c) is a proposition denial, the contrastive version tries to contrast two individuals and two properties one of which is a PPI. This is not possible.

(4.23) a. Max ist nicht ZIEMLICH müde, sondern / *aber   (er ist)
            Max is not   fairly   tired, butCORR/butCONTR he is
            SEHR müde.
            very tired.

        b. Max ist nicht ziemlich MÜde, sondern / *aber   (er ist)
            Max isn't   fairly   tired   butCORR/butCONTR he is
            etwas ABwesend.
            a.little absent-minded.

        c. MAX ist nicht ZIEMlich müde, sondern / *aber   MaRIa
            Max isn't   fairly   tired   butCORR/butCONTR Mary
            (ist) SEHR müde.
            is   very tired.

To summarize, coordinations with corrective *but* are a typical vehicle for expressing denials. They can be used to express metalinguistic negation, which can only occur in denials. Contrastive *but* does not share these characteristics. The negation in denials occurs in the form of an echo operator that scopes over the entire utterance, that is it is illocutionary negation and operates on the level of the speech act.

4.1.2 *The syntax of coordinations with corrective* but

In this section, I show that the negation in corrections takes a special surface position, both in stripping (which is well-known) as well as in gapping. I take this to be a reflex of the fact that corrections are denials with a substitution part. In structures like stripping or gapping, the part of the utterance that is to be corrected (which is a focus), is marked structurally by the position of the negation. Stripping underlies a c-command restriction which can be relaxed in some environments. In transitive gapping structures, the negation must c-command at least one of the correlates. I will discuss some accounts that have been given of corrective stripping structures and show that they are insufficient to account for the gapping data (of which there have been no accounts so far). What is important for my analysis of the wide scope readings in Section 4.2 is that the existing stripping, that is correction, accounts assume a high syntactic position of the negation—above TP. This is higher than propositional negation which I assume to be in the I-domain of the clause (see Chapter 2). I will not offer a new proposal of corrections in general because I believe that the full range of data—stripping, gapping, full clause corrections—have to be taken into account, which I cannot do here.

4.1.2.1 *The shape of corrections: Stripping*   The shape of corrections is characterized by their information structure, their prosody and the position the negation takes. In this section, I shall describe these features for stripping, subsection 4.1.2.3 looks at gapping. The first conjunct in correction structures with stripping typically contains a focus, which marks the element that is to be substituted by an alternative in the second conjunct. This substitute is a focus itself:

(4.24)   Peter is not [in LEIPZIG Foc] but [in BerLIN Foc].

Examples like this suggest that correction with substitution in general is restricted to narrow foci. This, however, is not the case. Example (4.25) illustrates that the whole clause can be in focus:

(4.25)   PEter ist nicht zu SPÄT gekommen sondern MaRIA hat am
         Peter is not   too late arrived   butCORR Maria has at.the
         falschen ORT gewartet.
         wrong   place waited
         'Peter wasn't late but Mary was waiting in the wrong place.'
         = not [Peter was late Foc] but [Mary was waiting in the wrong
         place Foc]

It is also possible to have several foci in a corrective-*but*-coordination, which is the case in gapping (see section 4.1.2.3):[11]

(4.26)   [PEter Foc] bewundert nicht [LuISE Foc] sondern [LuISE Foc]
         Peter   admires   not   Luise   butCORR Luise
         [PEter Foc].
         Peter
         'Peter does not admire Luise, Luise admires Peter.'

[11] Recall from Chapter 3 that I generally assume gapping to be a contrastive-topic–contrastive-focus structure. For corrections, this might be inappropriate.

It is not always necessary to mark the focus itself by overt phonological means:

(4.27) Er wohnt \NICHT in Berlin, sondern in \MÜNCHEN.
       he lives   not   in Berlin, butCORR in Munich
       'He doesn't live in Berlin but in Munich.'

In (4.27) there is an accent on the polarity of the first conjunct, which I characterized as typical of denials in the previous section. There is no accent required on the focus to be substituted by the alternative in the second conjunct (it is possible though). What *is* required is an intonational break with a low boundary tone after the first conjunct. I suggest that the pattern in (4.27) is licit because even in the case of narrow foci, what is denied is a whole utterance, or what one could call a potential utterance, an assumption that the speaker believes to be held by another discourse participant. This potential or real utterance is given and therefore can be deaccented. Only the polarity is accented. The first pattern, with an accent on the narrow focus (example (4.24)) makes explicit what part of the to-be-denied utterance the speaker disagrees with. The second clause then provides an alternative for it. This pattern is not available for most metalinguistic denials because the denied presupposition, implicature, etc. and the correction, or the reason offered for the denial, are normally not narrow focus alternatives. That this is not excluded, however, is shown by (4.28) (= (4.12a) repeated from above), which is an implicature denial:

(4.28) We don't have THREE children but FOUR.

I shall come back to the issue of intonation in denials in Section 4.2 and investigate the special intonation in wide scope gapping sentences: these have the main accent on the polarity, which signals the denial, and secondary accents on the contrast pairs.

    The interaction of focus and negation in corrective-*but*-coordinations involves specific structural relations between the negative marker and the focus it associates with. Jacobs (1982, 1991) says that the focus needs to be in the semantic scope of the negation, which in most cases boils down to syntactic c-command. In (4.29a) the definite DP *die Mutter* ('the mother') occurs before the negation. This is the normal word order in a simple clause— the definite has scrambled over the negation (see Chapter 2). It cannot be used in a correction where *die Mutter* is to be corrected, see (4.29b).[12] A correction of *die Mutter* requires the negation to c-command the DP, see (4.29c). Without the corrective conjunct, the first conjunct in this example would be degraded:

---

[12] Unless the negation carries a heavy accent, see ex. (4.27) above.

(4.29) a. Peter hat die Mutter nicht angerufen.
            Peter has the mother not   called
            'Peter hasn't called the mother.'

        b. *Peter hat [die MUTTER Foc] nicht angerufen, sondern
             Peter has the mother   not called   butCORR
            [den VAter Foc]
             the father
            'Peter hasn't called the mother but the father.'

        c. Peter hat nicht [die MUTTER Foc] angerufen, sondern
            Peter has not   the mother   called   butCORR
            [den VAter Foc].
             the father
            'Peter hasn't called the mother but the father.'

It is important to note in this connection that ordinary, that is non-corrective, clausal negation may also come with a focus, see (4.30a) and (4.30b).

(4.30) a. Peter hat die Mutter [von FRANZFoc] nicht angerufen.

        b. Peter hat [die MUTTERFoc] von Franz nicht angerufen.
            Peter has the mother   of   Franz not   called
            'Peter hasn't called Franz's mother {a: focus on Franz | b: focus on mother}.'

A continuation with corrective *but* is impossible in these cases, though, because the focus is not in the scope of the negation. Thus, the position of the negative marker in correction structures marks the first conjunct as a denial and singles out the element to be denied, which, by implicature, requires a substitute. There are some exceptions to the generalization about c-command, which I shall discuss in the next subsection.

Next to the restriction on c-command, it is assumed that the negation often takes a position quite close to its focus (e.g. Jacobs 1982). In English, McCawley (1991) identifies two forms that a corrective-*but*-coordination can take, which correspond to different realizations of the negation. He calls these forms the *basic form* and *the anchored form*:

(4.31) a. John put not gin but vodka in the punch.—*basic*

                                            (McCawley 1991: 191)

        b. John didn't put gin in the punch but vodka.—*anchored*

The basic form involves adverbial negation, which occurs close to the focus. The anchored form involves ordinary clausal negation, although McCawley assumes that the negative marker in both cases is one of ordinary clausal negation. The two forms differ in various ways, for instance with respect to 'extraposition' (this terminology depends on the syntactic analysis of these structures). Example (4.31a) above shows the basic form with a continuous *not–but* phrase. In (4.31b), the *but*-conjunct is extraposed. Example (4.32) shows the basic form with an extraposed focus, which results in ungrammaticality:

(4.32)   ??John put not gin in the punch but vodka.

We can make a similar observation in German: an extraposition of the corrective part is not always possible, see (4.33a) versus (4.33b) from Jacobs (1982: 276):

(4.33)   a.   Einige nicht uniformierte, sondern von   oben bis
              a.few not   in.uniform   butCORR from top   to
              unten   schwarz vermummte Polizisten   stürmten die
              bottom black   masked   policemen stormed the
              geschlossene Abteilung.
              closed   ward
              'A few policemen, not in uniform but heavily masked from top to toe, stormed the closed ward.'

         b.   *Einige nicht uniformierte Polizisten   stürmten die
              a.few not   in.uniform   policemen stormed the
              geschlossene Abteilung, sondern von   oben bis unten
              closed   ward   butCORR from top   to bottom
              schwarz vermummte (Polizisten).
              black   masked   policemen
              'A few policemen who were not in uniform stormed the closed ward, but who were heavily masked from top to toe.'

The best analysis for cases like the one in (4.33a) seems to be a small conjunct analysis, where *not–but* operates over a coordination of adjective phrases,[13] see

---

[13] With the negation in clause-initial position, extraposition seems to be possible:

(i)   Nicht einige uniformierte Polizisten stürmten die geschlossene Abteilung sondern einige von oben bis unten schwarz vermummte (Polizisten).

Note in this context that it is actually unclear to what projections the German marker for non-clausal negation can attach. Adjunction to DPs is unclear, compare (ii) versus (iii), where (ii) indicates that DP-adjunction is possible and (iii) indicates the opposite:

(ii)   Nicht Luise sondern Maria bewundert Peter.
       Not   Luise butCORR Mary admires   Peter.

(iii) *Peter wird von   nicht Luise, sondern Maria bewundert.
       'Peter is   admired by   not   Luise but   Mary.'

the next section, yet there has not been a successful analysis suggested for them as far as I am aware.

Next, consider example (4.34). The (a)-case is an instance of McCawley's base form, the (b)-case is an instance of the anchored form, that is here, the negation takes the position of clausal negation. Yet, it seems that it cannot associate with an element within a complex NP:

(4.34) a. John has drunk a quart not of beer but of whiskey.

(McCawley 1991: 193)

   b. ??John hasn't drunk a quart of beer but of whiskey.

Similar cases are investigated by Drubig (1994) and Moritz and Valois (1994). They show that reduction to the focus substitute in the second conjunct is not possible if the focus of the negation in corrections is contained within a syntactic island. The substitute must at least correspond to the island itself:

(4.35) John hasn't drunk a quart of beer but a quart of whiskey.

(4.36) He didn't interrogate the man who invited the ex-convict with the RED shirt, but

   a. *{the BLUE shirt / with the BLUE shirt / the ex-convict with the BLUE shirt}.

   b. the man who invited the ex-convict with the BLUE shirt.

(Drubig 1994)

(4.37) a. Max n'est   parti avant   personne mais *(après)
          Max NEG.is left   before nobody   but   after
          tout le monde.
          everybody
          'Max did not leave before anybody but (after) everybody.'

   b. Maradonna n'est   l'ennemi   de personne mais l'idole
          Maradonna NEG.is the.enemy of nobody   but   the.idol
          *(de tous).
          of all
          'Maradonna is nobody's enemy but everybody's idol.'

(*French*; Moritz and Valois 1994)

In the next section, I shall discuss a couple of accounts that have been proposed to accommodate these features of corrections with stripping and focus especially on the negation.

The difficulty of how to place a negative marker within a PP is paralleled by the difficulty of how to place focus particles like *only* or *even* in that position (see Section 3.4; also see Jacobs 1982).

4.1.2.2 *The structure of corrections: Stripping*   McCawley (1991) transfers the idea of the complex operator directly into the syntax. He proposes that the two conjuncts conjoined by *not–but* are positive sentences, where *not* is attached to the first sentence and *but* to the second. Thus, the negation in these constructions is a structurally high negation. The idea is that the semantics of the overarching coordination must (somehow) imply that the negation gets an interpretation in the first conjunct. The final form of the coordination is derived by conjunction reduction. This accounts for the complex character of *not–but*. In addition, under this proposal, ellipsis in corrective-*but*-structures is no different from ellipsis in other environments. I shall not go into the details of McCawley's account (which also contains an analysis of the extraposition facts) and instead turn to Drubig (1994), who gives an account in terms of focus movement.

Following Culivover (1991), Drubig (1994) assumes that a focus phrase, that is a phrase containing a focus such as the remnant in corrective-*but*-structures, moves into the specifier of a functional phrase Pol_2P, which is situated between IP and CP. Again this is a high negation as compared to 'ordinary' clausal negation, which is situated in the I-domain. Pol_2P is reserved for what Drubig calls *emphatic* negation/affirmation, by which he means negation that is associated with a focus phrase. Drubig (2003), which partly builds on Drubig (1994), speaks of 'contrastive [narrow] focus', that is to say that there is a closed set of alternatives under debate and the respective sentence can be followed 'by an enumeration of the excluded items in replacive constructions' (2003: 15). This is basically denial with substitution as in corrections with *but*.

The focus phrase must move to Spec,Pol_2P either overtly, or covertly at LF because the focus must be licensed there. In addition to Pol_2P, there is Pol_1P, which is situated between VP and IP and is the locus of sentence negation/affirmation. Pol_1 also carries a focus feature $[+F]$, and also accommodates the negative marker, affirmation, and the focus particles but only for cases with wide focus.

(4.38) $[_{Pol2P} SpecPol_2 \ldots [_{Pol1P} SpecPol_1 \ldots VP]]$

Evidence for the focus movement account comes from several sources. The first one is the island constraints in corrections with stripping observed in the previous subsection. The idea is that it is not just the focus that moves to Spec,Pol_2P but that the entire focus phrase is pied-piped (similarly Moritz and Valois 1994).[14] The second piece of evidence, which also bears on the

---

[14] For the semantic interpretation, it is not necessary to assume association with the focus phrase. Association with the focus itself is sufficient (Krifka 2006):

(i)   John didn't read [the book that MARY_F recommended]_FP, but [Moby DICK]_F.

position of the negation in these structures, comes from scope facts. We saw above that corrective-*but*-coordinations in English can occur in a basic and in an anchored form. The following examples show that these forms allow for different scope of the negation in complex clauses. The structure in (4.39a) is ambiguous in that it allows the negation to scope over the embedded clause (see (i)) or over the main clause (see (ii)). Examples (4.39b) and (4.39c), in contrast, have surface scope. Such effects were first discussed by Taglicht (1984) for focus particles.

(4.39)   a.   John allows Mary to drink not coffee but tea.

(McCawley 1991: 193)

   (i)   John allows Mary [NEG [to drink coffee] BUT [to drink tea]]
   (ii)   NEG [John allows Mary to drink coffee] BUT [he allows her to drink tea]

   b.   John allows Mary not to drink coffee but tea.

   c.   John doesn't allow Mary to drink coffee but tea.

To account for the ambiguity in (4.39a), it is often assumed that the focus operator (in this case the negation) combines with the focus phrase (e.g. the DP) and raises at LF to a position from which it can take scope over the entire sentence (for a discussion see, for instance, Bayer 1990, 1996; von Stechow 1991a). The third aspect Drubig (1994) discusses with respect to focus movement and a high position of the negation is that both focus particles and negation can elicit verb second structures in English if they are part of a fronted phrase. This indicates that they are indeed situated in a high position:

(4.40)   {Only WINE / No wine} does John allow Mary to drink.

We may conclude that the negation in corrective-*but*-structures takes a high position in the clause.

   Recall that we also encountered examples where *not–but* seemed to operate over non-clausal coordinations such as conjoined adjective phrases (example (4.33)). To account for these, Drubig (1994) adapts a proposal for *except*-phrases and general bare argument ellipsis (= stripping) put forward by Reinhart (1991) and assumes that the construction *not X but Y* is a coordination of small conjuncts. At the surface, these small conjuncts may also be a discontinuous constituent (e.g. McCawley 1982) yet on LF they move to the specifier of Pol_2P as a unit:

For this sentence to be felicitous, *Moby Dick* needs to be a book that was recommended by an alternative to Mary, so the alternative set evoked by the focus is what is important for the interpretation.

(4.41)   John sent not money to his friends but presents. (Drubig 1994: 35)

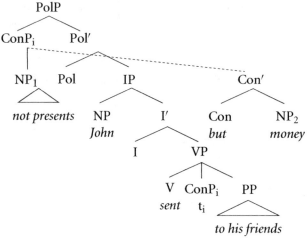

The negative marker behaves like an adverb in this structure, that is, it attaches to the NP. This analysis is not without problems. Drubig (1994: 35) speculates that the discontinuity arises from rightward movement at the surface 'to the point where it signals the closure of the propositional constituent over which the focused ConP has scope at LF'. He suggests that the movement might be restricted by a principle which disallows movement of a phrase over a constituent it does not c-command at LF. He further speculates that some island constraints might be related to this. Note, however, that island constraints are usually assumed to apply to leftward and not to rightward movement. Reinhart (1991) also argues against a parallel between extraposition and displacement of the corrective conjunct, as Drubig (1994) concedes. This is also a problem for the analysis of the data in example (4.33) discussed above, where extraposition of the *but*-phrase was impossible. For corrective-*but*-coordinations with clausal scope, Drubig (1994) suggests essentially the same structure as in (4.41) except that the negative marker is originally situated in the lower Pol, that is Pol$_1$, which is the position of ordinary sentence negation. It moves to Pol$_2$ at LF. I will come back to Drubig's account in the next subsection, when I discuss gapping.

4.1.2.3 The shape and structure of corrections: Gapping

I mentioned above that there are some exceptions to the rule-of-thumb that the negation c-commands the focus in its scope. There are cases, where c-command is not 'enough', that is where the negation c-commands a focus but the construction is still ungrammatical. There are also cases where focus can escape the c-command domain of the negation. I shall concentrate on the latter cases here as these are most relevant to gapping.[15]

To begin with, Jacobs (1991) points out that it is usually ambiguous whether the position before the finite verb in German and English is contained within the scope of an operator after the finite verb. A relevant example is (4.25) above, repeated below as (4.42), where the focus corresponds to the whole clause and the negative marker occurs further down in the structure. We find the same effects in gapping, recall (4.26), repeated below as (4.43).

(4.42) PEter ist nicht zu SPÄT gekommen sondern MARIA hat am
        Peter is not too late arrived   butCORR Maria has at.the
        falschen ORT gewartet.
        wrong   place waited
        'Peter wasn't late but Mary was waiting in the wrong place.'

(4.43) PEter bewundert nicht LuISE sondern LuISE PEter.
        Peter admires   not Luise butCORR Luise Peter
        'Peter does not admire Luise, Luise admires Peter.'

In both cases, the negation occurs right after the verb in C. It takes the highest position in the IP (the middle field). This is not the normal position of clausal negation, which for the first conjunct of the gapping sentence in (4.43) would be the one shown in (4.44a). This position is excluded in corrections with gapping, cf. (4.44b):

(4.44) a. PEter bewundert LuISE nicht.
            Peter admires   Luise not
            'Peter does not admire Luise.'

        b. *PEter bewundert LuISE nicht sondern LuISE PEter.
             Peter admires   Luise not   butCORR Luise Peter
             'Peter does not admire Luise: Luise admires Peter.'

On the other hand, it is not actually necessary for the negation to be the highest element in the IP. All that seems to be required is that in a transitive sentence with two names (or definite DPs) like (4.43) it occurs before the lower DP. This is evidenced by examples where the Spec,CP position is taken by an expletive and the foci remain in the middle field. The negation in the first conjunct can appear in a position right before the two foci, that is IP-initially, see (4.45a), and it can also occur between them, see (4.45b) (the sentences are easier to parse with the determiners added):

---

[15] For other examples, see Jacobs (1991).

(4.45)   a.   Es   bewundert nicht der P**ɛ**ter die Luɪse, sondern die
              E**xpl** admires   not   the Peter the Luise but**corr** the
              Luɪse den P**ɛ**ter.
              Luise the Peter

         b.   Es   bewundert der P**ɛ**ter nicht die Luɪse, sondern die
              E**xpl** admires   the Peter not   the Luise but**corr** the
              Luɪse den P**ɛ**ter.
              Luise the Peter
              'Peter does not admire Luise: Luise admires Peter.'

Another position available for the negation in corrections of the above sort is the one before a phrase in Spec,CP, see (4.46). Except for a few special cases involving quantifiers this is impossible in non-corrections.[16]

(4.46)   Nicht P**ɛ**ter bewundert Luɪse sondern Luɪse P**ɛ**ter.
         not   Peter   admires   Luise but**corr** Luise Peter
         'Peter doesn't admire Luise: Luise admires Peter.'

We find the same pattern in examples where the roles of agent and patient are not simply swapped but where the contrast between the conjuncts is non-reciprocal:

(4.47)   a.   Nicht M**ax** hat den K**rug** zerbrochen, sondern M**aria**
              not   Max has the jar   broken   but**corr** Maria
              das G**las**.
              the glass

         b.   M**ax** hat nicht den K**rug** zerbrochen, sondern M**aria** das G**las**.

---

[16] Note in this connection that the focus particle *only*, of which *nicht* is often assumed to be a close relative (Jacobs 1982), cannot take scope from a clause-initial position both over the element in Spec,CP and over an element further down in the clause, see (i) versus (ii):

(i)   Nur   der   \P**ɛ**ter bewundert die Maria, der   /K**laus** **nicht**.
       Only the**nom** Peter   admires   the Maria, the**nom** Klaus   not
       'Only Peter admires Maria, Klaus doesn't.'

(ii)   *Nur der /P**ɛ**ter bewundert die Ma\rɪa und **nicht** (auch) der \K**laus** die \A**nna**).
       Only the   Peter   admires   the Maria, and not   also   the Klaus the Anna
       Intended: 'It is only the case that Peter admires Mary, it is not the case that Klaus admires Anna.'

In clause-internal position, however, such a reading is available:

(iii)   Es bewundert nur der Peter die Maria und nicht auch der Klaus die Anna.

This speaks against a completely parallel analysis of *nicht* and *nur*, and in particular against an analysis of *nur* where the particle adjoins to CP if it occurs in clause-initial position (see Section 3.4 for more on this). Note that Kay (1990) discusses instances of *even* also associating with two foci:

(iv)   John would even sell reF**r**ɪgerators to the **ɛ**skimos!

c. *MAX hat den KRUG nicht zerbrochen, sondern MARIA das GLAS.
'Max did not break the jar: Mary broke the glass.'

The data show essentially the following:

(4.48) GENERALIZATION ABOUT THE NEGATION IN CORRECTIONS WITH
GAPPING
The negation in corrections with gapping (transitive structures) can
take several positions but it must c-command at least one of the
correlates.

Thus, it is possible for one of the foci to escape the c-command domain of the
negation as long as the other correlate stays in that domain. It is worth noting
in this context that in corrections with wider focus (e.g. VP-focus), parts of
the wide focus can, and sometimes must, leave the c-command domain of
the negation, as was observed by Jacobs (1982). This is for instance the case
with pronominal elements. Even though in (4.49) the whole VP is focused
(cf. the corrective conjunct), the direct object obligatorily occurs outside the
c-command of *nicht*.

(4.49) dass Dr. No (sie) nicht *(sie) impfte,   sondern einen
that Dr No her not   her vaccinated but$_{CORR}$ a
Kollegen zu Rate zog
colleague to advice pulled
'that Dr. No didn't vaccinate here but (that he) took advice from a
colleague'   (Jacobs 1982: 290)

Thus, the matter is more complicated than might be indicated by the gapping
examples.

Neglecting this difficulty for the moment, let us consider what Drubig
(1994) would have to say about corrections with gapping. The first thing to
be considered is the fact that we have two foci here. If they are treated as an
instance of narrow focus it is not clear how the two foci could move together
with the negation as one constituent to Pol$_2$P, which is what Drubig (1994)
envisages for narrow focus. One might assume a multiple specifier analysis
where the foci move independently. Still the idea that the foci of the first
and of the second conjunct form one constituent with the negation seems
hard to accommodate in the case of multiple foci. In addition, recall from
Chapter 1 that even though focus movement has been assumed to be at work
in gapping (e.g. Kim 1997; van den Wyngærd 1998), the restrictions on gapping
actually go beyond the island constraints, that is, it is impossible to gap across
complement clauses. This is different in stripping consider (4.50a) versus
(4.50b):

(4.50) a. John didn't say that he bought a Porsche, but ~~he said that he bought~~ a Maserati.

  b. *John said that he bought a Porsche and Pete ~~said that he bought~~ a Maserati.

Furthermore, stripping is different from gapping in that in stripping it is not usually[17] possible to focus a DP outside the c-command domain of the negation:

(4.51) a. *Max ist nicht Lehrer, sondern Markus.

  b. *Max isn't a teacher but Marcus.

Thus, although stripping at first sight looks like gapping with only one remnant left, the two constructions behave differently in these very interesting respects. The syntax of corrections still awaits a thorough investigation, both with respect to the data and with respect to their analysis. I will leave this open for future research.

By way of summary, let me again highlight the main characteristics of corrective-*but*-coordinations and the negation in them. Corrective-*but*-coordinations are used as denials of a contextually available or reconstructable previous utterance. They offer a substitute for that part of the previous utterance which gives rise to the denial. The negation in these constructions is different from ordinary sentence negation: it interacts with focus in specific ways, it can be used to express metalinguistic negation, it does not license NPIs and freely allows the occurrence of PPIs. The negative marker is assumed to be hosted in a high position in the C-domain of the sentence at LF. On the surface, the negative marker usually c-commands the elements to be corrected but there are notable exceptions such as that in gapping only one of the foci has to be c-commanded by the negation. These issues will be taken up again in the next section, where I discuss the wide scope readings in gapping. These share a large part of their characteristics with the corrections discussed in this

---

[17] The 'unusual' cases require a special intonation contour, which was termed *I-topicalization* by Jacobs (1982). It corresponds to the intonation of contrastive topics I investigated in Section 3.1. In (i), the first accent must be a (fall)–rise followed by a fall on the negative marker. In English, this construction requires asyndetic coordination. Stripping is highly marginal, at least VP ellipsis is required (McCawley 1991: 192), cf. (ii) and (iii):

(i)   /Max ist \nicht Lehrer, sondern \Markus.

(ii)   [??]/Max \isn't a teacher but \Marcus.

(iii) /Max \isn't a teacher, Marcus is.

I-topicalization (also bridge contour) in German has long been known to alter scope relations in the clause (e.g. Jacobs 1982, 1983, 1984; Krifka 1998; Lötscher 1983; Löbner 1990; Féry 1993; Höhle 1992; Büring 1997b). The effect observed in (i) might be another instance of this well-known scope effect.

section, not least of all, the position of the negation and the behaviour with respect to NPIs and PPIs.

4.2 The wide scope readings

In gapping sentences with wide scope of the negation, the negation which on the surface is situated in the first conjunct takes scope over both conjuncts. Thus, for the whole coordination to be true it is sufficient if one of the two conjuncts is false, see (4.52), although it is also possible for both of them to be false (in many of the examples below).

(4.52) WIDE SCOPE READING: ¬(A & B)
Kim DIDn't play bingo and Sandy sit at home all night. I am sure Sandy went to a club herself. That's what she always does when Kim plays bingo.

The intonation contour typical for this reading is a single intonational phrase for the whole coordination (Oehrle 1987) and the negative marker (plus auxiliary) in such constructions typically is stressed (Winkler 2005). I shall say some more about the intonation below.

The existence of wide scope readings has been the main motivation for the small conjunct analysis of gapping, for example Johnson (1996/2003), López and Winkler (2003), Winkler (2005), see Chapter 1. The idea in this kind of analysis is that the negation is situated above a coordination of conjuncts smaller than CPs for example vPs, and so can take scope over both conjuncts. This analysis has also been extended to the distributed scope readings and adjusted accordingly but, as I argued in Chapter 1, this extension faces considerable difficulties. The purpose of the present section is to demonstrate that the wide scope readings differ from the other readings in ways that make such an extension even less convincing. I shall argue that declarative gapping sentences with a wide scope reading of the negation are denials, which I argued in the preceding section to occur with illocutionary rather than propositional negation, which is the negation found in the other readings. Interrogative gapping sentences with a wide scope reading also involve illocutionary negation: they occur with what has been called *outer negation* by Ladd (1981), which I argue to be illocutionary negation, too. In sum therefore, wide scope readings come with illocutionary rather than propositional negation, which sets them clearly apart from the distributed and the narrow scope readings.[18]

---

[18] See Repp (2006) for a few remarks on imperatives.

The section is organized as follows. In Sections 4.2.1 and 4.2.2, I argue for an analysis of the negation as illocutionary negation in declaratives and interrogatives, respectively. In Section 4.2.3, I give an analysis of illocutionary negation in terms of the degrees of strength that are associated with the sincerity conditions of a speech act. Other elements that can express the degrees of strength are VERUM focus and some epistemic adverbs. We shall see that they behave like illocutionary negation, that is take wide scope in gapping. In Section 4.2.4, I propose that illocutionary negation can be represented syntactically as a Strength projection in the C-domain of the clause. The wide scope readings in gapping have one ForceP and one StrengthP and split up only below that into small conjuncts. The negation is situated above the coordination and thus has wide scope over both conjuncts.

4.2.1 *Declaratives*

My main claim in this section is that declarative gapping sentences with a wide scope reading of the negation are denials and involve illocutionary negation. The evidence supporting this claim is: declarative gapping sentences with a wide scope reading need a context appropriate for denials, they have the intonation of denials (Section 4.2.1.1), and the negation behaves to a very high degree like the negation in corrections (Section 4.2.1.2). None of these features is shared by gapping with a distributed or a narrow scope reading. Additional evidence comes from the behaviour of modals in negative gapping sentences (subsection 4.2.1.3).

4.2.1.1 *Context and intonation*   Wide scope declarative gapping sentences usually require a rather specific context. Winkler (2005) says that 'often the wide scope reading of negation over the conjuncts is rather difficult to obtain without contextual manipulation' (p. 200). Here is an example:

(4.53)   CONTEXT: *Everybody knows that chameleons can move their eyes inde-pendently, as picture (1) shows: [picture of chameleon]. But the situation is different for humans, as picture (2) shows [picture of boy trying to imitate a chameleon].*
The left eye can't go up and the other down!   (Winkler 2005: 202)

The sentence is essentially a reaction to something present in the (non)linguistic context. It denies the implicit assumption that humans might be able to do the same things with their eyes as chameleons. Winkler reports that two of the speakers to whom she presented this example judged it to express incredulity. Siegel (1984, 1987) also gives several examples of wide scope readings where the context suggests that the utterance must be a(n implicit) denial:

(4.54) a. Goodness! Ralph isn't in the den and the baby in the boiler room!
(Siegel 1987: 58)

b. Oh, no, John hasn't flown the coop and his wife simply enjoyed it!
(Siegel 1987: 56)

Indeed, for many English speakers such sentences only become grammatical if they have been offered the option of interpreting them as a denial.

Another characteristic supporting a denial analysis for wide scope gapping declaratives is their phonological make-up. Wide-scope readings typically have the prosody given in (4.55a), which is very different from the prosody of the distributed or the narrow scope readings. For comparison, I am giving the same example with a distributed scope reading in (4.55b):

(4.55) a. Leon CAN'T eat CAViar and Anna BEANS. (Winkler 2005: 200)
(H*) H* +L   H* +L H⁻   (H*) H* +L H%
'It is not possible that (Leon eats the caviar and Anna the beans).'

b. LEon can't eat CAViar and ANna   BEANS. (Winkler 2005: 201)
L* H   H* L-L%   L* H H* L-L%
'It is not possible that Leon eats the caviar and it is not possible that Anna eats the beans.'

Winkler (2005) conducted a pilot study with four native speakers of English where she elicited distributed and wide scope readings. She confirmed Oehrle's (1987) observation that for the wide scope readings, speakers form only one intonational phrase for the whole coordination. Furthermore, she found that the (negated) auxiliary is heavily accented and receives the highest pitch in the whole utterance. The other pitch accents, partly given in brackets above, are less pronounced (if they are realized at all). So what we get as the defining characteristic of these structures is a main accent on the negated auxiliary as well as rising or falling boundary tones on the conjunct-final elements. The heavy accent on the negated auxiliary is obviously what we also found to be typical of denials (see Section 4.1.1).[19] The fact that there are secondary accents is due to the underlying focus structure (more on this below).

4.2.1.2 *Negation, focus, and polarity items* The following example shows that the negative marker in the wide scope gapping sentences cannot take the

---

[19] Stress on the—negative or positive—polarity of a sentence has different functions. It can also simply highlight the polarity of the sentence, where the alternativeness with the polarity of a preceding sentence is at issue [p, ¬p]:

(i)   DID John come or did he NOT come?

The negative marker in (i) is focused. Its alternative is provided in the first conjunct.

position of ordinary clausal negation. I am giving a context here that aids a denial reading:

(4.56)   PICTURE DESCRIPTION. *The first speaker says something like: 'In this picture, Max is reading the book he is holding in his hands, and Mary is reading her magazine.' What the picture really shows, though, is that while Mary is reading her magazine, Max is playing with a paper ball by his feet instead of concentrating on his book. The second speaker answers:*

    a.   *Max liest   das Buch NICHT und Maria die Zeitschrift.
          Max reads the book not   and Maria the magazine

    b.   Max liest NICHT das Buch und Maria die Zeitschrift.[20]
          'Max isn't reading the book and Mary the magazine.'

In (4.56a), the negative marker takes its normal position for clausal negation. The definite DP has scrambled out of the *v*P and *nicht* occurs after it. This version is ungrammatical in the wide scope reading no matter whether the negative marker is stressed or not. The only option to produce a wide scope reading for a coordination like (4.56) is given in (4.56b), where the negative marker is placed before the definite DP. This is exactly the position I identified as typical in corrections with gapping in the previous section, that is at least one of the correlates must be c-commanded by the negative marker.[21] Similar effects obtain in main verb gapping with adverbials (example (4.57b)) and in auxiliary gapping (example (4.58b)). In neither case can the negative marker occur in its normal position (which is given in (4.57a) and (4.58a)). It must c-command one of the correlates, or in the case of auxiliary gapping, the *v*P:

(4.57)   a.   Klaus hat am Montag nicht angerufen.
          Klaus has on Monday not   called

    b.   Klaus hat (NICHT) am Montag (*NICHT) angerufen und
          Klaus has not   on Monday   not   called   and
          Maria am Dienstag.
          Maria on Thursday
          'It is not the case that Klaus called on Monday and Mary on Tuesday.'

---

[20] Recall that for a wide scope reading to be true, it is sufficient if one of the conjuncts is false. This is the case here: it is not the case that Max is reading the book but it is the case that Maria is reading the magazine.

[21] Jacobs (1982: 240) makes similar observations for the wide scope reading in (ii), which is an instance of left peripheral deletion (cf. (i) for the 'ordinary' word order):

(i) *Peter bewundert Dr. No {nicht/NICHT} und verehrt Luise.
     Peter admires   Dr. No not   and adores Luise

(ii) Peter bewundert NICHT Dr. No und verehrt Luise.   (Jacobs 1982: 240)
     'It is not the case that Peter admires Dr. No and adores Luise.'

(4.58) a. Die Tante hat die Suppe nicht gekocht.
            the aunt has the soup   not   cooked

       b.   Die Tante hat (NICHT) die Suppe (*NICHT) gekocht

            und die Mutter den Kuchen gebacken.
            and the mother the cake   baked

            'It is not the case that the aunt cooked the soup and that the
            mother baked the cake.'

The next set of data illustrates that it is possible to correct a whole gapping
coordination, and give a full clause substitute, see (4.59). In such structures,
too, the negative marker appears in a position where it c-commands one of
the correlates. One difference with the previous structures is that the negative
marker in (4.59) does not have to be accented (but it can be accented). Only
the foci are accented. I illustrated in the last section that this is a typical feature
of corrections.

(4.59) PEter liest nicht das BUCH und MARia die ZEITschrift,
        Peter reads not   the book and Maria the magazine
        sondern die beiden gucken aus dem FENster und schauen
        butCORR the both   look   out of.the window and watch
        den Vögeln zu.
        the birds   PART
        'Peter isn't reading the book and Mary the journal but the two of them
        are looking out of the window and are watching the birds.'

Example (4.59) involves a correction of both gapping conjuncts, and not 'just'
the coordination as a whole. The latter is possible as well, see (4.60). The
difference is made explicit in the *but*-conjunct, which shows that the first
conjunct of the corrected coordination in (4.60) is false whereas the second
one is true.

(4.60) PEter liest nicht das BUCH und MARia die ZEITschrift,
        sondern während SIE konzentriert   LIEST, spielt ER mit
        butCORR while   she concentratedly reads plays he with
        seinen STIFten.
        his   pencils
        'Peter isn't reading the book and Mary the magazine: while she is
        concentrating reading he is playing with his pencils.'

Apart from the intonational 'flexibility' of corrections (stress on the negative
marker or not), corrections on the one hand and denials without a corrective
part on the other also differ in their options for the negative marker to occur
in clause-initial position, which is possible in the former but not in the latter:

(4.61) a. Nicht P<small>ETER</small> bewundert L<small>UISE</small> und A<small>NNA</small> K<small>LAUS</small>, sondern
            not   Peter admires   Luise and Anna Klaus   but
            L<small>UISE</small> bewundert P<small>ETER</small> und K<small>LAUS</small> A<small>NNA</small>.
            Luise admires   Peter and Klaus   Anna
            'Peter doesn't admire Luise and Anna Klaus: Luise admires Peter
            and Klaus Anna.'

       b. *{Nicht/N<small>ICHT</small>} P<small>ETER</small> bewundert L<small>UISE</small> und A<small>NNA</small> K<small>LAUS</small>.

I am not sure why the two sorts of denials differ in this aspect. If *not–but* indeed is a complex operator (also syntactically, see subsection 4.1.2.3), this might be responsible for it (however it is spelt out).

The data discussed so far show that (apart from the case in (4.61)), the negation in wide scope gapping sentences (corrective or not) takes the same position as in 'simple' corrections (Section 4.1.2): the negative marker c-commands at least one correlate in the first conjunct. At first sight, this might seem surprising given that single-clause denials without a correction part do not require the negation to occur in a position any different from ordinary sentence negation (see Section 4.1.1 for many examples). Nevertheless, as (4.62a) shows, even in single-clause denials it is actually possible to have the *accented* negative marker in the 'correction position' (compare unacceptable (4.62b) for the alternative intonation pattern):

(4.62) a. Max liest N<small>ICHT</small> das Buch.
            Max reads not   the book

       b. ^{??}B: Max liest nicht das B<small>UCH</small>.
            'Max <small>ISN'T</small> reading the book.'

Example (4.62a) would usually be uttered in a context where reading *the book* and not an alternative to *the book* was at issue. It carries the implicature that Max might be reading something else. This can be cancelled, as is illustrated in (4.63a), where speaker B suggests that Max might be doing something completely different from reading. With the intonation pattern given in (4.62b) a cancellation is not possible, see (4.63b). A suitable continuation would have to involve reading.

(4.63) I thought Max was reading the B<small>OOK</small> (and not the magaz<small>INE</small>).

       a. B: Max liest N<small>ICHT</small> das Buch. I don't know what he's doing.

       b. *B: Max liest nicht das B<small>UCH</small>. I don't know what he's doing.

I suggest that the sentence in (4.63a) is a kind of multiple focus structure as it is found in sentences with several focus particles (Krifka 1992), for example:

(4.64) a. John only introduced B<small>ILL</small> _{Foc} to Sue.

  b. John also$_2$ only$_1$ [introduced B<small>ILL</small>$_{Foc1}$ to M<small>ARY</small>$_{Foc2}$]

Whereas one focus (*Bill*) is associated with *only*, the other focus (*Mary*) is associated with *also*. Sentences containing multiple foci are best in the context of an antecedent that already contained one of the foci.[22] Similarly, in (4.63a) the contrastive focus on *book* is inherited from the previous utterance. This is indicated by the position the DP takes with respect to the negative marker. In addition, the proposition expressed by the previous utterance is denied: the focus and thereby the scope of the denial correspond to that proposition. This is marked by a pitch accent on the negative marker, which signals a wide focus over the entire utterance.

It is pretty straightforward now to see why the negative marker in wide scope gapping sentences needs to c-command one of the correlates even in cases where no correction is offered. The antecedent sentence—even if it is only recoverable and not actually present in the context—contains narrow foci on the remnants and their correlates, which is simply due to the contrastive relations in gapping structures. This structure is inherited in the denial.[23]

This point of view is also supported by the intonational structure of the wide scope gapping sentences I described at the beginning of this section. It has been suggested that in secondary occurrence expressions (see example (4.64)), the focus 'inherited' from a previous utterance typically is marked with a somewhat less prominent accent than the first occurrence focus (Krifka 1997). This is exactly what we find in gapping. I repeat below the intonation contour Winkler (2005) found for English wide scope readings:

(4.65) Leon C<small>AN'T</small> eat C<small>AVIAR</small> and Anna   (= example (4.55a) above)
  (H*) H*+L   H* +L H⁻ (H*)
  B<small>EANS</small>.
  H* +L H%

There are focus accents both on the auxiliary as well as on the contrast pairs but the auxiliary receives the highest pitch in the utterance. The other accents have smaller pitch excursions. See Winkler (2005: 200) for the pitch contour that shows this.

The evidence discussed so far has shown that the negative marker in gapping with a wide scope reading of the negation takes the same position as the

---

[22] It is necessary to restrict this to foci focus particles associate with, and to contrastive foci as in (4.63). Otherwise, new information focus would always elicit a multiple focus structure in the next clause, which clearly overgenerates.

[23] I shall not offer a syntactic implementation of this in this study as this presupposes a proper analysis of corrections, which is not available (see Section 4.1.2 for discussion).

negative marker in (narrow scope) corrections. This suggests that wide scope gapping sentences, like corrections, involve illocutionary negation. Importantly, distributed and narrow scope readings are not good with the negative marker in that position even if it is not accented (here illustrated for distributed readings):

(4.66)   a.   *PEter hat nicht LuIse bewundert und KLAUS ANna.
              Peter has not   Luise admired   and Klaus Anna
                                            distributed scope intended
              'Peter didn't admire Luise and Klaus didn't admire Anna.'

         b.   *JOHN put not GIN in the punch and MAry voDka.
                                            distributed scope intended

This suggests that distributed and narrow readings always involve ordinary clausal negation.

To finish the section and further support the assumption that wide scope gapping involves illocutionary negation, I will demonstrate next that wide scope gapping sentences behave like denials when it comes to polarity-sensitive items. Recall from Section 4.1.1 that illocutionary negation in denials does not license negative polarity items. In the wide scope readings in gapping, NPIs like *ever* are bad, see (4.67a). They force a distributed reading of the negation, which is only possible with the appropriate intonation, see (4.67b):

(4.67)   a.   *Oh, come on, John DIDN'T ever touch snails and Mary slugs.
                                            wide scope intended

         b.   JOHN didn't ever touch SNAILS and MAry SLUGS. *distributed scope*

Thus, wide scope gapping sentences behave like all denials with respect to NPIs. NPIs are not allowed because they are not licensed in the positive (implicit or explicit) utterance that is denied.

4.2.1.3 *Modal verbs and the negation*   There has been a claim that different modals come with different scope of the negation in gapping (Siegel 1987; Moltmann 1992*a*). This is only true to some extent: all kinds of modals are compatible with a wide scope of the negation in gapping. However, for different modals, this takes different marking (e.g. an accent on the negation or not), depending on the scope the modal takes with respect to the negation in a simple clause. The findings in this section further corroborate the view that the negation in wide scope readings is illocutionary negation, which syntactically is a high negation.

In a footnote, Siegel (1987: 72, fn. 6) suggests that if wide scope gapping sentences contain a modal this modal always gets an epistemic reading. Moltmann (1992*a*: 142f., fn. 6) suggests that wide scope readings allow both

epistemic and deontic[24] modal readings. Modals of physical modality, according to Moltmann, cannot take wide scope. She gives the following examples
that also involve negation:

(4.68) a. weil   Hans nicht reich sein kann und Maria arm
            because Hans not   rich   be   can   and Maria poor
                                                    (Moltmann 1992a: 143)
            'because Hans cannot be rich and Mary poor'

        b. weil   Hans nicht in Afrika leben kann und Maria
            because Hans not   in Africa live   can   and Maria
            in Amerika
            in America
            'because Hans cannot live in Africa and Mary in America'

        c. weil   Hans nicht über die Hürde springen kann und
            because Hans not   over the hurdle jump   can   and
            Maria über die Kiste
            Maria over the box
            'because Hans cannot jump over the hurdle and Mary over the
            box'

Moltmann says that the modal and the negation in (4.68a) and (4.68b) obligatorily have a wide scope reading and that (4.68a) obligatorily receives an
epistemic reading; (4.68c) in contrast does not receive a wide scope reading. A
potential distributed scope reading is highly marginal (a fact Moltmann does
not discuss).

There are several things to be said about these examples. First, (4.68c)
improves and does allow a wide scope reading if the negative marker receives
a pitch accent, which produces a straightforward denial reading. In addition,
the example in (4.68a) contains an (incorporated) predicate (reich 'rich'). Such
cases are probably quite similar to auxiliary gapping: the predicate, like the
main verb in auxiliary gapping, introduces a new event (in the wide sense of
the word), which comes with its own polarity (see Chapter 3). Therefore
distributed readings are not readily available here, which makes a wide scope
reading more likely (to make sense of the sentence at all, as it were; the
same holds for (4.68c)). Finally, the negative marker in (4.68b) is in a position
typical of correction negation, which calls for a wide scope rather than a
distributed scope reading. Thus, I would like to argue that the reasons for the

[24] On a deontic interpretation, modals express permission, obligation, recommendation, etc. per-
ceived to originate from outside the speaker. On a dynamic interpretation, modals (including what
Moltmann calls physical ability modals) express internal conditions or dispositions of the subject of
the clause.

wide scope interpretations in (4.68) are quite different from those Moltmann (1992*a*) suspected. Nevertheless, as the discussion in this section will show, it is worth taking a look at the interaction of modals and negation in gapping. In what follows I shall first look at epistemic modals and then at root modals. We shall see that they behave slightly differently in the gapping context.

A good criterion to differentiate the different kinds of modal verbs is the complements they can take (see Erb 2001: 93 ff. for extensive discussion). For instance, an epistemic reading can be more or less forced if the complement of the modal is a perfective infinitive:[25]

(4.69)   Susie muss den Rasen gemäht haben.
          Susie must the lawn   mown   have
          'Susie must have mown the lawn.'

In (4.70a), which has a neutral sentence accent,[26] the necessity modal scopes over the negation. A gapping sentence with (4.70a) as the first conjunct is marginal, see (4.70b). The modal itself can take wide scope but the negation does not do so. The sentence is marginal because German does not normally allow distributed readings (see Chapter 2).

(4.70)   a. Max muss das rote Schild nicht gesEHen haben.
             Max must the red sign   not   seen   have
             'Nec (Not (Max hasn't seen the red sign)).'

          b. ??MAX muss das ROte Schild nicht gesehen haben und
             Max must the red sign   not   seen   have and
             MARIA das GRÜne.
             Maria the green
             'Nec (Not (Max has seen the red sign) & Not (Mary has seen the green one)).'

Again, however, what saves this sentence is letting the negative marker c-command one of the correlates and stressing it, see (4.71). Importantly, this results in a scope reversal so that the negation scopes over the epistemic modal. As a consequence, the negation can also take the widest scope over the whole coordination, together with the modal:

(4.71)   Max muss NICHT das rote Schild gesehen haben und Maria das grüne.
          'Not (Nec (Max has seen the red sign & Mary has seen the green one)).'

---

[25] Unless the sentence receives a future interpretation:

(i)   Susie must have mown the lawn by next week.   *deontic*

[26] It is actually far from clear what the 'neutral' intonation of such sentences is. It does not necessarily fall on the complement of the verb, as shown above.

Once more, this sentence can only be understood as a denial. The negation involved is illocutionary negation.

The scope relations between modal verbs and negation are complicated and depend on several factors such as the position of the negative marker, the intonation, the type of modality involved and the expression of necessity versus obligation. I shall concentrate on the intonation aspect here as this is directly pertinent to the present problem. In the following example with epistemic modality, an accent on the negative marker—quite independently of its position—produces a reading where the modality scopes over the negation, see (4.72a), (4.72b). An accent on the modal, the main verb, or the object, on the other hand, results in the negation taking wide scope, see (4.73a), (4.73b).

(4.72) a. Max kann das Haus doch NICHT gekauft haben.[27]
            Max can   the house PART not   bought have

        b. Max kann doch NICHT das Haus gekauft haben.
            'Poss (Not (Max bought the house)).'

(4.73) a. Max KANN das Haus doch nicht gekauft haben.

        b. Max kann das Haus doch nicht GEKAUFT haben.
            'Not (Poss (Hans bought the house)).'

I do not have an explanation for the above effects at present but we can use them fruitfully to explore the behaviour of the negation in gapping with modals. In a gapping sentence building on the above examples the negative marker must not be stressed:

(4.74) Max kann doch {nicht/*NICHT} das Haus gekauft haben und
        Max can   PART not   the house bought have   and
        Maria die Wohnung!
        Maria the apartment
        Unstressed: Not (Poss (Max bought the house and Maria the apartment)).
        Stressed: Poss (Not (Max bought the house and Maria the apartment)).

So, the negative marker in a wide scope gapping sentence must not carry a pitch accent if that pitch accent results in the negation taking narrow scope

---

[27] Without the discourse particle *doch* the data are slightly different but still confirm the generalizations made above.

with respect to the modal. In wide scope readings in gapping, the negation must scope over the modality.[28]

Syntactically, epistemic modals are often assumed to have a high position in the clause such as in the CP, or at least over TP (e.g. Brennan 1997; Butler 2003; Cinque 1999; Erb 2001; McDowell 1987). If the negation is to scope over them, it must be very high. I shall come back to this in Section 4.2.4.

To close the discussion of epistemic modals, let me return to one of Moltmann's (1992a) examples of epistemic modality—(4.68b). I've substituted present tense with present perfect, which eases the epistemic reading:

(4.75)   weil Hans nicht in Afrika gelebt haben kann und   = (4.68b)
          Maria in Amerika.
          'Not (Poss (Hans lived in Africa and Mary in America)).'

Here again, we have a wide scope reading without stressing the negative marker. The negation scopes over the modal. In this particular example, the negation can be stressed and a wide scope reading is still possible (for whatever reason[29]). Importantly, stressing the negation does not result in a scope reversal here but in highlighting the denial reading.

As for deontic and dynamic modals, we find that, contra Moltmann (1992a), they too can occur in wide scope negation gapping sentences. I indicated this above, when discussing Moltmann's original examples in (4.68). I said that wide scope readings are possible with these modals provided the negative marker c-commands one of the correlates and is stressed, which invariably produces a straightforward denial reading. The same can be said for the examples below. Example (4.76a) can receive a deontic or a dynamic interpretation but not an epistemic one since the modal's complement is a directional PP, which is excluded in the latter reading (Erb 2001). In (4.76b), the modal's

---

[28] Note that the wide scope of the negation over the modality precludes the occurrence of negative polarity items even in simple clauses, e.g. *jemals* ('ever') in (i) or *keiner Menschenseele* ('not a single soul') in (ii). This corroborates the status of this negation as illocutionary negation.

(i)   ??Max kann doch nicht jemals solche Pillen geschluckt haben.
      Max can PART not ever such pills swallowed have
      'Not (Poss (Max ever ate such pills)).'

(ii) ??Max kann keiner Menschenseele Bescheid gesagt haben.
      Max can no   soul   notice   told have
      'Not (Poss (Max told a single soul)).'

Also note, however, that these data are reminiscent of certain interveners for PPIs/NPIs (Kroch 1979; Linebarger 1987; Szabolsci 2004):

(iii) John didn't always call someone / *anyone.

[29] As I said above, the factors on the scope interaction of modals and negation are manifold and need further research.

complement is a DP so we can be sure it is a dynamic modal. In both examples, the negation scopes over the whole coordination as illocutionary negation. The modals, in contrast, take distributed scope:

(4.76)   a.   Susie kann NICHT ins   Schwimmbad   und   *deontic*
              Susie can   not   in.the swimming.pool and
              Max in die Sporthalle!
              Max in the gymnasium
              'Not ((Susie may go to the pool) & (Max may go to the gymna-
              sium))'.

         b.   Susie kann NICHT das Alphabet und Max das Einmaleins.
              Susie can   not   the alphabet and Max the tables
                                                              dynamic
              'Not ((Susie can say the alphabet) & ((Max can say his tables).'

Stressing the negation in these examples does not (necessarily) have the effect of a scope reversal. Indeed, even if the negation is unaccented it scopes over the modals. The fact that it is obligatory to place an accent on the negation in the wide scope gapping sentence indicates that the negation is propositional negation if it is not stressed but illocutionary negation if it is stressed.

This assumption is compatible with the different syntactic positions that are often assumed for epistemic versus root modals.[30] I have already mentioned that it has been argued that epistemic modals take a high position in the clause. Root modals, on the other hand, are situated in a lower position such as V or Asp (see Butler 2003; Erb 2001 for two recent accounts and summaries). This distinction might also be responsible for the observed effect that it is easier for the epistemic modals to scope over the entire coordination than for the root modals to do so. As we saw in the above examples, the root modals tend to receive a distributed reading, which indicates that they are interpreted in each conjunct individually.

To summarize, the claims of Siegel (1987) and Moltmann (1992a) could not be confirmed. It is not the case that only some of the modals allow wide scope of the negation over the entire coordination in gapping: all modals allow such a reading provided some conditions are met. A general prerequisite for the negation taking wide scope over both conjuncts in gapping is that it takes wide scope over the modal(s), which is a clear indicator for the high position of the negation in these sentences. In some cases, such a scope relation can only

---

[30] The matter is not undisputed. Looking at non-English Germanic modals, Barbiers (1995), Haider (1993) and Thráinsson and Vikner (1995), for instance, assume that all modals occur in V. Schütze (1997, also for English) and Wurmbrand (2001) take all modals to occur in I.

be obtained through intonational means, for instance by placing an accent on the negative marker. If, however, placing an accent on the negative marker obligatorily results in a scope reversal, that is if the negation comes to take narrow scope with respect to the modal, wide scope in gapping is not possible. For gapping with root modals, we found that they always require stress on the negative marker, which produces a clear denial reading. The differences between root modals and epistemic modals correspond to the different syntactic positions that have been suggested for them and which, due to reasons of space, I could not discuss in any detail here.

On the larger picture, I found that the negation in declarative sentences with a wide scope reading differs from the negation found in the other two readings in gapping. This suggests that the wide scope readings are truly different from the distributed and the narrow scope readings. This assumption will be further confirmed by the data investigated in the next section, where I look at interrogatives. These must also come with illocutionary negation if they are to receive a wide scope interpretation.

4.2.2 *Interrogatives*

Interrogative gapping sentences with a wide scope reading share many features with the declaratives discussed in the previous section. I propose that they also involve illocutionary negation, that is a negation that operates on the level of the speech act. Interrogatives obviously are not used as denials but they can also express certain expectations/opinions of the speaker with respect to the truth of an assumed proposition. Negative interrogative gapping sentences with a wide scope reading express the fact that the speaker had assumed that a positive belief s/he held was true. The speaker wants to check this again because in the context some negative evidence came up. The negation used in such 'checking contexts' has been termed *outer negation* by Ladd (1981). I will argue that it is an instance of illocutionary negation. The evidence I will discuss is essentially the same as the evidence I used for denials: contextual restrictions, the position of the negation in the clause and its behaviour with respect to polarity-sensitive items. All these show precisely the characteristics that we expect if illocutionary negation is involved: just as in denials, the context must license the use of outer negation, the negation must c-command one of the correlates and polarity-sensitive items are neither licensed nor disturbed. I also discuss the intonation of the interrogative gapping sentences, which differs from that of denials. It is still the case that the two conjuncts must be uttered as one intonational phrase but the negation and/or auxiliary are usually not accented. Finally, interrogatives offer a nice way to show that wide scope readings in contrast to the other readings involve only one speech act and are indeed a coordination of smaller conjuncts: wide scope interrogatives contain only one question operator rather than two. The section is structured as follows. After presenting some basic data, I introduce the concept of outer negation (4.2.2.1). Then I show that outer negation shares many features with illocutionary negation in denials (4.2.2.2), and investigate this for gapping (4.2.2.3). Finally, I discuss the issue of the number of question operators in the wide scope versus distributed scope readings (4.2.2.4).

To begin consider the following interrogatives, where the negation takes wide scope over both conjuncts. Example (4.77) shows polarity questions and (4.78) shows constituent questions. To avoid confusion with the distributed readings, the examples have been constructed with auxiliary gapping, which never allows distributed readings. Note, however, that this results in the English examples looking like left peripheral deletion, which blurs the scope facts because a small conjunct analysis is readily available. I shall present main verb gapping, which does not have this problem, later on. The German data are clearer here because the negation occurs in a non-peripheral position.

(4.77)　a.　Can't John eat caviar and Mary eat beans? (Siegel 1987: 73, fn. 16)

　　　　b.　Hat Hans nicht Fisch gegessen und Maria Wein getrunken?
　　　　　　has Hans not　fish　eaten　　and Maria wine drunk
　　　　　　'Is it not the case that Hans ate fish and Mary drank wine?'

(4.78)　a.　Why didn't John eat fish and (*why) Mary drink wine?

　　　　b.　Warum hat Hans nicht Fisch gegessen und (*warum)
　　　　　　why　　has Hans not　fish　eaten　　and　why
　　　　　　Maria Wein getrunken?
　　　　　　Maria wine drunk

　　　　c.　Wer hat denn Maria NICHT was　　　vom　Eis
　　　　　　who has PART Maria not　something of.the ice.cream
　　　　　　weggegessen und (*wer) Paul was　　　vom　Shake
　　　　　　eat.steal　　and　who Paul something of.the shake
　　　　　　weggetrunken?
　　　　　　drink.steal
　　　　　　'Who didn't eat some of Mary's ice cream and drink some of Paul's shake?'

Polarity questions and constituent questions differ in that the former seem generally fine whereas the latter are only felicitous if the *wh*-phrase occurs in the first conjunct only. If the *wh*-phrase also occurs in the second conjunct a distributed reading is attempted. This fails because auxiliary gapping does not allow distributed readings. This difference between polarity questions and *wh*-questions is only apparent. In polarity questions, the question-marking element, that is the clause-initial finite verb, is absent in the second conjunct, too. This is simply due to the fact that we are dealing with gapping so it does not strike us as unusual.

4.2.2.1 *Outer negation versus inner negation*   Polarity questions come in two varieties: they can be positive or they can be negative. In a traditional account of the meaning of questions, where the meaning of a question is the set of possible answers to that question (e.g. Hamblin 1973; Groenendijk and Stokhof 1984), positive and negative polarity questions mean the same: for a polarity question, the set of possible answers contains two elements: a positive answer and a negative answer (compare Büring and Gunlogson 2000):

(4.79)   ⟦Has John drunk beer?⟧ (w_0)/ ⟦Has John not drunk beer?⟧ (w_0) =
          { w_0|John has drunk wine in w_0; w_0|John has not drunk wine in w_0}

This analysis does not reflect some peculiar characteristics of negative polarity questions, which have been shown to be able to give rise to implicatures that positive polarity questions do not have (Ladusaw 1980; and especially Ladd 1981 and subsequent literature).

    In English negative polar questions, the negative marker can take two positions. It can either move along with the auxiliary to the beginning of the clause (= preposed negation) or it can stay in situ (= non-preposed negation). These two varieties give rise to different interpretations. Preposed negation in a negative polar question carries the epistemic implicature that the speaker believed or expected the positive answer to be correct. Non-preposed negation does not necessarily have this effect. Here is an example from Romero and Han (2004):

(4.80)   SCENARIO: *The speaker is organizing a party and she is in charge of supplying all the non-alcoholic beverages for teetotalers. The speaker is going through a list of people who are invited. She has no previous belief or expectation about their drinking habits.*

          A: Jane and Mary do not drink.
          S: OK. What about John? Does he not drink (either)?
          #S′: OK. What about John? Doesn't he drink (either)?

                                                    (Romero and Han 2004: 610)

Answer S′ is pragmatically inappropriate in this unbiased context because it carries the implicature that the speaker believed that John does actually drink.

Negative polar questions with preposed negation can be further distinguished by whether they express what Ladd (1981) called *inner* or *outer* negation. Consider the following examples:

(4.81)   A: I'd like to take you guys out to dinner while I'm here—we'd have
         time to go somewhere around here before the evening session tonight,
         don't you think?
         B: I guess but there's not really any place to go to in Hyde Park.
         A: Oh really, isn't there a vegetarian restaurant around here?

(4.82)   A: You guys must be starving. You want to get something to eat?
         B: Yeah, isn't there a vegetarian restaurant around here—Moosewood,
         or something like that?

Ladd says that in (4.81) speaker A originally had assumed that there would
be a vegetarian restaurant nearby. From B's answer, however, A concluded
that this is false. With the negative polar question, A checks that the original
assumption is indeed false. Thus, what is being questioned is the inference ¬p
(Ladd 1981: 165). This is what Ladd calls inner negation. In (4.82), in contrast, B
checks that the proposition he or she believes to be true actually *is* true. What is
being questioned is the speaker's belief p. This is Ladd's outer negation. Thus,
outer negation—like the negation in a negative denial—'embeds' a positive
proposition whereas inner negation is part of a negative inference.[31]

4.2.2.2 *Outer negation has the characteristics of illocutionary negation*   Having
introduced the concept of outer negation, let me go through the evidence that
suggests that outer negation is illocutionary negation, just like the negation
in denials. The first piece of evidence concerns the context. Outer negation
and inner negation occur in different contexts. Büring and Gunlogson (2000)
show that what they call neutral contextual evidence and negative contextual
evidence are acceptable for the use of outer negation, whereas positive contextual evidence is pragmatically inappropriate:

(4.83)   *A and S want to go out for dinner. S has been to Moosewood a couple of
         years back.*

         S': Where do you want to go out for dinner?   *neutral*
         #S": I bet we can find any type of restaurant you can think of in this
         city. Make your choice!   *positive contextual evidence*
         S''': Since you guys are vegetarians, we can't go out in this town, where
         it's all meat and potatoes.   *negative contextual evidence*
         A: Isn't there some vegetarian restaurant around here?

---

[31] A similar example was discussed by Cattell (1973: 616–19).

Example (4.83) shows that checking a positive proposition if that proposition was just confirmed in the context makes little sense. It is just like rejecting a negative proposition if one believes that the proposition should indeed be negative.

The second piece of evidence is found in examples with polarity-sensitive elements. Romero and Han (2004) show that outer negation comes with positive polarity items and inner negation, with negative polarity items. Example (4.84) is an example where the belief p is checked. It contains the PPI *too*. In (4.85) an inference ¬p is checked. It contains an item that requires a negative clause (*either*).

(4.84) Ok, now that Stephan has come, we are all here. Let's go!
        S: Isn't Jane coming too?   *outer negation*

(4.85) SCENARIO: *Pat and Jane are two phonologists who are supposed to be speaking in our workshop on optimality and acquisition.*

        A: Pat is not coming. So we don't have any phonologists in the program.
        S: Isn't Jane coming either?   *inner negation*
                                                    (Romero and Han 2004: 610 f.)

In German, the difference between (84) and (85) has a syntactic reflex in the relative position of the additive particle *auch* ('too') and the negative marker:

(4.86) Kommt Jane nicht auch?   *outer negation*
        Kommt Jane auch nicht?   *inner negation*

Otherwise, we find the same effects with PPIs as in English. In (4.87), the PPI *schon* ('already') is embedded under outer negation:

(4.87) Hat Meyer nicht schon bei   uns publiziert?
        has Meyer not   already with us   published
        'Hasn't Meyer already published with us?'

Thus, outer negation behaves like illocutionary negation when it comes to polarity items whereas inner negation behaves like propositional negation.

Finally, consider the position of the negative marker, which in corrections with multiple focus as well as declarative gapping sentences with wide scope, must c-command at least one focus, and in corrections with one focus, that one focus. For English, we have already seen that preposing is more or less a prerequisite for outer negation. Romero and Han (2004) suggest that the same holds for German:

(4.88) a. Hat Hans Maria nicht gesehen?   *no implicature*
            has Hans Mary not   seen

        b. Hat nicht Hans Maria gesehen?   *outer negation*
            'Hasn't Hans seen Mary?'

In (4.88b), the negation occurs immediately after the auxiliary. This is, how-ever, not necessary, as (4.89) illustrates:

(4.89) Hat Hans nicht Maria gesehen?   *outer negation*

The difference between (4.88b) and (4.89) is one of focus. In (4.88b), either only *Hans* or both *Hans* and *Mary* can be focused: the speaker believes either that it was Hans who saw Mary rather than, for example, Paul who saw Mary; or that it was Hans who saw Mary rather than, for example, Paul who saw Ann. In (4.89), only *Mary* can be in focus, that is the speaker believes that Hans saw Mary and not some other woman. Thus, the data pattern with corrections involving stripping rather than gapping: the negative marker c-commands (all) the element(s) that elicit(s) an alternative.[32] In sum, outer negation behaves like the negation in corrections/denials. I assume that this is due to its status as illocutionary negation.

4.2.2.3 *Interrogative gapping sentences with a wide scope reading*   In what follows, I demonstrate that wide scope interrogative gapping sentences always involve outer negation and never inner negation. I shall discuss both polarity questions here and *wh*-questions. As far as negative *wh*-questions are con-cerned, it is not so clear that they should differ from their positive counterparts in the same way as negative polarity questions differ from positive ones. Never-theless, we shall see that the negation in *wh*-interrogatives can also scope over the whole coordination and if it does so it has all the features of illocutionary negation.[33] The tests I will use are those familiar from the previous sections: the position of the negative marker, intonation, polarity-sensitive items and, in addition, what one could call the *no*-test: the fusion of the negation with an indefinite determiner producing *no*, which is not allowed in outer negation.

First, the position of the negative marker: in the coordinated polarity ques-tion in (4.90a) the negative marker c-commands one of the correlates, that is it takes the position of illocutionary negation. The resulting reading is a wide scope reading. In (4.90b) the negation occurs in its ordinary position.

---

[32] This also means that when (4.88a) is read with a focus accent on the main verb participle *gesehen* ('seen') this can elicit an outer negation reading if the speaker has been confronted with the idea that Hans maybe spoke to Mary over the phone rather than saw her in person. Thus, it is no precondition in German for the negation to occur in a 'preposed' position in order to elicit an outer negation reading. What is required is c-command of the focus by the negation.

[33] I will not explore the function of illocutionary negation in *wh*-interrogatives in this study but see a few remarks in Section 4.2.3. See Creswell (2000) for the functions of polarity focus in *wh*-questions.

A distributed reading arises. The result is marginal because German does not allow distributed readings with an elided negative marker.

(4.90)   a. Hat Max nicht den Club organisiert und Maria die Bar?
              has Max not   the   club organized and Maria the bar
              'Is it not the case that Max organized the club and Maria the bar?'

         b. ⁇Hat Max den Club nicht organisiert und Maria die Bar?
              'Did Max not organize the club and did Mary not organize the bar?'

Wh-questions behave in the same way. In (4.91a), the negative marker takes the position of illocutionary negation in gapping and in (4.91b), that of propositional negation.

(4.91)   CONTEXT: *Some game where the participants have to hand various toys to two kids.*

         a. Wer hat denn NICHT dem Jungen den Ball gegeben und
              who has PART not   the boy   the ball given   and
              dem Mädchen das Seil?
              the girl   the rope

         b. *Wer hat denn dem Jungen den Ball NICHT gegeben und dem
              Mädchen das Seil?
              'Who DIDN'T give the boy the ball and the girl the rope?'

Note that the negative marker needs to be stressed in (4.91a). This is probably due to the fact that negative *wh*-questions are not as 'unusual' as negative polarity questions, as I mentioned above. It seems that the high position of the negation needs to be signalled by intonational means in addition to the changed position of the negative marker just as the denial reading in declaratives often needs to be signalled by intonational means.[34]

For the behaviour of polarity items consider the data in (4.92) and (4.93). The examples in (4.92), which contain the PPI *schon* ('already'), receive a wide scope reading. The examples in (93) with the NPIs *keine müde Mark* ('not a penny') and *ever* can only be read with a distributed scope of the negation.[35, 36]

---

[34] The particle *denn* is also important in the above example. Together with *nicht* it signals that a positive state-of-affairs (i.e. the kids were given their respective toys) is really what anybody would have expected.

[35] Which is acceptable in German because of the NPI, see Chapter 2.

[36] There are some data in English which are slightly curious. The PPI in (i) can be left out in the second conjunct whereas the NPI in (ii) cannot:

(i)   Didn't John eat some caviar and Pete (some) salmon?

(ii) Did John not eat any caviar, and Pete *(any) salmon?

In (i), we have outer negation which scopes over two positive conjuncts. The presence or absence of the positive polarity item does not interact with that. In (ii), on the other hand, we have inner

Also note that it is possible in (4.92a), and (4.92c) and necessary in (4.92b) to place an accent on the negative marker. In (4.93), on the other hand, the negative marker must not be accented, which is what we would expect in illocutionary versus propositional negation.

(4.92) a. Hat Kurtz nicht schon bei uns publiziert und Schmidt
            has Kurtz not   already with us   published and Schmidt
            bei Springer?
            with Springer
            'Is it not the case that Kurtz already published with us and Schmidt with Springer?'

        b. Wer hat denn NICHT schon   bei Hofmanns Bier gekauft
            who has PART not   already with H.   beer bought
            und bei   Vino Italia Wein?
            and with Vino Italia wine
            'Who HASn't already bought beer at Hofmanns and wine at Vino Italia?'

        c. Why hasn't Max already bought beer at Thresher's and Mary wine?

(4.93) a. Hat Max dem Kellner keine müde Mark Trinkgeld gegeben
            has Max the waiter not.a.penny   tips   given
            und Maria dem Barkeeper?
            and Maria the bar.man
            'Is it the case that Max didn't give the waiter a penny in tips and is it the case that Mary didn't give the bar man a penny in tips?'

        b. *Why hasn't Max ever bought beer at Thresher's and Mary wine?

Another way to test wide scope gapping structures for inner (propositional) versus outer (illocutionary) negation is the above-mentioned *no*-test. Büring and Gunlogson (2000) argue that in German negative polar questions involving indefinites, NEG does not merge with the indefinite (or zero) determiner to *kein* ('no') if outer negation is involved. It does so, however, with inner negation.[37] Similarly, English *no* only allows inner negation. Now, in gapping with a wide scope reading, only *nicht* can be used and not *kein*, that is only

negation—otherwise the NPI in the first conjunct would not be licensed. It seems that inner negation itself actually requires the presence of the negative polarity item in this particular case. Leaving it out results in an outer negation reading. This produces a curious kind of contrast with the first conjunct and violates the PBC (see Chapter 3).

[37] Note that illocutionary negation in corrections is fine with *kein*:

(i) Max isst keine Birnen sondern Äpfel.
     Max eats no   pears butCORR apples
     'Max isn't eating pears but apples.'

outer negation is possible as (4.94a) versus (4.94b) and (4.95a) versus (4.95b) illustrate:

(4.94) a. Hat Hans nicht Wein getrunken und Maria Fisch gegessen?

b. *Hat Hans keinen Wein getrunken und Maria Fisch
has Hans not/no wine drunk   and Maria fish
gegessen?
eaten
'Wasn't it the case that Hans drank wine and Mary ate fish?'

(4.95) a. Wer hat denn (NICHT) Hans (NICHT) einen Ball
who has PART not   Hans not   a   ball
zugeworfen und Maria einen Reifen?
thrown   and Maria a   hoop
'For whom isn't it the case then, that s/he did do the following: throw a ball to Hans and a hoop to Mary?'

b. *Wer hat denn Hans {keinen/KEINen} Ball zugeworfen und Maria einen Reifen?

The argument is weakened by the fact that *kein*—except for cases of narrow scope—is bad in gapping. Note, though, that a distributed reading can be saved by the repetition of *kein* in the second conjunct, which, of course, is not possible in the wide scope readings.

In sum, the evidence clearly supports the view that questions with a wide scope reading of the negation in gapping always contain illocutionary negation.

4.2.2.4 *One coordination—one speech act* In the introductory paragraphs to this section on interrogatives, I pointed out that the second conjunct in the wide scope interrogatives may not contain a *wh*-word, consider the following example repeated from above, as well as the examples in the previous section:

(4.96) Why didn't John eat fish and (*why) Mary drink wine?

In Chapter 1, I showed that it is perfectly possible to have a *wh*-phrase in run-of-the-mill gapping, see (4.97a) and (4.97b). And even though negative *why*-questions cannot be coordinated in the distributed readings, negative *who*-questions can, see (4.98):

(4.97) a. Who gave the boy the ball and who the girl the rope?

b. Why did John eat the fish and why Mary the tofu?

(4.98) a. Who didn't give the boy the ball and who the girl the rope?

b. *Why didn't John read the book and why Mary the magazine?

I will leave the reasons for the difference between *why*-questions and *who-* or *what*-questions open. *Why*-questions are different from the other questions in many ways. For instance, *why* takes clausal scope. It asks for an event that causes another event. *Who* or *what* only ask for arguments. Also, *why* gives rise to negative islands (the so-called inner island effects) for which both syntactic, semantic, and pragmatic reasons have been given. Argument *wh*-phrases do not give rise to inner islands. As (4.96) above illustrates, a negative *why*-question is fine if the negation takes wide scope. The negative marker must not be accented in this case.

I indicated above that the ban on the occurrence of *wh*-words in the second conjunct of the wide scope readings is essentially a ban on the occurrence of the question marking element, which in polarity questions cannot be seen as clearly because the only question-identifying element—the finite verb in its clause-initial position—is elided in gapping. This indicates that we are dealing with only one question in the wide scope readings: the question takes scope over the whole coordination. This is another feature wide scope interrogatives share with wide scope declaratives: in the declaratives there is only one denial that rejects the whole coordination. So, for the wide scope readings, we may say that the coordination corresponds to one speech act. This finding is crucial for the syntactic analysis of the wide scope readings versus the other readings. I shall argue in Section 4.2.4 that there is only one Force projection in wide scope gapping whereas in the distributed and the narrow scope readings, there are two.

4.2.3 *Epistemic speech act operators*

In the previous sections I argued that outer negation in interrogatives shares very many characteristics with the negation used in denials and suggested that both are instances of illocutionary negation, that is a negation that operates on the speech act level. For denials, this was implemented for example, by van der Sandt (1991) in the form of an echo operator that scopes over the entire utterance, non-propositional parts included. In this section, I shall review an account of outer negation in interrogatives, Romero and Han (2004), which proposes that outer negation scopes over an illocutionary epistemic operator (VERUM). I will depart from this and propose that illocutionary negation is itself an illocutionary operator.

Ladd's (1981) original idea for outer negation was that the difference with inner negation is due to a difference in scope: that in the case of outer negation, the negation indeed is outside the questioned proposition. Romero and Han (2004) also assume a scopal difference to be behind the two different kinds of negation but the elements involved are different. They propose that the general epistemic implicature that negative polar questions give rise to is a conversational epistemic implicature which at Logical Form introduces the conversational (i.e. illocutionary) epistemic operator VERUM. VERUM, according to Romero and Han, is used by the speaker to assert that s/he is certain that in all the worlds conforming to the hearer's and speaker's knowledge where all the conversational goals of speaker and hearer are fulfilled, the proposition VERUM embeds, should be added to the Common Ground.[38] It is the VERUM operator that interacts with the negation, that is scopes over it in the case of inner negation, or scopes under it in the case of outer negation (see below for examples).

The term VERUM comes from the study of VERUM focus, a concept which was first introduced by Höhle (1988, 1992). VERUM focus can be expressed by stress on an auxiliary in a positive sentence. The effect is that the utterance is understood as something like a positive denial, that is a negative proposition is rejected. In (4.99), B rejects the assertion made by A.

(4.99)   A: Peter wasn't in last night.

         B: He WAS in, you just didn't hear him coming.

Höhle also assumes that VERUM is an illocutionary operator. He argues that the meaning of the contrastive focus on the finite element of the clause is that the speaker insists on the truth of the proposition. The focus is on the assertion of the sentence, or, as Klein (1998) puts it, the actual 'claim' is highlighted. Erb (2001) takes a slightly different position and suggests that VERUM indicates the speaker's opinion on the truth of the proposition, that is, like Romero and Han (2004), she considers VERUM as having an epistemic component. Höhle (1992) also gives examples for VERUM focus where the alternatives to the focus involve epistemic expressions. Consider the following examples from Erb (2001):

(4.100)   A: The book is not on the table.   (Erb 2001: 65)

          B: Of COURSE the book is on the table.

---

[38] Formally, this reads as follows (x is a free variable whose value is contextually identified with the addressee/speaker):

$[\![\text{verum}_i]\!]^{gx/i} = \lambda p_{<s,t>} \lambda w. \forall w' \in \text{Epi}_x(w)[\forall w'' \in \text{Conv}_x(w')[p \in CG_{w''}]] = \text{FOR-SURE-CG}_x$

$\text{Epi}_x(w)$ is the set of worlds that conform to x's knowledge in w. $\text{Conv}_x(w')$ is the set of worlds where all the conversational goals of x in w' are fulfilled (according to the Maxims of Quantity and Quality). $CG_{w''}$ is the set of propositions that the speakers assume in w'' to be true (= common ground).

(4.101) A: Peter was not at the party yesterday.

B: SURE he was at the party.

VERUM focus is not restricted to declaratives. It also occurs in interrogatives, imperatives, and expressive counterfactuals (Höhle 1992):

(4.102) Who DID come to the party, then?

(4.103) NÄHME   er sich doch einen Stuhl!   (Höhle 1992: 120)
took.SUBJUNCT he REFL PART a   chair
'If only he took a chair!'

Obviously, VERUM in questions, imperatives, or counterfactuals can hardly mean that the speaker insists on the truth of the proposition or that s/he highlights the claim. It seems that VERUM does different things in declaratives versus questions and other sentence types. Höhle (1992) proposes that VERUM in *wh*-questions means something like 'for which x is it really the case that. ....' This paraphrase suggests that Erb's (2001) and Romero and Han's (2004) proposal that an epistemic component might be relevant is the correct kind of analysis.

I said above that in the Romero and Han (2004) account, VERUM is an illocutionary epistemic operator which signals that the speaker is sure that the proposition at hand should be added to the common ground, and interacts with the negation in polarity questions. Applied to an example of outer negation, this yields the following (tense and polarity item ignored):

(4.104) Isn't Jane coming (too)?   (= ex. (4.84), outer negation)
LF: [$_{CP}$ Q not [VERUM [$_{IP}$ Jane is coming]]]
{it is not for sure that we should add to CG that Jane is coming;
it is (not not) for sure that we should add to CG that Jane is coming}

The first answer in the set of answers to the question says that it is not the case that the proposition *Jane is coming* is (= should be) in the common ground. The second answer says that it is the case that the proposition *Jane is coming* is in the common ground. Inner negation is interpreted as follows:

(4.105) Isn't Jane coming (either)?   (= ex. (4.85), inner negation)
LF: [$_{CP}$ Q VERUM [not [$_{IP}$ Jane is coming]]]
{it is for sure that we should add to CG that Jane is not coming;
it is not for sure that we should add to CG that Jane is not coming}

Here, VERUM and the negation exchange places. One answer says that it is the case that the proposition *Jane is not coming* is in the common ground, the other answer says that it is not the case that the proposition *Jane is not coming* is in the common ground. Thus, for outer negation, we have a positive proposition whose addition to the common ground is evaluated, and for inner negation, we have a negative proposition whose addition to the common ground is evaluated. The analysis carries over to declaratives expressing positive denials:

(4.106)   She DID go to the Himalayas.   (Han and Romero 2004: 630)
          LF: [$_{CP}$ VERUM [$_{IP}$ she went to the Himalayas]]

To account for negative denials, Romero and Han (2004) define a negative version of VERUM, which they call NOT or FOR-SURE-CG$_x$-NOT, and which basically[39] says that the speaker is sure that a negative proposition should be added to the common ground. In other words, the negation operates on the proposition, as in inner negation (with the exception, of course, that the meaning is not a set of propositions but a single proposition). Now, in Section 4.1.1 I argued at length that a negative denial rejects a positive proposition (and with it the entire utterance). This is not captured by this account. Quite the opposite, it is claimed that a negative proposition should be added to the common ground, that is only the substitution aspect of denials is captured, not the denial aspect itself. For such an approach, the observed parallel behaviour of denials and questions with outer negation with respect to context, polarity items, and positioning of the negative marker (see previous sections), remains completely mysterious.[40] What we need is a high negation and not a low one.

The most straightforward way to implement a high negation in the LF of denials is probably to take over the analysis from outer negation. Nevertheless, I would like to argue that a slightly different analysis is more attractive. Let us examine the idea of a conversational epistemic operator a little more closely. Apart from VERUM, there are other epistemic operators at the level of the speech act. Romero and Han (2004) suggest that the adverb *really* is such an operator. *Surely* is also a good candidate. So are the German adverbs *sicherlich* ('possibly') (Krifka 2004) and *wohl* ('possibly') (Krifka 2004; Zimmermann 2008). All these adverbs clearly have epistemic content. What I need to

---

[39] Here is the definition:

$[\![\text{NOT}_i]\!]^{gx/i} = \lambda p_{<s,t>}\lambda w.\forall w' \in \text{Epi}_x(w)[\forall w'' \in \text{Conv}_x(w')[\neg p \in \text{CG}_{w''}]]$ = FOR-SURE-CG$_x$-NOT

[40] The inability of outer negation in interrogatives to license NPIs, and their failure to block PPIs is regarded by Romero and Han (2004) to be a consequence of the intervention of the VERUM operator between the licensing negation and the polarity item. This does not carry over to negative denials, however, because there the negation scopes under VERUM.

demonstrate is that they operate on the speech act and not on the proposition. I will build on earlier work by Krifka (2004) and Zimmermann (2004, 2008) here.

First, whereas epistemic speech act operators cannot occur in the antecedent of conditionals, epistemic propositional operators can (Krifka 2004; Zimmermann 2008):

(4.107) a. Wenn es {sicher /   vielleicht / *sicherlich /*wohl}   regnet,
             if   it   certainly perhaps   surely   possibly rains
             nehme ich einen Schirm   mit
             take I   an   umbrella PART

         b. If it is {certainly/ *surely} going to rain I must take an umbrella.

The reason for this effect according to Krifka (2004) is that the antecedent of conditionals cannot embed a speech act (Frege 1919; Horn 1989). Note that if we have a focus on the negation in such environments this can only be understood as being an ordinary focus on the polarity, marking the alternativeness, without the denial element (as in *Did he come or did he* NOT *come?*, cf. footnote 19):[41]

(4.108) Wenn es NICHT regnet, brauche ich keinen Schirm
         If   it not   rains   need   I   no   umbrella
         mitzunehmen.
         to.take
         'If it doesn't rain, we don't need to take an umbrella.'

A second piece of evidence pointed out by Zimmermann (2008) is that the adverb *wohl* must be deaccented due to lexical blocking by accented *wohl* functioning as an affirmative particle.[42] Therefore, in a focus-background structure, unaccented *wohl* is expected to be part of the background (i.e. to be given). This also means that the background information should be an epistemically modified assumption because the meaning contribution of *wohl* is 'possibly'. Yet, this expectation is not borne out, as is illustrated by the following example. A propositional relative of *wohl*, *womöglich*, is fine in this context.

[41] Corrections can occur in such environments. I have no explanation for this difference:

(i) Wenn Paul nicht beide Kugeln   findet, sondern nur   eine, kriegt er Probleme.
     If   Paul not   both marbles finds   butCORR only one   gets   he problems
     'If Paul does not find both marbles but only one, he's in trouble.'

[42] Accented *wohl* looks itself very much like a VERUM operator:

(i) Hein ist WOHL auf See.
     'Hein IS at sea.'

(4.109)   PETER_{Foc} ist {#wohl / womöglich} gestern   nach Hamburg
Peter   is   possibly possibly   yesterday to   Hamburg
gefahren, auch wenn ich nicht ganz sicher bin, dass
gone   also if   I   not   quite sure   am   that
überhaupt jemand   nach Hamburg gefahren ist.
at.all   somebody to   Hamburg gone   is
'Peter possibly went to Hamburg yesterday, although I am not sure
that anybody went to Hamburg at all.'

The adverb *wohl* ('possibly') does not take part in the information structuring
of the proposition. Zimmermann concludes from this that it must be outside
the proposition.

   Another feature that sets epistemic speech act operators apart from propositional ones is that the former cannot be picked up in a correction and be
embedded under another speech act operator while the latter can, see (4.110a)
versus (4.110b). Zimmermann (2008) discusses these data with *wohl* and
attributes the effects to the adverb's obligatory deaccented status. Yet note that
accented *wohl*, which, as I said above, means something like *surely*, can also
not be corrected and substituted by an appropriate alternative like *perhaps*,
which indicates that accented *wohl* is an epistemic speech act operator itself.
Example (4.110c) shows that *sicherlich* and *surely*, which can both be accented,
are not good in correction contexts either. All this only holds, of course, if
the adverbs are not read as quotes, which would be a case of metalinguistic
negation.

(4.110)   a.   *Er hat nicht WOHL   das Haus verlassen,
                sondern {definiTIV/ vieLLEICHT}.

          b.   Er hat nicht möglicherwEIse das Haus   verlassen,
               he has not   possibly   the house left
               sondern definiTIV.
               but_{CORR} definitely perhaps
               'He didn't possibly leave the house but definitely perhaps.'

          c.   *Er hat nicht sicherlich das Haus verlassen, sondern definiTIV.
               'He didn't surely leave the house but definitely.'

          d.   He didn't {*surEly / cerTAINly leave the house but perHAPS.

To sum up, adverbs like *wohl* and *surely* are epistemic operators that operate
on the speech act.

   What does it mean for an operator to work on the level of the speech
act? Searle and Vanderveken (1985) and Vanderveken (1990) have proposed
that speech acts come with certain sincerity conditions. A sincerity condition

determines the 'psychological modes of the mental states that the speaker must have if he is sincerely performing a speech act with that force in a possible context of utterance' (Vanderveken 1990: 117). A sincerity condition for an assertion would be that the speaker believes the truth of the proposition in question.

The mental states that are relevant for a sincerity condition come in varying degrees of strength, for example how strongly is a speaker committed to the proposition uttered. The degree of strength is essentially a notion of epistemic modality on the level of the speech act. I suggest that all the epistemic speech act operators that we have seen, including VERUM, are operators that are best considered in terms of degree of strength.[43] VERUM itself signals a very high degree of strength, namely that the content of the proposition at stake should indeed be added to the common ground. English *surely* and German accented *wohl* also express a high degree of strength. German *sicherlich* and unaccented *wohl* express a lower degree of strength. It is a natural step from here to assume that there should also be operators that signal an extremely low degree of strength, such as zero degrees of strength. I would like to argue that illocutionary negation is an instance of this. Thus, instead of analyzing outer negation as a negation that outscopes VERUM, and negative denials as VERUM outscoping clausal negation like Romero and Han (2004) do, I propose that in both cases, we are dealing with a strength operator, call it FALSUM, that signals that the sincerity conditions for an assertion cannot be upheld:

(4.111) $[\![$FALSUM p$]\!]$ = zero degrees of strength for adding p to the common ground[44]

Questions with outer negation can be taken to ask for the degrees of strength, consider:

(4.112)   Isn't Jane coming too?   (= ex. (4.35))
            LF: [$_{CP}$ Q [FALSUM [$_{IP}$ Jane is coming]]]

---

[43] Another means to qualify the degree of strength in an assertion is evidential modality (Krifka 2004). Also see Zaefferer (2001) on this topic.

[44] Formally this could be captured as follows (borrowing from Romero and Han's formalization, see note 39):

$[\![$FALSUM$_i$$]\!]^{gx/i} = \lambda p_{<s,t>} \lambda w. \neg \exists w' \in \text{Epi}_x(w)[\forall w'' \in \text{Conv}_x(w')[p \in CG_{w''}]]$

In none of the worlds that conform to x's knowledge in w such that all the conversational goals of x in w' are fulfilled (according to the Maxims of Quantity and Quality), is the proposition in question in the common ground. This formula gives us a different semantics for illocutionary negation in comparison to propositional negation, which is something that has been rejected in many accounts, see note 4 in this chapter. However, in view of the suggestion elaborated in the coming paragraphs—to view the common ground not as a collection of propositions but rather of speech acts, this would be warranted.

{There are zero degrees of strength for adding Jane is coming to CG; There are not zero degrees of strength for adding Jane is coming to CG}

VERUM signals that the degrees of strength of the sincerity conditions are very high:

(4.113)   ⟦VERUM p⟧ = high degree of strength for adding p to the common ground

Inner negation can be represented as VERUM scoping over propositional negation, as in Romero and Han (2004). For the epistemic operators investigated above, I suggest that they signal degrees of strength that lie between VERUM and FALSUM. This reflects Vanderveken's (1990) idea that the degrees of strength for the same illocutionary point come in scales. In the present case, I suggest the following scale, where a high degree of strength is on the left of the scale, and a low degree of strength on the right.

(4.114)   VERUM, *surely*, WOHL > neutral assertion > *sicherlich* > *wohl* >
           FALSUM

In essence FALSUM, VERUM, and the other epistemic illocutionary operators operate on the speech act in that they qualify the status of a proposition with respect to its role in the common ground. It is worth dwelling on this momentarily because it is not quite clear what 'the status of a proposition with respect to the common ground' is supposed to mean, if the common ground contains (just) propositions. As Zimmermann (2008) points out, it might be useful to consider the common ground not as containing only propositions but also 'social commitments that come in the form of illocutionary acts such as assertions, questions, directives, etc.' (fn. 7). Following Vanderveken's (1990) position that illocutionary acts are the primary meaning of sentences, Zimmermann suggests that a 'generalized common ground' should contain (amongst other things) 'all illocutionary acts that the discourse participants mutually accept as successful and still valid at any given stage of the discourse.' From this point of view, we can assume that in the case of denials not only the negative proposition that is eventually expressed by a negative denial is in the common ground (which is what Romero and Han's (2004) definition of the operator FOR-SURE-CG$_x$-NOT does) but a record of the speech act that brought this about, that is a denial that rejected a positive utterance.

In this sense, a denial is not a speech act that 'removes' a proposition from the common ground, as I, following van der Sandt (1991), assumed throughout this chapter. Rather, a denial marks a proposition as having such a low degree of strength (zero) that it should not be in the common ground.

But, since the proposition in question already was in the common ground, speakers would (obviously) not erase all memory of it but mark it as having been rejected. Thus the common ground would really be a history of speech acts rather than a set of propositions.

If the negation in the wide scope readings in gapping is illocutionary negation, which is an epistemic operator that signals that there are zero degrees of strength of the sincerity conditions required for adding the proposition in question to the common ground, that is, that those sincerity conditions are not met, we get the following for the wide scope readings in gapping. In the case of declaratives, the coordination as a whole is marked as being wrongly in the common ground. Consider the LF for the sentence in (4.115). FALSUM takes a high position and scopes over the entire coordination.

(4.115) Max liest NICHT das Buch und Maria die Zeitschrift.
         Max reads not   the book and Maria the magazine
         'Max isn't reading the book and Mary the magazine.'
         LF: [$_{CP}$ FALSUM [$_{\&P}$ Max liest das Buch und Maria liest die Zeitschrift]]
         = There are zero degrees of strength for adding to CG: Max is reading the book and Mary is reading the magazine.

In interrogatives, FALSUM ALSO takes a high position. In interaction with the question operator, it is the zero degrees of strength for adding a positive proposition to the common ground that are at issue. The exact structure of the coordination will be explored in the next section.

4.2.4 *The syntax of the wide scope readings*

Starting from the assumption that illocutionary information is represented in the C-system of the language (Rizzi 1997) I assume that FALSUM—as well as the other speech act operators I discussed—is situated in the C-system. Being an illocutionary operator which interacts with the illocutionary force of an utterance, FALSUM must stand in a direct relation to force information, which in Rizzi's (1997) system is contained in Force. One way to represent this is to assume that there is a head, call it *Strength*, at Logical Form, which hosts strength operators and which is directly under Force. It is important that Strength is situated below Force because the inverse order would mean that the speech act would be negated, in the sense that there is no denial, or no question, etc. This is impossible (for a discussion of this, e.g. for imperatives, see Han 2001; Zeijlstra 2006, also see Repp 2006 for a few remarks).[45]

---

[45] *Wohl* seems to differ from the other speech act operators considered here. Zimmermann (2008) suggests that *wohl* is situated in the specifier of ForceP because it can scope over the question operator.

(4.116)   [$_{ForceP}$ Force [$_{StrengthP}$ Strength [$_{TopP}$ Top [$_{FocP}$ Foc [$_{FinP}$ Fin [$_{IP}$ ...]]]]]]

Turning to gapping, I propose the following. If Strength is to scope over the entire coordination, the coordination must split up below Strength. This means, that there is only one Force projection for the entire coordination, which is very welcome, because it accounts for the fact that in wide scope interrogatives there is only one question operator, and in wide scope declaratives, an entire coordination is denied. Operators pertaining to the speech act (and the sentence type) are situated in Force. This gives us the following LF for the wide scope gapping readings:

(4.117)

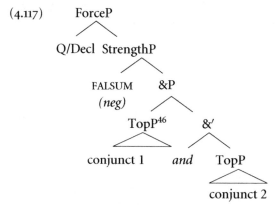

Distributed scope readings, recall from Chapter 2, have the following structure:

(4.118)

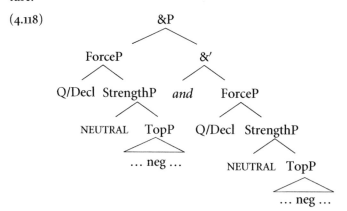

Thus, the wide scope readings are coordinations of small conjuncts with one ForceP and one StrengthP for the whole coordination. The distributed scope

---

[46] I said earlier (see note 11) that corrections are probably better analysed as multiple focus structures. This presumably carries over to denials.

readings are large conjuncts with two ForcePs and two StrengthPs—one of each in every conjunct.

Applied to a concrete example, we have an LF like the one given in (4.119). Compare this to the LF of the same sentence (with different intonation) with a distributed reading in (4.120). Again, we see that the wide scope reading is a small conjunct coordination, and the distributed scope reading, a large conjunct coordination. For better readability I am using traces here instead of copies, although I take the latter to be the proper derivation of movement (see Chapter 2). Shaded material has no phonology at PF (but recall that this is an LF representation anyhow).

(4.119)   Max isn't reading the book and Mary the magazine.   *wide scope*
          [$_{\&P}$ [$_{ForceP}$ D [$_{StrP}$ FALSUM [$_{TopP}$ Max$_1$ [$_{FocP}$ the book$_2$ [$_{TP}$ t$_1$ is [$_{PolP}$ not [$_{vP}$ t$_1$ reading t$_2$]]]]]]]]
          [$_{\&'}$ and [$_{TopP}$ Mary$_3$ [$_{FocP}$ the magazine$_4$ [$_{TP}$ t$_3$ is [$_{PolP}$ [$_{vP}$ t$_3$ reading t$_4$]]]]]]]]

(4.120)   MAX isn't reading the BOOK and MAry the magaZINE.
          distributed scope
          [$_{\&P}$ [$_{ForceP}$ D [$_{StrP}$ NEUTRAL [$_{TopP}$ Max$_1$ [$_{FocP}$ the book$_2$ [$_{TP}$ t$_1$ is [$_{PolP}$ not [$_{vP}$ t$_1$ reading t$_2$]]]]]]]]
          [$_{\&'}$ and [$_{ForceP}$ [$_{StrP}$ NEUTRAL [$_{TopP}$ Mary$_3$ [$_{FocP}$ the magazine$_4$ [$_{TP}$ t$_3$ is [$_{PolP}$ not [$_{vP}$ t$_3$ reading t$_4$]]]]]]]]]

Now, the negative marker in (4.119) is obviously not situated in Strength in overt syntax. On the other hand, its surface position must not be interpreted because this would produce a negative reading for the first conjunct, which does not correspond to the wide scope interpretation of the negation. I suggest that we are dealing with a sort of negative concord between a silent element in Strength and the negative element in the IP domain of the clause here. The agreement must be such that if FALSUM is situated in Strength, the negation further down in the clause must not receive an interpretation, and if a different operator such as NEUTRAL in the distributed readings is situated in Strength, the negation further down in the clause is interpreted—this holds for both conjuncts. There are of course many questions that remain open here but the details of this must await future research.[47]

The assumption that there is a strength operator above the coordination and not 'just' negation is supported by the behaviour of the other strength operators in gapping. Here is *wohl*:

---

[47] Similarly, the position of the negative marker with respect to the correlates in the first conjuncts, which I argued to be a reflex of the information structure of gapping (or corrections more generally) requires closer scrutiny.

(4.121)   Max hat wohl   ein Haus gekauft und Maria eine
           Max has presumably a   house bought   and Maria a
           Wohnung.
           apartment
           'I assume: Max has bought a house and Mary an apartment.'

The adverb scopes over the entire utterance. Distributed scope is impossible.[48]
Similarly, and maybe surprisingly from the point of view of the distributed
scope readings, the positive polarity on an auxiliary can be focused in the wide
scope readings:

(4.122)   Max HAT ein Haus gekauft und Maria eine Wohnung.
           'It is indeed the case that Max bought a house and Mary an apart-
           ment.'

The sentence might not be perfect but it certainly is possible. Recall that stress
on the finite verb is impossible in the distributed scope readings (cf. Hartmann
2000). Here, however, the stress indicates the presence of VERUM, which can
scope over the entire coordination.

  The present proposal that illocutionary negation is situated in a high syntactic position builds on earlier accounts of the negation in denials and in
corrections. I discussed the latter in Section 4.1.2. To close the present discussion, consider a few proposals that have been made for denials without a
correction part. Several authors have proposed that there is a specific syntactic
position for the negation in denials (which comes under very different names,
all of which I collapse under the term 'illocutionary negation'), see for instance
Cormack and Smith (1998), Kim (1991), Piñon (1991), Weiß (2002), Zanuttini
(1997). As in the present account, this negation is usually assumed to be higher
than ordinary sentence negation.

  Cormack and Smith (1998), for instance, argue for an 'Echo' position,
which can be positive or negative, above C (and below Q). This assumption
is mainly fed by the scopal behaviour of what they call echoic negation with
respect to modals in English, that is that echoic (= illocutionary) negation
always scopes over modals (also recall the discussion mainly of German

---

[48] Curiously, in contrast to illocutionary negation, *wohl* can occur in coordinated questions:

(i) Wer hat wohl   das Haus gekauft und wer die Wohnung?
     who has possibly the house bought   and who the apartment
     'Who do you think bought the house and who the apartment?'

Zimmermann (2008) suggests that *wohl* is situated in the specifier of ForceP. The example in (i)
supports such an analysis: it is possible to have two question operators here. *Wohl* scopes over them. It
takes wide scope over the coordination in this example. So, the conclusion that all epistemic operators
eventually are situated at Strength might be premature.

modals in subsection 4.2.1.3). For instance, the modal *should*, which usually takes wide scope over the negation, can also take narrow scope in echoic contexts:

(4.123)   a.   Shouldn't you be at work?   (Cormack and Smith 1998: 26)
            'Is it not the case that you should be at work?'

         b.   A: You should eat more vegetables.
            B: No, I shouldn't.
            'It is not the case that I should eat more vegetables.'

Furthermore, in various languages the difference between ordinary sentence negation and illocutionary negation has a lexical reflex. This is for instance the case in Korean (Kim 1991) and in Piedmontese, a Romance variety spoken in north-western Italy (Zanuttini 1997, 2000). The latter language distinguishes between the marker *pa* for illocutionary negation and the marker *nen* for ordinary sentential negation. The two markers take different positions in the clause: *pa* appears above adverbs like *gia* ('already'), *nen* below. If, however, *nen*, is in the 'wrong' position—as below—which is normally ungrammatical, stressing it will produce a denial interpretation:

(4.124)   *[?]A   l'   e   nen   gia   *(Piedmontese;* Zanuttini 1997: 70)
          s.cl. s.cl. is neg already
          andait a   ca.
          gone to home
          'He HASN't already gone home.'

More evidence for a differential syntactic representation of illocutionary negation comes from Hungarian (Piñon 1991). The examples in (4.125) demonstrate that the preverb in Hungarian, which normally occurs in post-verbal position ((4.125a)) occurs before the negation ((4.125b)) if it receives an illocutionary interpretation. In addition, it receives heavy stress:

(4.125)   a.   Nem megyek be   a   lakásba.
            neg go.I   PREVERB the flat.into
                                        (*Hungarian;* Piñon 1991: 246)
            'I won't go into the flat.'

         b.   BE   nem megyek a   lakásba.
            PREVERB neg go.I   the flat.into
            'I WON'T go into the flat.'

Piñon (1991) notes that focus in Hungarian is realized in the preverbal position (Kiss 1987), which is the reason for the preverb moving there in the denial contexts. Note in this connection that in German it is possible to stress the auxiliary rather than the negation to express a negative denial:

(4.126)   Er   HAT   das   nicht   gemacht.
          He   has   that   not   done
          'He DIDN'T do it.'

Also, it often seems to be elements that are not very likely to be stressed for 'ordinary' focus, that are highlighted in denial contexts (M. Krifka, p.c.).

Finally, Weiß (2002) proposes a high position for illocutionary negation in Bavarian German. This negation, for which he posits a Neg_2P above IP, differs from ordinary clausal negation in that it does not induce negative concord, seems to be 'preposed', that is it occurs before definite DPs, see (4.127a), and can precede PPIs, e.g. *schō* ('already'), (4.127a) versus (4.127b):

(4.127)   a.   daß ja   ned da Beda schō   gejd
               that PART not the Peter already goes
               'I hope Peter is not leaving!'

          b.   daß da Beda schō   (*ned) kema is
               that the Peter already   not   come is

This selection of examples and the discussion in the preceding sections should suffice to motivate a differential treatment of illocutionary and propositional negation in the syntax.

Let me summarize my proposal for the wide scope reading gapping sentences. I assume that wide scope gapping sentences are indeed coordinations of small conjuncts. Thus, I follow Johnson (1996/2003), López and Winkler (2003) and Winkler (2005). Yet, I do not assume that this small conjunct analysis should be transferred to the distributed scope readings or the narrow scope readings. Wide scope readings are clearly distinct from the other readings. They occur in different discourse situations and have a different phonology, syntax, and semantics. The negation in the wide scope readings is illocutionary negation whereas in the other readings, we have propositional negation. This difference is reflected in different positions for the two types of negation at LF.

5

Finiteness in gapping

What is gapping from a semantic-pragmatic point of view? Is there more to it than the descriptive generalization that it drops the finite verb? Hartmann (2000) suggests that gapping elides the assertion (see Chapter 1). I shall argue in this chapter that this proposal cannot be upheld (Section 5.1). Therefore, I shall explore the notion of finiteness in greater detail (Section 5.2) and also look at the relation between finiteness and the complementizer system, which will ultimately lead me to the following definition of gapping:

(5.1) DEFINITION OF GAPPING (SEMANTIC-PRAGMATIC)
       Gapping is the coordination of two sentences where the elliptic conjunct copies the anchoring of the proposition to the factual world from its non-elliptic antecedent.

Syntactically, this means that the head that expresses this anchoring is gapped. The anchoring is realized by the C-system of a language, which through the encoding of finiteness, binds the tense, mood, and aspect information contained in the I-system. Heads c-commanded by the highest head in the C-system must also be gapped if they are identical to an antecedent in the first conjunct. This is basically Wilder's (1995, 1996) head condition on forward deletion (see Chapter 1), which says that an ellipsis site may not be c-commanded by a non-deleted head in the same conjunct. Of course, I proposed a copying account and not a deletion account, so I will take the head condition just as a descriptive generalization which states which heads are gapped. In view of this condition, the data to be discussed in the following sections are not remarkable at all—they support the head condition. We expect that gapping of the finite verb presupposes gapping of the complementizer if the latter c-commands the former, which is the case in languages such as German or English. What I want to explore here is whether there might be a semantic motivation that comes with this syntactic generalization.

5.1 Assertion

Hartmann (2000) suggests that gapping elides the assertion. The term assertion has been used in the literature in two different but related ways. On the one hand, assertions have been defined as speech acts which represent 'how things are, and the propositional content of the speech act is supposed to match a state of affairs existing in general independently in the world' (Vanderveken 1990: 104; see also Searle 1969). On the other hand, the term assertion has played an important role in the study of VERUM focus. As we saw earlier (Chapter 4), it has been argued that the focus on the finite verb of a sentence focuses the assertion (apart from the possibility of focusing the lexical content or the tense expressed by the finite verb). I gave a different account for VERUM in Chapter 4, which is based on the degrees of strength of the sincerity conditions of a speech act. Recall that an assertion comes with the sincerity condition that the speaker believes the propositional content of his/her utterance (to varying degrees of strength). The degrees of strength are the alternatives elicited by VERUM focus.

Hartmann's (2000) proposal for gapping is built on the assumption that finiteness is connected with the assertion as it is defined in the VERUM focus studies, in particular Klein (1998). The idea for gapping is that the finite verb is the carrier of the assertion and that with the verb, the assertion is elided too. However, now that I have argued that the original approach to VERUM focus is not appropriate we obviously need to reconsider. We also need to reconsider in view of the data that I investigated in Chapter 3, that is, the narrow scope readings. The assumption that the assertion somehow is connected with the truth of a proposition usually goes hand in hand with the assumption that it is tightly linked with the polarity of the sentence. The alternative evoked by focusing the finite verb is usually taken to be 'being not the case' (Erb 2001). Thus, positive polarity is contrasted with negative polarity. This, however, means that if gapping elides this kind of assertion, the polarity in the first and in the second conjunct of a gapping coordination should always be the same because gapping in the general case requires semantic identity of gap and antecedent. The narrow scope readings are notable exceptions to this. Whereas the first conjunct is negative, the second one is positive. In a sense, then, we expect the second conjunct in a narrow scope reading to have its own 'assertion'. This undermines the position that finiteness hosts assertion in the sense of Klein (1998) and Hartmann (2000).[1]

---

[1] Klein's (1998) assertion is not exclusively tied to finiteness. He observes that there are non-finite structures that seem to host an assertion, e.g.:

(i) * [DP Der von Bunsen erfundene Brenner] wurde nicht von Bunsen erfunden.
         The by Bunsen invented   burner] was   not by Bunsen invented
      'The burner invented by Bunsen was not invented by Bunsen.'

An interesting observation in the discussion around the gapping of the assertion concerns the fact that in embedded gapping sentences the complementizer must be left out:

(5.2)   Ich glaube [$_{C'}$ dass Peter mit   seiner Frau nach Indien reist],
        I   believe   that Peter with his   wife to   India   travels
        und [$_{C'}$ (*dass) Martin mit   seinen Kollegen in die
        and   that Martin with his   colleagues to the
        Schweiz.]
        Switzerland
        'I believe that Peter will travel with his wife to India and Martin with
        his colleagues to Switzerland.'   (Hartmann 2000: 161)

Note that the coordination in such cases only involves the embedded sentences. Gapping is not usually possible across clause boundaries (see Chapter 1 for exceptions):

(5.3)   *[$_{CP}$ Herr Meyer glaubt   dass Peter mit   seiner Frau nach
               Mr   Meyer believes that Peter with his   wife to
        Indien reist,]
        India   travels
        und [$_{CP}$ Herr Pin ~~glaubt~~ ~~(dass)~~ Martin mit   seinen Kollegen
        and   Mr   Pin ~~believes~~ ~~that~~ Martin with his   colleagues
        in die Schweiz   ~~reist.~~]
        to the Switzerland ~~travels~~

        'Mr Meyer believes that Peter will travel with his wife to India and Mr
        Pin believes that Martin will travel with his colleagues to Switzerland.'

Also note that the problem is due to the ellipsis and not to the inability to conjoin two clauses that start with *that*:

(5.4)   Ich glaube [$_{C'}$ dass Peter mit seiner Frau nach Indien reist], und [$_{C'}$ dass
        Martin mit seinen Kollegen in die Schweiz reist.]

Now, Hartmann (2000) observes that the C-position has been associated with assertion. One of the reasons is that in embedded clauses, a focus on the complementizer has also been suggested to elicit a VERUM focus reading. Höhle (1992) gives the following example (but is himself not so clear on the association of VERUM focus with C):

(5.5)   A: Hört   er   ihr denn   überhaupt ZU?   (Höhle 1992: 124)
             Listens he   her PART actually   PART

(i) is ungrammatical because it is a contradiction. Klein concludes that even though the modified DP is not finite it contains an (embedded) assertion.

B: Ich denke, er HÖRT ihr zu.
    I   think he listens her PART

B': Ich denke, DASS er ihr zuhört,
    I   think that he her listens

    aber ob er sie versteht,   ist eine andere   Frage.
    but if he her understands is a   different question
    'A: Is he actually listening to her? B: I think he IS listening. B':
    I think that he IS listening but if he understands her is a different
    question.'

What is interesting about the version with the complementizer is that there is a
'desire to continue' the sentence (Höhle 1992: 125). This desire does not arise if
the focus occurs on the finite verb. This phenomenon still awaits explanation.
Nevertheless, there seems to be a certain parallelism between the sentence with
the focus on the finite verb and the one with the focus on the complementizer.
Consequently, Hartmann (2000) suggests that the idea that it is the assertion
that is elided in gapping accounts both for finite verb gapping in main clauses
and complementizer gapping in embedded clauses: they are both situated in
C. Hartmann actually says that the complementizer is the first element to go
in embedded clauses as it carries the assertion there, and that the verb follows
after.

A connection of C—and verb-second—with assertion, or force marking
in general, has also been suggested on the basis of independent evidence for
instance by Bayer (2004), Brandner (2004), Gärtner (2001, 2002), Lohnstein
(2000), Meinunger (2004), and Wechsler (1990, 1991). Note, however, that
most of these authors assume that verb-second only enables force-marking
and does not necessarily determine the actual type of force (see Bayer 2004;
Brandner 2004 for details). Also, the application of this reasoning to the
gapping data has a couple of drawbacks. To start with, we cannot assume
that in all languages which allow gapping the verb is actually situated in C.
In English clauses, for instance, finite main verbs are assumed to remain in V
(or v). However, if we take a closer look at the English gloss for (5.2), we find
that the complementizer must be left out here, too:

(5.6)   I believe [$_{C'}$ that Peter will travel with his wife to India]
        and [$_{C'}$ (*that) Martin with his colleagues to Switzerland].

Thus, whereas in German the C-position is assumed to contain the assertion,
which accounts for the fact that the verb in main clauses and the complementizer in embedded clauses is elided in gapping, in English this seems to be the
C position for complementizers but I for main clause verbs. We end up with

an asymmetry. As I shall show below (Section 5.2.2), this is a problem we have to deal with anyhow. It is not peculiar to Hartmann's (2000) approach. Let me therefore turn to some other considerations that do not quite conform to the idea of assertion drop.

An examination of the semantic contribution of the complementizer *that* in sentences like the one above can give us a first clue. Usually, it is assumed that an embedded clause containing *that* is semantically and pragmatically equivalent to the same sentence without *that*:[2]

(5.7)   a.   I believe that Peter will travel with his wife to India.

   b.   I believe Peter will travel with his wife to India.

On the other hand, it has been noted that the deletion of *that* is not compatible with all matrix clause predicates (Bolinger (1972) and subsequent literature[3]). For instance, predicates of physical manipulation of text (*write down, record, publish*) or predicates of occurrence (*to happen, to come about*) never take a complement without *that*. On the basis of a very detailed overview of such data, Dor (2005) takes up a proposal by Searle and Vanderveken (1985) according to which *that*-clauses are 'the characteristic form of isolating the propositional content' (1985: 9). Dor (2005) suggests that clauses without *that* are structurally marked as 'asserted propositions' meaning that they are propositions which are asserted by a cognitive agent to be true. Therefore, they can only be embedded under verbs that make such a truth claim. *That*-clauses, on the other hand, are isolated propositions and need not be asserted. Consequently, they can be embedded under verbs that do not make a claim with respect to the truth of the embedded proposition. This is quite interesting considering that the complementizer *that* does not actually seem to contribute the truth claim which is part of an asserted proposition. In other words, it does not actually seem to carry the assertion in these contexts (if we associate the assertion with truth).[4]

Note, however, that *that* nevertheless must have some semantic content of its own apart from its function of isolating the proposition. This becomes

---

[2] *That*-deletion underlies syntactic restrictions which I cannot even begin to discuss here. See e.g. Bošković and Lasnik (2004), Doherty (1997), Grimshaw (1997), Pesetsky (1992), Postal (1974), Stowell (1981), and the references cited therein.

[3] For syntax-oriented works on this, see for instance Erteschik (1973), Giorgi and Pianesi (2004), Hegarty (1992), and Stowell (1981).

[4] For more on the semantic-pragmatic conditions on *that*-deletion, see for instance Thompson and Mulac (1991). In V2-languages, complementizer deletion obviously goes hand in hand with I-to-C movement of the finite verb. So the above sentences without *that* in German or Scandinavian would be realized as verb-second structures. These are assumed to have force-features of their own, even though they occur in embedded contexts (see for instance Bayer 2004; Gärtner 2001; Meininger 2004), thus essentially supporting Dor's (2005) analysis.

obvious once *that* is substituted by other complementizers in otherwise identical sentences:

(5.8)   a.   I want to hear that he's coming tomorrow.

      b.   I want to hear if he's coming tomorrow.

Example (5.8a) certainly has an assertoric flavour in comparison with (5.8b) with the complementizer *if*, which introduces an indirect question.

It is actually the comparison with other complementizers in gapping that truly shows that it cannot be the assertion which is at stake in gapping. Complementizers, no matter what meaning they convey, have to be elided in this ellipsis type. To start with, let us look at the complementizers *ob/if* and *whether*. Hartmann (2000) gives the following example (which really is an instance of stripping).

(5.9)   a.   Ich weiß   nie,   ob   die Inder   mehr Atomtests
            I   know never whether the Indians more nuclear.tests
            gemacht haben, oder (*ob)   die Pakistani.
            done   have   or   whether the Pakistani
      b.   I never know whether the Indians did more nuclear tests or
         (*whether) the Pakistani.

Obviously, as I just said, the complementizers *ob/whether* do not introduce an assertion, they introduce an indirect question.

Similarly, if gapping occurs in embedded conditional clauses the complementizer has to be dropped:

(5.10)   Helga wollte   kommen, wenn Frau Meyer den
        Helga wanted come   if   Mrs Meyer the
        Kindergeburtstag   organisiert und (*wenn) Herr Schulz
        children's.birthday.party organizes and   if   Mr   Schulz
        die Dinnerparty.
        the dinner.party
        'Helga wanted to come if Mrs Meyer organizes the children's birthday party and Mr Schulz the dinner party.'

We cannot assume that the antecent of a conditional hosts an assertoric feature. Nevertheless, the complementizer must be left out in the second clause. Further recall that gapping can also occur in questions or imperatives, which do not host assertoric features. Thus in sum, there is little reason to believe that it is the assertion that is elided in gapping—no matter how we define it.

5.2 Anchoring

Observe the following. A complementizer which introduces a non-finite (!) clause must be elided if the non-finite verb in that clause is elided. Thus, the German complementizer *um* (roughly 'in order to', 'so as to'), which occurs with *to*-infinitives, needs to be left out in embedded elliptic coordinations such as those investigated in the previous section even if it is a non-finite verb that is elided:

(5.11) Hans ging, [[um   dem Schwiegervater das Haus   zu zeigen]
        Hans left   COMP the   father.in.law   the house to show

        und [(*um) dem Kollegen   die Wohnung ~~zu zeigen~~]].
        and COMP the colleague   the flat   to show

        'Hans left to show his father-in-law the house and his colleague the flat.'

Again, the coordination can only involve the embedded clauses because ellipsis is not possible here across clause boundaries (in contrast to non-finite control structures without *um*, see Chapter 1):

(5.12) *[[Hans ging, um dem Schwiegervater das Haus zu zeigen]
         und [Robert ~~ging~~ (um)   dem Kollegen   die Wohnung ~~zu~~
         and Robert left COMP the   colleague   the flat   to
         ~~zeigen~~]].
         show
         'Hans left to show his father-in-law the house and Robert left to show his colleague the flat.'

So, there is no finite verb in the embedded coordination in (5.11) that can be elided. Instead it is the complementizer and the non-finite verb that are left out. Is this still an instance of gapping? I would like to argue that it is. Note that it is still verbal ellipsis and importantly, the other types of verbal ellipsis—pseudogapping and VP ellipsis—require the presence of a finite auxiliary. In the elliptic conjunct of (5.11) there is no finite verb.

Similar examples can be found with other non-finite complementizers both in English and in German:

(5.13) a. Max ging ins   Kino,   statt   Maria beim Malern   zu
            Max went to.the cinema instead.of Maria with painting to
            helfen oder (*statt)   Paul beim Packen.[5]
            help   or   instead.of Paul with packing

---

[5] These sentences are better with *or* due to the negative content of the complementizer.

'Max went to the cinema rather than helping Mary painting or Paul packing.'

b. Max ging, ohne   dem Mädchen das neue Buch zu zeigen
   Max left without the girl   the new book to show
   oder (*ohne)   dem Jungen das neue Auto.
   or   without the boy   the new car
   'Max left without showing the girl the new book or the boy the new car.'

(5.14)   The party should be excellent, with Al buying the food and (*with) Ann the drinks.

All of the above non-finite complementizers introduce adjunct clauses. As a matter of fact, German non-finite complement clauses may not occur with a complementizer at all (see Wöllstein 2004 for an account of this). English has the complementizer *for*, which subordinates complement clauses. Again, *for* must be left out in the relevant constellation:

(5.15)   I would prefer for Sue to buy this book and (*for) John this paper.

Dutch *om* (similar in meaning to German *um*) also is a complementizer that introduces non-finite complement clauses:

(5.16)   Hij probeert om   een comic voor zijn neef   te vinden
         He tries   COMP a   comic for his nephew to find
         en (*om)   een bal voor zijn nicht.
         and COMP a ball for his niece
         'He is trying to find a comic for his nephew and a ball for his niece.'

Thus, it seems that gapping is not dependent on the elision of the finite verb after all. If the complementizer is gapped, a non-finite verb further down in the clause can also be gapped. So, what features do complementizers and finite verbs share? In the following I shall first look at the notion of finiteness and then approach the question of what role complementizers play in a clause. I shall argue that both finiteness and complementizers anchor the clause in the previous discourse.

5.2.1 *Finiteness*

As Maas (2004) observes, the notion of finiteness goes back to the late Latin grammarians. Priscian (Institutio grammatica 17, 89 [1981: 157]) uses the term *finire* 'to define (something)'. Prisican is mainly interested in reference so that a sentence is non-finite 'if it can be made [de]finite by adding a referring pronoun' (cited in Maas 2004: 363). The modern use of finiteness is different, yet, as we shall see below, the notion of defining something is still important.

Finiteness has been viewed from a number of different angles. Lasser (1997) points out that it is important to distinguish between morphological (= morphosyntactic) and semantic finiteness (also see Erb 2001 or Maas 2004).[6] Morphological finiteness means the form variability of verbs, which in their finite form, for example in the indicative, subjunctive, imperative, and optative, take different affixes for tense, mood, aspect, and/or agreement.[7] This kind of finiteness is not important for the present purposes but it is worth pointing out that finiteness does not have to be expressed on the verb itself but can also be expressed on other elements in the clause. Lasser (1997), citing Klein and Hendriks (1995), proposes that in Chinese, which does not have finiteness marking on the verb, particles, or adverbs express finiteness. Similarly, Classical Arabic has particles expressing tense, which are sometimes seen as finiteness markers (see Maas 2004). Amritavalli and Jayaseelan (2004) suggest that in Dravidian, negative morphemes, being situated in a MoodP, can contribute finiteness. Finiteness markers can also be distributed according to prosodic factors. Maas (2004) shows that in Mundari (Munda language, India), person markers occur on the word preceding the predicate if the clause contains several verbs. Semantic aspects can also play a role. Jung (1984) reports on Paez (an isolated language in Columbia) where person marking can appear on a complement rather than on the predicate for the purposes of focus marking. It seems then that finiteness can be marked in quite diverging ways. Therefore, it is important to find a definition that abstracts away from the formal realization. Let us turn to semantic notions of finiteness.

The most straightforward semantic characterization of finiteness would obviously take into account the semantic categories that are respresented by the morphological markers for tense, mood, aspect, and person/number agreement. Lasser (1997) proposes that finiteness is a composite notion that comprises the features of tense, mood, and aspect. She also includes assertion in her definition of semantic finiteness (see also Erb 2001). I shall not discuss

---

[6] Some authors claim that finiteness is a purely syntactic notion and consists in the ability to license structural case on the subject and agreement marking on the verb (e.g. Cowper 2002; Philippaki-Warburton 1987).

[7] The division into non-finite and finite forms is actually not as clear-cut as one might expect: infinitives in Portuguese (e.g. Raposo 1987, 1989), Romanian and some varieties of Italian and Spanish (see e.g. Ledgeway 1998) can occur with agreement endings. Infinitives in Old Greek can have tense endings (Maas 2004). In the Balkan languages (e.g. Modern Greek, Albanian, Romanian), subjunctives occur in environments where Germanic and Romance languages use infinitives (e.g. in control and raising structures), e.g. Roussou (2001).

assertion here anymore as this notion was treated in sufficient detail in the previous section. The idea that finiteness has something to do with tense is quite pervasive. Aspect is not usually considered systematically, mood is considered as relevant by some authors.

What do tense, mood, and aspect do for a sentence? Holmberg and Platzack (1995) point out—quite in line with the definition of Priscian quoted above—that *finite* means something like 'restricted to the particular situation' (1995: 23). They say that a predication needs to be related to the time of utterance, which is the basis for expressing the speaker's attitude to the situation in question. Therefore, 'finiteness is a prerequisite for tense and mood' (Holmberg and Platzack 1995). Similarly, Tsoulas (1995) suggests that finite propositions are temporally definite, referring to specified points in time whereas non-finite propositions refer to unspecified temporal points. Maas (2004) considers semantic finiteness as a prerequisite for an independent interpretation of a sentence. It maps the sentence onto the context of utterance: it grounds the sentence in the context in terms of reference and temporal anchorage (see also Roberts and Roussou 1998; Roussou 2001), or anchorage of the event (see also Bayer 2004: 81–2).

All of the above definitions of finiteness make reference to the particular situation. This seems to exclude generic, gnomic, or habitual sentences. Note, however, that such sentences are usually minimally marked for tense and aspect, that is they lack overt tense and aspect marking or they use the least marked form available in a system (Dahl 1995). For instance, in Swahili generic and habitual sentences, the verb is prefixed by *hu-*, while personal affixes and temporal affixes are not realized:

(5.17)   a.   Watoto   huenda   shule.   (*Swahili*)
              children habit.go school
              'The children go to school.'

         b.   Watoto   walikwenda   shule.
              children 3ps.pl.past.go school
              'The children went to the school.'

Thus, these sentences seem to be less finite, if you will, than episodic sentences (thanks to M. Krifka for pointing this out to me).

With respect to temporal anchorage, it is quite instructive to take a brief look at non-finite structures. Stowell (1982) suggests that non-finiteness corresponds to the absence of tense specification, or at least of the [+past] specification. Indeed, it is often assumed that infinitives, for instance in control structures, have future tense or describe hypothetical, unrealized events

(Bošković 1997*b*; Bresnan 1972; Landau 2000; Portner 1997; Stowell 1982, and many others):

(5.18)   I promised her yesterday to come (next week).

Nevertheless, it is not the case that non-finite structures can never be specified for past tense. The non-finite clause in the following West Flemish sentence is modified by the temporal adverb *gisteren* ('yesterday') whereas the matrix clause has future tense.

(5.19)   mee ik da   gisteren   te zeggen goa-se   dat   (*West Flemish*)
          with I   that yesterday to say   goes-she that
          hus   kopen.
          house buy
          'Because of my saying that yesterday, she will buy that house.'

(Haegeman 1985: 132)

Other infinitives do not generally allow temporal adverbs which are not compatible with the embedding finite verb (as long as that is not a modal, see Erb 2001):

(5.20)   a.   * Heute wird das Buch gestern/letzte   (Erb 2001: 27)
                today is   the book yesterday/last
                Woche gelesen.
                week   read
                'Today, the book is read yesterday/last week.'

          b.   (*)Heute hat sie das Buch gestern/letzte Woche gelesen.
                today has she the book yesterday/last week   read
                'Today (she says), she read the book last week.'

Example (5.20a) is impossible. Example (5.20b) can only be read with a so-called opaque interpretation (Cremers 1983), which means that the adverb *heute* ('today') modifies an implicit utterance, like: *Today, she said that she read the book last week.*[8]

---

[8] The temporal, or more correctly, aspectual specification of an infinitival clause depends on the type of non-finite form that is used. Past participles are different from bare infinitives and so on. Thus, bare infinitives in German are assumed to express durative aspect, *to*-infinitives prospective aspect, and the past participle perfective aspect (e.g. Lohnstein and Wöllstein-Leisten 2001, cited in Wöllstein 2004; Wurmbrand 2001):

(i)   Der Computer ist zu reparieren.   (Wöllstein 2004: 497 f.)
       the computer is to fix
       'The computer has to be fixed.'

(ii)   Der Computer ist repariert.
       the computer is fixed
       'The computer has been fixed.'

Thus control structures, or *to*-infinitives seem to be more like finite verbs than the other infinitives in that they can be modified temporally independently of the embedding verb. In another aspect, though, they are less like finite structures. Consider the following paradigm given for Dutch by Verkuyl (2003):

(5.21)   a.   Els zei de oplossing te hebben   (*Dutch*; Verkuyl 2003: 7)
              Els said the solution   to have
              gevonden.
              found.

         b.   Els zei dat ze de oplossing heeft gevonden.
              Els said that she the solution   has   found

         c.   Els zei dat ze de oplossing had   gevonden.
              Els said that she the solution   had   found
              'Els said {a: to have found | b: that she has found | c: that she had found} the solution.'

Whereas in a finite embedded clause it is possible to have a reference time that is different from the speech time ((5.21c)), this is not possible in the non-finite clause ((5.21a)).

Outside the temporal domain, Wöllstein (2004) suggests that it is not possible to refer to an embedded *to*-infinitive by means of an anaphoric pronoun, which is perfectly fine if the embedded clause is finite, see (5.22a) versus (5.22b).

(5.22)   a.   Maria hat behauptet, dass sie den Hund geschlagen hat.
              Mary has claimed   that she the dog   beaten   has.
              Ich bedaure das.
              I   regret that
              'Mary claimed that she beat the dog. I regret that.'
              that = Mary's claim *or* Mary's beating the dog

         b.   Maria hat behauptet, den Hund geschlagen zu haben. Ich
              Mary has claimed   the dog   beaten   to have.   I
              bedaure das.
              regret that
              'Mary claimed to have beaten the dog. I regret that.'
              that = Mary's claim   (Wöllstein 2004: 503)

Wöllstein argues that whereas finite structures are referential, *to*-infinitives are not. This conclusion seems to be correct but the underlying reason might be different (M. Krifka p.c.). The verb *bedauern* ('to regret') selects for a proposition. The infinitive in (5.22b) does not denote a proposition but an event and therefore cannot serve as an argument of *bedauern* (the pronoun itself can pick up events[9]). Again, this means that finite structures are anchored whereas non-finite structures are not (see especially the discussion of auxiliary gapping in Chapter 3 on the distinction of events and propositions).

The behaviour of non-finite root clauses is also quite instructive with respect to the function of finiteness. Root infinitives are a somewhat rare phenomenon. There are different types whose grammaticality differs depending on the language. Root infinitives come in the form of mad magazine sentences (Akmajian 1984; Etxepare and Grohmann 2005, 2007; Grohmann and Etxepare 2003; Lambrecht 1990), see (5.23a); *wh*-root-infinitives, see (5.23b) and non-*wh*-root-infinitives (see especially Fries 1983; Lasser 1997; Reis 2002; Weuster 1983 for German non-finite root clauses), see (5.23c):

(5.23)   a.   Me—wash the dishes? Never!

       a′. Ich—(und) das Geschirr waschen? Niemals!
           I   and the dishes   wash   never

       b.   Wohin fahren?
           where go
           'Where should we go?'

       c.   Den Pullover umdrehen.   (Fries 1983)
           the   sweater turn.over
           'Let me turn over this sweater.'

The foremost difference between mad magazine sentences and the other two types, which do not exist in English, is that the former allow a subject and the latter do not.[10]

It has been claimed that these root infinitives can occur with all temporal specifications (Lasser 1997) but these specifications are highly context-dependent. In addition, what kind of temporal specification is allowed depends on the particular structure as well as on the language. For instance, (5.23c), the non-*wh*-root infinitive, can describe an ongoing event or it can describe a future action. What it cannot do, however, is describe a past event (see (5.24a)).[11] The same holds for *wh*-root infinitives:

---

[9] The pronoun *das* ('this') can refer to a proposition (as in (5.22)) or to an event:

(i)   Peter hat das mit eigenen Augen gesehen.
    Peter has this with own   eyes   seen
    'Peter has seen this with his own eyes.'

[10] Other differences are discussed in Reis (2002).

[11] Lasser (1997) gives a few examples which seem to describe events in the past (determined by context), see (i) below for a Dutch example. This structure involves a subject although it does not seem

(5.24) a. * Gestern   den Pullover umdrehen.
            yesterday the sweater turn.over
            'Yesterday, to turn the sweater over.'

        b. * Was gestern   / damals / in jenen Tagen tun?
            what yesterday / then   / in those days do
            'What to do yesterday / then / in those days?'

        c. Wohin morgen   fahren?
            where tomorrow go
            'Where should we go tomorrow?'

What's more, *wh*-root-infinitives and non-*wh*-root-infinitives cannot express completed events even in contexts that support a past tense reading (Lasser 1997).

Mad magazine sentences are quite different from the other root infinitives (see fn. 10) and we find that in general they can be temporally modified for past reference:

(5.25) John read that sort of thing back in the old days?! No way! (Etxepare and Grohmann 2007)

Whether temporal modification to a deictic point is possible seems to be language-dependent. Thus, whereas English does not allow the adverb *yesterday* in a mad magazine sentence, Spanish does:

(5.26) a. * John read that sort of thing yesterday?! No way!
                                        (Etxepare and Grohmann 2007)

        b. Juan leer   eso ayer?! Ya   me extraña! (*Spanish*)
            Juan read.INF that yesterday already me amazes

Etxepare and Grohmann (2007) give a syntactic account of this, the details of which are not important to us here. Note, however, that even in Spanish, temporal modification is restricted when it comes to modal contexts:

(5.27) * Juan poder   leer   un libro ayer?!   (*Spanish*)
        John can.INF read.INF a book yesterday
        'John be able to read a book yesterday?!'

to have the exclamatory character of mad magazine sentences. Also, there is no temporal adverb in the non-finite clause.

(i) De conducteur floot   al   voor het vertrek,   dus ik rennen.   (*Dutch*)
     the conductor whistled already before the departure so I run.INF
     'The conductor had already blown his whistle so I ran.'   (Wijnen 1997: 8)

English and German do not allow these structures.

Thus, overall, we find that non-finite root clauses are restricted when it comes to temporal reference. This is what we would expect if the finite element is missing and if finiteness is the temporal anchoring of a proposition in the utterance context, or referential anchoring in general. This anchoring is missing in non-finite root clauses.

According to Reis (2002), all root infinitives (apart from mad magazine sentences) contain a modal component. Thus a sentence like (5.23b) *Wohin fahren?* means something like *Where should/can/could we go?* Reis suggests that the reason for this lies in the anchoring function of finiteness: a sentence lacking finiteness is not anchored with respect to time or with respect to the factual world. Every independent sentence must have communicative force, which presupposes that it must be referentially anchored. Non-finite root clauses are obviously meant to be independent sentences and therefore they must have communicative force. Consequently, their literal meaning must be enriched by referentially anchoring the proposition to the set of possible worlds, which then results in the modal interpretation.

Mad magazines sentences do not necessarily have a modal interpretation. Yet, as Etxepare and Grohmann (2007) point out, they have a very specific communicative (exclamatory) force, which is tightly linked to the construction and which typically is expressed by what they call the coda, that is the utterance of exclamations like *Never!*, *No way!*, etc.

Comparing non-finite root clauses with non-finite embedded clauses, we may say that an embedded non-finite clause receives its anchoring via the matrix clause. It is dependent on the matrix clause and is not linked directly to the extrasentential discourse. A non-finite root clause, on the other hand, must be linked directly to the discourse but the kind of linking that is chosen is subject to particular restrictions because of the lack of finiteness features.

Taking the discussion back to gapping, observe that in the cases where the anchoring function is not visible at the surface—that is in the non-finite root clauses—gapping of the non-finite verb is possible:

(5.28)   a. Wohin das Kind bringen und wohin den
           where the child take.INF and where the
           Erwachsenen _?
           adult   take.INF
           'Where should we take the child and where the adult?'

        b. Ich die Küche putzen   und du das Schlafzimmer
           I   the kitchen clean.INF and you the bedroom
           ?   Vergiss es!
           clean.INF forget it

b′. Me clean the kitchen and you the bedroom? Forget it!

c. Den Pullover auf die Heizung legen und die Hose   auf
   the sweater on the radiator put and the trousers on
   den Tisch _.
   the table put
   '(I'm putting) the jumper on the radiator and the trousers on the
   table.'

In none of the above examples is there a finite verb, yet the non-finite verb can
be gapped. Again, we see that gapping does not rely on the elision of the finite
verb. Instead, the (modal) anchoring to the previous discourse is taken over
from the first conjunct. The second conjunct in the above examples has the
same modal quality as the first.

Before I turn to the relation between finite verbs and complementizers in
the next section, I will briefly digress here and sketch a possibility in which
syntax and semantics might interact with respect to finiteness as a device
to anchor a proposition in the factual world. In event semantics, we can
interpret finiteness as the existential closure of the event. Note, however, that
the definition of event in this system usually includes temporal specifications,
that is it is different from the one I used in the discussion of auxiliary gapping
in Chapter 3:

(5.29) Bill came

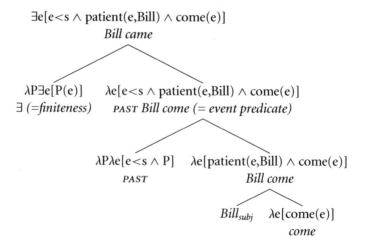

Let me relate this to the system Butler (2004) envisages, which I used in the
discussion of auxiliary gapping. Recall that every phase in Butler's system

(V-phase, T-phase, D-phase) has an event variable which is subject to existential closure. Existential closure is represented by the ∃-head of a phase's CP.

(5.30)

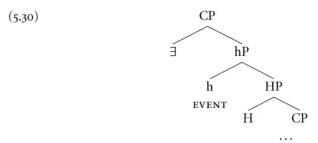

Finiteness, I would like to argue, can be linked to the existential closure of the T-phase.

For the interaction of T-phase and V-phase Butler follows an idea by Stowell (1996), who assumes that there is a ZP (a *Zeit*-phrase) above *v*P which serves as the event-time[12] denoting argument of T, and which gives the event variable in *v*P its denotation. In Butler's system this ZP phrase is the CP of the V-phase. It hosts an operator-like element which fixes the event variable in *v*P and gives the *v*P referential status. This gives us the event time. T takes this event time as its argument. At the same time it hosts an event variable itself, which is closed off by ∃ in the CP of the T-phase. This gives us the speech time. The function of T is to order speech time and event time. Thus, we could also say that ∃ in the CP of the T-phase relates its referential argument to the outside world, that is to say, it expresses finiteness.

In what follows, I shall use the better-known Rizzi-style analysis of the C-system. We can probably assume that the existential closure of the T-phase can be connected with the Fin-head. I shall not investigate the details of this here. I hope to have shown that the existential closure of an event in time can be a useful way of looking at finiteness as an anchoring function.

5.2.2 *Finiteness and complementizers*

I said above in connection with the verb-second characteristic of Germanic languages that the C-system has been associated with force-marking, that

---

[12] Tense can be roughly characterized as a predicate that describes the temporal relation between the event time (= the time at which the event described by the verb is assumed to hold), the speech time, and, for relative tenses, a reference or topic time (= the point of view from which the event is seen, or the time that is relevant in the description of the event). For details and semantic analyses of tense see for instance Bäuerle (1979), Enç (1987), Klein (1994), Kratzer (1978), Musan (1997), Partee (1973), Reichenbach (1947), or von Stechow (1992). Syntactically, it has been suggested that the C domain is related to the speech time and that the T domain is related to the event time (Enç 1987; Stowell 1982, 1996 and others; for a different view see Erb 2001 and Klein 1998).

is the classification of a sentence to function in the discourse as a question, an exclamative, a comparative, etc., realized by different sentence types. More generally, Rizzi (1997)[13] says that the C-system functions as an interface between a propositional clause and a superordinate structure. That superordinate structure can be the previous discourse or a higher clause. Thus, the C-system like finiteness seems to have the function of connecting the clause to the 'outside world' (see chapter 4 for more discussion of the C-domain).

Finiteness obviously has been suggested to be an articulated part of the C-system in Rizzi (1997) but in this account finiteness is seen more as a function that looks to the propositional content of a clause rather than to the superordinate structure. The finiteness head is mainly responsible for the selection of a finite or non-finite embedded clause, which—as I showed above—interacts with the choice of complementizer. Rizzi assumes this interaction to derive from the C system containing 'rudimentary' temporal properties as it was suggested for verb-second languages by Den Besten (1983) and much subsequent literature: the temporal specifications in C are assumed to account for the asymmetries of finite versus non-finite structures with respect to tense (see the previous section for details).

Let us take a brief look at the relation between the C system and finiteness in verb-second languages—for instance German, Dutch, and the Scandinavian languages. In these languages, both complementizers and main clause finite verbs are assumed to be situated in C, basically because they occur in complementary distribution. Thus, either there is a complementizer in C (audible or zero) and the verb stays in I, or the verb moves to C. There have been various accounts of this. I shall only look at one example, namely Holmberg and Platzack (1995 (which builds on earlier work of theirs)). Holmberg and Platzack (1995) propose that in verb-second languages, there is a finiteness feature in C whereas in non-verb-second languages the finiteness feature is in I. Furthermore, they assume that finiteness must be made overt through lexicalization (basically for case reasons, see Holmberg and Platzack (1995: 46). Therefore, in verb-second languages either the verb moves to C (via I), or finiteness is lexicalized by a complementizer, which is base-generated in C. Thus, in this account there is a clear connection between finiteness, the finite verb, and the complementizer (position).

Although in non-verb second languages, the finiteness feature is in I and the finite verb is not assumed to move to C, there are clear connections

---

[13] For earlier proposals to split the CP, see for instance Culicover (1991), Müller and Sternefeld (1993), Koizumi (1994), and Vikner (1995).

between finiteness and the complementizer. To start with, non-verb-second languages display the same sensitivity of complementizer choice to the finite–non-finite distinction and the temporal restrictions this distinction brings with it. Rizzi (1997) notes for instance that Italian *che*, which subcategorizes for finite clauses, co-occurs with present, past, and future indicative as well as present and past subjunctive and conditional, whereas non-finite clauses are more restricted. In addition, he points out that the C-system replicates many features that are found in the IP. For instance, in Polish there are complementizers that are specified for subjunctive. In Irish, some complementizers can express tense (Cottell 1994). Negation is found on complementizers (Latin, Celtic), and there is the familiar complementizer agreement found in several Dutch and German varieties (Bayer 1984; Haegeman 1992 and many others). Furthermore, Roberts (2004) suggests that in Welsh, complementizer-like affirmative particles at the beginning of a clause indicate the clause type in a similar way to the finite verb in verb-second structures:

(5.31)   a.   Fe/mi welais i John.   (*Welsh*; Roberts 2004: 298)
             PART   saw   I John
             'I saw John.'

         b.   Pa   ddynion a   werthodd y   ci?
             which men   PART sold   the dog
             'Which men sold the dog?'

The relation between complementizer and finiteness also works the other way round, as it were. In languages like Hungarian, for instance, (also Kashmiri, Bengali, Korean, Japanese, and other languages, see Bhatt and Yoon 1991), the sentence type—that is a force marking—can be indicated on the verb and the complementizer has a purely subordinating function:

(5.32)   a.   Tudod,   hogy el   mentem.
             know.2sg that away went.1sg
                                  (*Hungarian*; Koopman and Szabolcsi 2000: 114)
             'You know that I left.'

         b.   Tudod,   hogy el   mentem-e   Mari-hoz.
             know.2sg that away went.1sg-INTERROG Mari-to
             'You know whether I visited Mari.'

In recent accounts (Pesetsky and Torrego 2000), this two-ways dependency has been made explicit by assuming that the complementizer *that* might actually originate in I and MOVE to C. The idea is that we might have to do with a kind of tense doubling, similar to *wh*-movement that leaves resumptive pronouns.

In sum, judging from this (short) description of rather diverse phenomena I conclude that the finiteness features associated with the C-domain are not dependent on the verb-second phenomenon but that they are an integral part of that domain in non-verb-second languages, too. This is what has been assumed since Rizzi (1997).

As we would expect, non-verb second languages also show complementizer drop in gapping, as was observed for English[14] above (see example (5.6)), and as is shown for French and Russian below:

(5.33) Je crois   que Jean voyagera à Strasbourg et   (*French*)
        I believe that Jean travel.FUT to S.   and
        (*que) Maria à   Paris.
          that Maria to Paris
        'I believe that Jean is travelling to Strasburg and (that) Mary to Paris.'

(5.34) Ja dumaju, chto Petr ezdit v Indiju a   (*chto)   (*Russian*)
        I think   that Peter go.FUT to India and that
        Pavel v   Švejcariju.
        Pavel to Switzerland
        'I think that Peter will go to India and Pavel to Switzerland.'

Also, in Hungarian, for which I observed that sentence mood is not necessarily indicated on the complementizer, the complementizer in such sentences must be left out, so it clearly is the anchoring function of finiteness that has to go in gapping and not the actual force marking.

(5.35) Tudod,   hogy János meglátogatta-e   a lányokat (*Hungarian*)
        know.2sg that Janos visited-INTERROG the girls
        és Péter a   fiúkat.
        and Peter the boys
        'I know whether John visited the girls and Peter the boys.'

From what I have said so far, one might conclude that complementizers generally occur in Fin. Yet this is not the case. Rizzi (1997) points out that complementizers can occur in two positions: in Force and in Fin. The distribution is reflected in word order facts. So, for instance, whereas Italian *di*, which introduces non-finite clauses and must occur after a topic, its finite counterpart *che* occurs before a topic:[15]

---

[14] English is considered a residual verb-second language as in some environments it shows verb-second effects, e.g. in negative preposing:

(i)   Under no circumstances will I go out in this wheather.

[15] Benincà (2001) and Cardinaletti (2004) say that *che* can actually occur after topics.

(5.36)   a.   Penso a Gianni, di dovergli parlare.   (*Italian*; Rizzi 1997: 304)
             'I think to Gianni, 'of' to have to speak to him.'

         b.   *Penso di a Gianni, dovergli parlare.
             'I think ('of') to Gianni I have to have to speak to him.'

         c.   *Penso, a Gianni, che gli dovrei parlare.
             'I think, to Gianni, that I should speak to him.'

         d.   Penso che a Gianni, gli dovrei parlare.
             'I think that, to Gianni, I should speak to him.'

Topics are situated in a TopP that is situated between ForceP and FinP. Therefore, Rizzi concludes that *di* occurs in FinP and *che* occurs in ForceP. As it
turns out, most non-finite complementizers seem to occur in FinP whereas
finite complementizers occur in ForceP, although Rizzi, citing some evidence
from West Flemish, points out that this does not necessarily have to be so:

(5.37)   Mee   (?gisteren) zie   niet   te   kommen,...
         With   yesterday   she   not   to   come

                                          (*West Flemish*; Rizzi 1997: 302)

He suggests that the main reason for the observed distribution is case assignment to the subject of the embedded non-finite clause by the non-finite
complementizer, for which a local configuration is necessary. The details are
not important here.

   This poses the question why in gapping all kinds of complementizers must
be elided. If we compare English finite *that* with non-finite *for*, for instance,
which must both be elided in gapping, we observe that the former seems
to occur in Force whereas the latter occurs in Fin, that is we have the same
distribution as in the Italian case above:

(5.38)   a.   that (tomorrow,) John will leave (tomorrow)   (Rizzi 1997: 301)

         b.   for (*tomorrow,) John to leave (tomorrow)

         a'. [$_{ForceP}$ that [$_{TopP}$ tomorrow Top [$_{FinP}$ [$_{IP}$ John will leave]]]]

         b'. [$_{ForceP}$ [$_{TopP}$ tomorrow Top [$_{FinP}$ for [$_{IP}$ John to leave]]]]

Since topics are sandwiched between ForceP and FinP, *that* in (5.38a) must be
in Force, above the topic. *For*, on the other hand, must be in Fin: it cannot
precede a topic.

   Examining the realization of the force-finiteness system by single versus
separate items, Rizzi argues that in order to express force, a complementizer
must be in Force. In order to express finiteness, on the other hand, it must be
situated in Fin, adjacent to IP. The behaviour of English *that* above suggests

that this cannot always be guaranteed. The same holds for other finite complementizers in English:

(5.39)   a.   If, tomorrow, John doesn't turn up in time, we'll have to take more drastic measures.

b.   Because on Monday, John didn't turn up in time, the project failed.

c.   When in Berlin the weather is good, people sit outside.

In all these cases, a topicalized phrase intervenes between the complementizer and the IP. Rizzi (1997) only examines the case of *that*, which can alternate with a zero complementizer under particular circumstances. He proposes that for the cases where force and finiteness cannot both be expressed on *that* because a topic intervenes, *that* occurs in Force and Fin hosts a zero C head. In sentences where there is no topic (or focus), *that* is assumed to be specified both for force and finiteness. Rizzi assumes that in the absence of topics or foci, the relevant projections are absent. This means that in these cases there can be a syncretic Force–Fin head. Rizzi discusses this solution with respect to economy notions and suggests that a syncretic head is preferred over two heads because it avoids structure. He assumes that the contents of numerations is determined by lexical items (and their feature specifications) rather than by functional elements, which allows *Avoid Structure* to be a derivational economy principle that opts for a derivation with a syncretic and not two heads.

Note however, that in the case of the split of force and finiteness features, the two categories must still be linked in some way because the lexical item in Force can only co-occur with a Fin that fits its finiteness specifications: if a non-finite complementizer like the West Flemish *mee* occupies Force (see example (5.37) above), Fin must be non-finite, if a finite complementizer like *that* occupies Force, Fin must be finite. This connection must be established across the Top and Foc projections. Rizzi suggests that Fin can move head to head to Top for independent reasons. So we might assume that a complementizer is base-generated in Fin and can move as high as Force, which would produce the necessary configuration. This means that the head positions of other intervening functional projections which are assumed to reside above FinP, such as FocP or StrengthP (Chapter 4) must be empty. This seems to be given for Strength, as speech act operators cannot occur in embedded clauses introduced by a complementizer. As for FocP, it is usually assumed that focus-moved phrases move into the specifier.[16]

---

[16]   I indicated above (example (5.5)) that what looks like VERUM focus on the complementizer itself might have to be treated in slightly different terms.

Roberts (2004) makes a similar proposal. He compares the Force–Fin situation to that of the finite verb which is also associated with two positions. On the one hand, the finite verb has properties of V (its thematic structure) and on the other, it has properties of T/I (tense). As we know from the discussion of English negation in Chapter 2, it has been assumed (Pollock 1989) that main verbs raise to I in French but stay in V in English. The tense features are transferred onto the English verb by lowering. Likewise, Roberts suggests that complementizers in some languages may occur in Force whereas in others they stay in Fin. He qualifies this idea to account, amongst other things, for the different behaviour of finite versus non-finite embedded clauses in different contexts. The details are not important to us here. Basically, his suggestion is that complementizers originate in Fin and, under particular circumstances, move to Force.[17]

To sum up, finiteness and complementizers are tightly linked both in verb-second languages and in non-verb-second languages. They are both associated with the Fin-position—either because they have moved there as in the case of the finite verb in root clauses, or because they were base-generated there as in the case of complementizers. Both can be viewed as anchoring devices: they anchor a proposition in the factual world. A complementizer does this for an embedded clause via the matrix clause. A finite verb anchors a root clause directly, or via previous discourse.

5.3 Anchoring and gapping

Applying the insights from the previous sections to gapping, I propose to define gapping as given at the beginning of this chapter:

(5.40)   DEFINITION OF GAPPING (SEMANTIC-PRAGMATIC)
         Gapping is the coordination of two sentences where the elliptic conjunct copies the anchoring of the proposition to the factual world from its non-elliptic antecedent.

In a root clause, the finite verb anchors the proposition and therefore is gapped. In a coordinated subordinated clause, the complementizer anchors the subordinate clause to the matrix clause and therefore is gapped. The finite or non-finite verb in such a clause is elided if it is identical to its antecedent. Whether the verb is finite or non-finite is immaterial at this stage. The fact that tense, mood, and aspect have to be identical in the second conjunct of a

---

[17]   Roberts links this system with the verb-second phenomenon and suggests that the Welsh particles he investigates (see example (5.31) in the main text) fulfil the same function as the finite verb in verb-second root clauses.

gapping sentence falls out naturally from this view on gapping because these are means to anchor a proposition in the factual world.

The relation between the elliptic conjunct in gapping and its antecedent clause differs from that between a subordinated clause and its matrix clause.[18] In gapping, there is nothing there in the elliptic conjunct that anchors it to its antecedent. It must copy the anchoring function from its antecedent and that way gets anchored to the factual world (and the previous discourse). The subordinated clause is anchored to its matrix clause by means of a complementizer. This view on gapping opens up a way to explain why gapping might be restricted to coordinations without having to appeal to ATB-movement as in Johnson (1996/2003). The following is an attempt at gapping in a subordinated clause that has the matrix clause as its antecedent:

(5.41)   * John gave me the book because Mary the card.

In (5.41), the embedded clause is anchored to its matrix clause by the complementizer *because*. This means that the subordinating clause IS anchored, and in addition, it is anchored in a different way from its potential antecedent. Consequently, the anchoring of the matrix clause cannot be copied. Alternatively, if the complementizer is gapped, the subordination relation is no longer marked:

(5.42)   John gave me the book(,) Mary the card.

With an appropriate intonation this sentence comes over as ordinary gapping, that is as a coordination. To summarize, finiteness in its anchoring function is at the heart of gapping. The second clause of a gapping sentence essentially is an unanchored sentence, which needs to borrow its anchoring from the preceding sentence.

As for the difference between the wide scope readings, on the one hand, and the narrow and distributed scope readings, on the other hand, I proposed in Chapter 4 that the wide scope reading gapping sentences contain only one ForceP and a StrengthP below it. Further down, the structure divides. I argued that this accounts for the fact that these sentences come with illocutionary rather than propositional negation, as well as the fact that the question and the denial here take scope over the whole coordination. Note that the gapping construction itself is licensed as in the other readings: the head carrying the

---

[18] This does not conflict with the idea that coordinations in modern theories are assumed to have an internal structure which takes the first and second conjuncts to be asymmetrical—be that as specifier and complement in a &P (Collins 1988; Grootveld 1994; Johannessen 1998; Kolb and Thiersch 1991; Munn 1987; Zoerner 1995; and others), or in an adjunction structure where the second conjunct is adjoined to the first (Munn 1993, 1999) or the first to the second (Kayne 1994), or both conjuncts to an abstract phrase (Progovac 1997).

finiteness feature is gapped. For the wide scope structures, I assume that this head is always situated in Fin as these structures, due to their discourse status, cannot be embedded. So there will never be a complementizer in Force. To see this for the complementizer *dass* ('that'), compare the following examples. In (5.43a), the accented negative marker takes a position it can only take in denial readings, in (5.43b) it takes the position of ordinary sentence negation:

(5.43) a. ??Ich glaube, dass Max NICHT das Haus   gekauft hat.
        b. Ich glaube, dass Max   das Haus NICHT gekauft hat.
            I   believe that Max not   the house not bought has
            'I think that Max DIDN'T buy the house.'

Neither of these sentences can be used as a denial. The only reading that is available is one where a 'simple' polarity alternative is elicited (see Chapter 4 for this difference). A denial would have to be construed with the matrix clause:

(5.44) Ich glaube NICHT, dass Max das Haus gekauft hat.
        I   believe not   that Max the house bought has
        'I DON'T think that Max bought the house.'

Distributed and narrow scope readings are the coordination of full ForcePs, which is why they can be coordinations of full questions and so on. If a complementizer in Force is elided here, this is due to the finiteness features it brings with it from the Fin position.

6

Summary

In this study, I investigated the following interpretation patterns in gapping sentences which contain a negative marker in the first conjunct but not in the second:

(6.1) a. distributed scope of the negation: $(\neg A) \wedge (\neg B)$

      b. narrow scope of the negation: $(\neg A) \wedge (B)$

      c. wide scope of the negation: $\neg(A \wedge B)$

I found that the emergence and grammatical felicity of these readings depends on syntactic, semantic, discourse-pragmatic, and prosodic factors. The type of examples relevant for each of these readings are listed below:

(6.2) $(\neg A) \wedge (\neg B)$

      a. *English (and other languages where the negative marker is a head)*

         JOHN didn't buy the BOOK and MARY the magaZINE.
         L* H   L* H H% L* H   H* L L%

      b. *German (and other languages where the negative marker is an adjunct)*
         ??HANS hat das BUCH nicht gekauft, und MARIA die ZEITschrift.

(6.3) $(\neg A) \wedge (B)$

      a. *gapping with contrastive* but *(in English restricted)*

         HANS hat das BUCH NICHT gekauft, aber MARIA die ZEITschrift
         L* H   L* H   H* L L- L%   L* H   H* L L%

      b. *gapping with corrective* but *(in English restricted)*
         HANS hat nicht das BUCH gekauft, sondern MARIA die ZEITschrift.
         (H*)   L*H   H-H%   L*+H   H*L L%

      c. *gapping with a focus particle in the second conjunct*
         JOHN didn't buy ANYthing, and MARY only a cheap magaZINE.
         L* H   L* H H-H%, L* H (L* H)   H* L L%

d. *auxiliary gapping*
HANS hat das BUCH nicht gekauft
L* H   L* H   H- H%,
und MARIA die ZEITUNG vergessen.
    L* H   H* L   L- L%
'Hans didn't buy the book and Mary forgot the magazine.'

(6.4)   ¬(A ∧ B)

a. *Denials (and corrective-but-coordinations)*
John DIDN'T buy a BOOK and Mary (sell) a magazINE.
(H*) H* +L   H* +L H⁻ (H*)   H* +L H%

b. *Interrogatives with outer negation*
Didn't MAX drink WINE and MARY eat FISH?
    (H*)   L*+H H⁻ (H*)   L+H* H%

The study of the negation in gapping has been a fruitful enterprise in several respects. It has uncovered a whole new set of data which heretofore were largely unknown—many of the above. It has furthered our understanding of ellipsis, and it has furthered our understanding of negation.

I started from the assumption that the distributed scope readings are something like the default readings in gapping: elements that are (apparently) gapped are underlyingly present. As it turned out, narrow scope readings can be default as well in the sense that from the point of view of semantic parallelism they are often the readings that are the 'most parallel'. I captured this by the principle of balanced contrast (PBC), which says that the two conjuncts in a gapping sentence with *and* must make the same kind of contribution to an overarching discourse topic. So, what seemed a most natural assumption to make from the point of view of ellipsis—that a distributed scope reading would be the default reading—is not the most natural assumption anymore.

The principle of balanced contrast is a very important principle in gapping. It is not only at work in the narrow scope readings but also in the distributed scope readings, where the syntax in certain languages does not provide a structure that conforms to the PBC, that is a negative second conjunct, which results in the unacceptability of the respective structures. The principle is different from more general conditions on semantic parallelism and from conditions on syntactic parallelism because the reasons for semantic-pragmatically unbalanced contrast, especially in the narrow scope readings, can be extremely subtle.

The study of negation in gapping has led to an analysis of this ellipsis type in terms of syntactic copying. Gapping is derived by copying of material from the first conjunct to the second in conjunction with a condition on the numeration of the elliptic conjunct, rather than by deletion or in terms of multiple dominance. This analysis sets gapping clearly apart from other ellipsis types on the one hand, and from non-elliptic structures on the other, neither of which share the behaviour gapping shows with respect to negation.

The different scope options of the negation in gapping led me to investigate the features of the negation involved very closely. I concluded that different scope can go hand in hand with a different interpretation of the negation and proposed that we need to distinguish propositional negation and illocutionary negation, which are represented in different domains in the syntactic structure. I also argued that predicate negation, which describes an event in negative terms and whose differentiated semantic contribution is often difficult to pin down does actually make a clear appearance in auxiliary gapping.

References

ABE, J. and H. HOSHI (1995). 'Gapping and the Directionality of Movement', *Proceedings of FLSM 6*: 82–93.

—— —— (1997). 'Gapping and P-Stranding', *Journal of East Asian Linguistics* 6: 101–36.

—— —— (1999). 'Directionality of Movement in Ellipsis Resolution in English and Japanese', in S. Lappin, and E. Benmamoun (eds), *Fragments. Studies in Ellipsis and Gapping*. New York, Oxford: Oxford University Press, 193–226.

ACQUAVIVA, P. (1995). 'Operator Composition, and Negative Concord', *Geneva Generative Papers* 3: 72–105.

—— (1997). *The Logical Form of Negation*. New York: Garland.

ADAMÍKOVÁ, M. (2004). *Kontrast oder Korrektur? Prosodische Disambiguierung bei negationshaltigen Adversativ-Konstruktionen in den Westslavinen*. PhD book. Humboldt University Berlin.

AGBAYANI B. and E. ZOERNER (2004). 'Gapping, Pseudogapping and Sideward Movement', *Studia Linguistica* 58: 185–211.

AKMAJIAN, A. (1984). 'Sentence Types and the Form-Function Fit', *Natural Language and Linguistic Theory* 2: 1–23.

ALTMANN, H. (1976). *Die Gradpartikeln im Deutschen. Untersuchungen zu ihrer Syntax, Semantik und Pragmatik*. Tübingen: Niemeyer.

AMRITAVALLI, R. and K. A. JAYASEELAN (2004). 'Finiteness and Negation in Dravidian', in R. Kayne and G. Cinque (eds), *Handbook of Comparative Syntax*. Oxford: Oxford University Press, 178–220.

ANDERSON, S. (1972). 'How to get "even"', *Language* 48: 893–906.

ANSCOMBRE, J. C. and O. DUCROT (1977). 'Deux *mais* en français?', *Lingua* 43: 23–40.

—— —— (1983). *L'Argumentation Dans la Langue*. Brussels: Pierre Mardaga.

ASHER, N. (1993). *Reference to Abstract Objects in Discourse*. Dordrecht: Kluwer.

ASBACH-SCHNITTKER, B. (1979). 'Die adversativen Konnektoren *aber, sondern* und *but* nach negierten Sätzen', in H. Weydt (ed.), *Die Partikeln der deutschen Sprache*. Berlin, New York: Walter de Gruyter, 457–68.

ATLAS, J. D. (1977). 'Negation, Ambiguity, and Presupposition', *Linguistics and Philosophy* 1: 321–36.

BACH, E. (1983). 'Generalized Categorial Grammars and the English Auxiliary', in F. Heny and I. Richards (eds), *Linguistic Categories: Auxiliaries and Related Puzzles*, vol. ii. Dordrecht: Reidel, 101–20.

BACH, K. (1999). 'The Myth of Conventional Implicature', *Linguistics and Philosophy* 22: 327–66.

BAKER, C. L. (1971). 'Stress Level and Auxiliary Behavior in English', *Linguistic Inquiry* 2: 167–81.

—— (1991). 'The Syntax of English *Not*: The Limits of Core Grammar', *Linguistic Inquiry* 22: 387–429.

BALTIN, M. (1993). *Negation and Clause Structure*. Ms. New York University.

BARBIERS, S. (1995). *The Syntax of Interpretation*. PhD book. HIL, University of Leiden. The Hague: Holland Academic Publishers.

BARTSCH, R. and T. VENNEMANN (1972). *Semantic Structures*. Frankfurt: Athenäum.

BARWISE, J. and J. PERRY (1983). *Situations and Attitudes*. Cambridge: MIT Press.

BÄUERLE, R. (1979). *Temporale Deixis, temporale Frage*. Tübingen: Narr.

BAYER, J. (1984). 'COMP in Bavarian', *The Linguistic Review* 3: 209–74.

—— (1990). 'What Bavarian Negative Concord Reveals about the Syntactic Structure of German', in J. Mascaro and M. Nespor (eds), *Grammar in Progress. Glow-Essays for Henk van Riemsdijk*. Dordrecht: Foris, 13–24.

—— (1996). *Directionality and Logical Form*. Dordrecht: Kluwer.

—— (1999). 'Bound Focus or How can Association with Focus be Achieved without Going Semantically Astray?', in G. Rebuschi and L. Tuller (eds), *The Grammar of Focus*. Amsterdam: Benjamins, 55–82.

—— (2004). 'Decomposing the Left Periphery. Dialectal and Cross-Linguistic Evidence', in H. Lohnstein and S. Trissler (eds), *Syntax and Semantics of the Left Periphery*. Berlin, New York: Mouton de Gruyter, 59–97.

BECK, S. (1995). 'Negative Islands and Reconstruction', in: U. Lutz and J. Pafel (eds), *Extraction and Extraposition in German*. Amsterdam: Benjamins, 121–43.

BECKMAN, M. E. and J. B. PIERREHUMBERT (1986). 'Intonational Structure in English and Japanese', *Phonology Yearbook* 3: 225–309.

BELLERT, I. (1972). 'On Certain Properties of the English Connectives *And* and *But*', in S. Plötz (ed.), *Transformationelle Analyse*. Frankfurt/Main: Athenäum, 327–56.

BENINCÀ, P. (2001). 'The Position of Topic and Focus in the Left Periphery', in G. Cinque (ed.), *Current Studies in Italian Syntax: Essays Offered to Lorenzo Renzi*. Amsterdam: Elsevier, 39–64.

BENNETT, J. (1982). 'Even If', *Linguistics and Philosophy* 5: 403–18.

BEUKEMA F. and P. KOOPMANS (1989). 'A Government-Binding Perspective on the Imperative in English', *Journal of Linguistics* 25: 417–36.

BHATT, R. and J. YOON (1991). 'On the Composition of COMP and Parameters of V2', in R. Bates (ed.), *Proceedings of the Tenth West Coast Conference on Formal Linguistics*. Stanford, CA: CSLI, 41–53.

BIANCHI, V. (1995). *Consequences of Antisymmetry for the Syntax of Headed Relative Clauses*. PhD book. Scuola Normale Superiore, Pisa.

BLAKEMORE, D. L. (1987). *Semantic Constraints on Relevance*. Oxford: Blackwell.

—— (2000). 'Indicators and Procedures: *Nevertheless* and *but*', *Journal of Linguistics* 36: 463–86.

BLAKEMORE, D. L. and R. CARSTON (2005). 'The Pragmatics of Sentential Coordination with *And*', *Lingua* 115: 569–89.

BŁASZCZAK, J. (2001). *Investigation into the Interaction between Indefinites and Negation*. Berlin: Akademie Verlag.

BLAU, U. (1977). *Die dreiwertige Logik der Sprache*. Berlin.

BOLINGER, D. (1972). *That's That*. The Hague: Mouton.

—— (1977). *Meaning and Form*. London: Longman.

BOŠKOVIĆ, Ž. (1997a). Fronting *Wh*-Phrases in Serbo-Croatian, in M. Lindseth and S. Franks (eds), *Proceedings of the V. Annual Workshop on Formal Approaches to Slavic Linguistics*. Ann Arbor: Michigan Slavic Publications, 86–107.

—— (1997b). *The Syntax of Nonfinite Complementation: An Economy Approach*. Cambridge, MA: MIT Press.

—— and H. LASNIK (1999). 'How Strict is the Cycle?', *Linguistic Inquiry* 30: 691–703.

———— (2004). 'On the Distribution of Null Complementizers', *Linguistic Inquiry* 34: 527–46.

BOZSAHIN, C. (2000). *Gapping and Word Order in Turkish*. Proceedings of 10th International Conference on Turkish Linguistics. Istanbul.

BRANDNER, E. (2004). 'Head-Movement in Minimalism, and V2 as FORCE-Marking', in H. Lohnstein and S. Trissler (eds), *The Syntax and Semantics of the Left Periphery*. Berlin: de Gruyter, 97–138.

BRENNAN, V. (1997). 'Modalities'. Ms. Vanderbilt University, Nashville, Tennessee.

BRESNAN, J. (1972). *Theory of Complementation in English*. PhD book. MIT. Published 1979, New York: Garland Press.

BÜRING, D. (1994). 'Mittelfeldreport', in V. B. Haftka (ed.), *Was determiniert Wortstellungsvariation?* Opladen: Westdeutscher Verlag, 79–96.

—— (1997a). *The Meaning of Topic and Focus. The 59th Street Bridge Accent*. London, New York: Routledge.

—— (1997b). 'The Great Scope Inversion Conspiracy', *Linguistics and Philosophy* 20: 175–94.

—— (2003). 'On D-Trees, Beans and B-Accents', *Linguistics and Philosophy* 26: 511–45.

—— and C. GUNLOGSON (2000). 'Aren't Positive and Negative Polar Questions the Same?' Ms. available at semanticsarchive.net

—— and K. HARTMANN (1998). 'Asymmetrische Koordination', *Linguistische Berichte* 174: 172–201.

———— (2001). 'The Syntax and Semantics of Focus-Sensitive Particles in German', *Natural Language and Linguistic Theory* 19: 229–81.

BURTON-ROBERTS, N. (1989). 'On Horn's Dilemma: Presupposition and Negation', *Journal of Linguistics* 25: 95–125.

—— (1999). 'Presupposition-Cancellation and Metalinguistic Negation: A Reply to Carston', *Journal of Linguistics* 35: 347–63.

BUTLER, J. (2003). 'A Minimalist Treatment of Modality', *Lingua* 113: 967–96.

BUTLER, J. (2004). *Phase Structure, Phrase Structure, and Quantification*. PhD book. University of York.

BUTULUSSI, E. (1989). *Studien zur Valenz kognitiver Verben im Deutschen und Neugriechischen*. PhD thesis. Tübingen University. Appeared 1991 at Tübingen: Niemeyer.

CARDINALETTI, A. (2004). 'Toward a Cartography of Subject Positions', in L. Rizzi (ed.), *The Structure of CP and IP. The Cartography of Syntactic Structures Vol. 2*. Oxford: Oxford University Press, 115–65.

CARLSON, K. (2001a). 'The Effects of Parallelism and Prosody in the Processing of Gapping Structures', *Language and Speech 44*: 1–26.

—— (2001b). *Parallelism and Prosody in the Processing of Ellipsis Sentences*. New York: Routledge.

CARPENTER, B. (1993). 'Sceptical and Credulous Default Unification with Applications to Templates and Inheritance', in T. Briscoe, V. de Paiva, and A. Copestake (eds), *Inheritance, Defaults, and the Lexicon*. Cambridge: Cambridge University Press, 13–37.

CARSTON, R. (1996). 'Metalinguistic Negation and Echoic Use', *Journal of Pragmatics 25*: 309–30.

—— (1998). 'Negation, "Presupposition" and the Semantics/Pragmatics Distinction', *Journal of Linguistics 34*: 309–50.

—— (1999). 'Negation, "Presupposition" and Metarepresentation: A Response to Noel Burton-Roberts', *Journal of Linguistics 35*: 365–89.

CATTELL, R. (1973). 'Negative Transportation and Tag Questions', *Language 49*: 612–39.

CHAO, W. (1988). *On Ellipsis*. New York and London: Garland Publications.

CHIERCHIA, G. (1995). 'Individual-Level Predicates as Inherent Generics', in G. N. Carlson and F. J. Pelletier (eds), *The Generic Book*. Chicago: University of Chicago Press, 176–223.

CHOMSKY, N. (1970). 'Remarks on Nominalization', in R. A. Jacobs and P. S. Rosenbaum (eds), *Readings in English Transformational Grammar*. London: Ginn, 184–221.

—— (1981). *Lectures on Government and Binding*. Dordrecht: Foris.

—— (1991). 'Some Notes on Economy of Derivation and Representation', in R. Freidin (ed.), *Principles and Parameters in Comparative Grammar*. Cambridge, MA: MIT Press, 417–54. Also in I. Laka and A. Mahajan (eds), *Functional Heads and Clausal Structure*. MIT Working Papers in Linguistics 1989, 43–74.

—— (1993). 'A Minimalist Program for Linguistic Theory', in K. Hale and S. H. Keyser (eds), *The View From Building 20: Essays in Linguistics in Honour of Sylvain Bromberger*. Cambridge, MA: MIT Press, 1–52.

—— (1995). *The Minimalist Program*. Cambridge, MA: MIT Press.

—— (2000). 'Minimalist Enquiries: The Framework', in R. Martin, D. Michaels, and J. Uriagereka (eds), *Step by Step: Essays on Minimalist Syntax in Honour of Howard Lasnik*. Cambridge, MA: MIT Press, 89–155.

—— (2001). 'Derivation by Phase', in M. Kenstowicz (ed.), *Ken Hale—A Life in Language*. Cambridge, MA: MIT Press, 1–52.

CHUNG, S., W. LADUSAW, and J. McCLOSKEY (1995). 'Sluicing and Logical Form', *Natural Language Semantics* 3: 239–82.

CINQUE, G. (1999). *Adverbs and Functional Heads*. New York: Oxford University Press.

CITKO, B. (2005). 'On the Nature of Merge: External Merge, Internal Merge, and Parallel Merge', *Linguistic Inquiry* 36: 475–97.

COHEN, A. (1999). 'How are Alternatives Computed?', *Journal of Semantics* 16: 43–65.

COLLINS, C. (1988). Part1: *Conjunction Adverbs*, Part 2: *Alternative Analyses of Conjunction*. Ms., Cambridge, MA: MIT.

COMOROVSKI, I. (1996). *Interrogative Phrases and the Syntax–Semantics Interface*. Dordrecht: Kluwer.

COPPEN, P.-A., R. VAN DER BORGT, S. VAN DREUMEL, E. OLTMANS, and L. TEUNISSEN (1993). 'Een implementatie van gapping', *Gramma/TTT* 2–1: 31–45.

COPPOCK, E. (2001). 'Gapping: in Defense of Deletion', *Chicago Linguistics Society* 37: 133–148. University of Chicago.

CORMACK, A. and N. SMITH (1998). 'Negation, Polarity and V Positions in English', *UCL Working Papers in Linguistics* 10: 285–322.

COTTELL, S. (1994). *The Representation of Tense in Modern Irish*. Ms. University of Geneva.

COWPER, E. (2002). *Finiteness*. Ms. University of Toronto.

CREMERS, C. (1983). 'On the Form and Interpretation of Ellipsis', in A. G. B. ter Meulen (ed.), *Studies in Modeltheoretic Semantics*. Dordrecht: Foris.

CRESTI, D. (1995). *Indefinite Topics*. PhD thesis. Cambridge, MA: MIT.

CRESWELL, C. (2000). 'The Discourse Function of Verum Focus in Wh-Questions', *Proceedings of North East Linguistics Society 30*.

CULICOVER, P. W. (1991). 'Topicalization, Inversion and Complementizers in English', in D. Delfitto, M. Everaert, A. Evers, and F. Stuurman (eds), *Going Romance, and Beyond: Fifth Symposium on Comparative Grammar*. Utrecht: OTS Working Papers 91–002, 1–43.

—— (1997). *Principles and Parameters*. Oxford: Oxford University Press.

DAHL, Ö. (1979). 'Typology of Sentence Negation', *Linguistics* 17: 79–106.

—— (1995). 'The Marking of the Episodic/Generic Distinction in Tense–Aspect Systems. in G. N. Carlson and F. J. Pelletier' (eds), *The Generic Book*. Chicago: University of Chicago Press, 412–25.

DAYAL, V. (1996). *Locality in Wh-quantification*. Dordrecht: Kluwer.

DEN BESTEN, H. (1983). 'On the Interaction of Root Transformations and Lexical Deletive Rules', in W. Abraham (ed.), *On the Formal Syntax of the Westgermania*. Amsterdam: Benjamins, 47–131.

DIESING, M. (1992). *The Syntactic Roots of Semantic Partition*. PhD book. University of Massachusetts, Amherst.

DIK, S. (1968). *Coordination: Its Implications for the Theory of General Linguistics.* Amsterdam: North Holland.

—— (1989). *The Theory of Functional Grammar. Part I: The Structure of the Clause.* Dordrecht: Foris.

DOHERTY, C. (1997). 'Clauses without Complementizers: Finite IP-Complementation in English', *The Linguistic Review* 14: 197–220.

DOR, D. (2005). 'Towards a Semantic Account of *That*-Deletion in English', *Linguistics* 43: 345–82.

DOWTY, D. (1994). 'The Role of Negative Polarity and Concord Marking in Natural Language Reasoning', in M. Harvey and L. Santelmann (eds), *SALT IV.* Cornell University. Ithaca, NY, 114–45.

DRUBIG, H. B. (1994). *Island Constraints and the Syntactic Nature of Focus and Association with Focus.* Arbeitspapiere des SFB 340, Nr. 51. Tübingen.

—— (2003). 'Toward a Typology of Focus, and Focus Constructions', *Linguistics 41*, 1–50.

DRYER, M. (1994). 'The Pragmatics of Focus-Association with Only', Unpublished paper delivered at the 1994 Annual Meeting of the Linguistic Society of America. Ms. SUNY Buffalo.

DUCROT, O. (1973). *La Preuve et la Dire.* Paris: Mame.

ENÇ, M. (1987). 'Anchoring Conditions for Tense', *Linguistic Inquiry 18*: 633–57.

ERB, C. (2001). *Finite Auxiliaries in German.* Tilburg Dissertation in Language Studies.

ERNST, T. (1992). 'The Phrase Structure of English Negation', *The Linguistic Review 9*: 109–44.

—— (2002). *The Syntax of Adjuncts.* Cambridge: Cambridge University Press.

ERTESCHIK, N. (1973). *On the Nature of Island Constraints.* PhD book. Cambridge, MA: MIT.

ETXEPARE, R. and K. K. GROHMANN (2005). 'Toward a Grammar of Adult Root Infinitives', in J. Alderete, C.-h. Han, and A. Kochetov (eds), *Proceedings of WCCFL 24*, 129–37.

—— —— (2007). 'Temporal and Aspectual Variation in Adult Root Infinitives', in J. Moschler, L. de Saussure, and G. Puskás (eds), *Recent Advances in the Syntax and Semantics of Tense, Mood and Aspect.* Berlin: Mouton de Gruyter, 147–68.

EVERS, A. (1975). *The Transformational Cycle in Dutch and German.* Bloomington: Indiana Linguistics Club.

FANSELOW, G. and D. ĆAVAR (2001). 'Remarks on the Economy of Pronunciation', in G. Müller and W. Sternefeld (eds), *Competition in Syntax.* Berlin: de Gruyter. 107–50.

—— —— (2002). 'Distributed Deletion', in A. Alexiadou (ed.), *Theoretical Approaches to Universals.* Amsterdam: Benjamins, 65–107.

—— and A. MAHAJAN (2000). 'Towards a Minimalist Theory of *Wh*-Expletives, *Wh*-Copying, and Successive Cyclicity', in U. Lutz, G. Müller, and A. von Stechow (eds), *Wh-Scope Marking.* Amsterdam: Benjamins, 195–230.

FAUCONNIER, G. (1975). 'Pragmatic Scales and Logical Structure', *Linguistic Inquiry* 6: 353–75.

FELSER, C. (2004). '*Wh*-Copying, Phases, and Successive Cyclicity', *Lingua* 114: 543–74.

FÉRY, C. (1993). *German Intonational Patterns*. Tübingen: Niemeyer.

—— (2001). 'Phonologie des Deutschen: Eine optimalitätstheoretische Einführung. Teil 2', *Linguistics in Potsdam* 11.

—— and K. HARTMANN (2005). 'The Focus and Prosodic Structure of German Right Node Raising and Gapping', *The Linguistic Review* 22: 69–116.

FIENGO, R. (1974). *Semantic Conditions on Surface Structures*. PhD thesis. Cambridge, MA: MIT.

FOGELIN, R. (1967). *Evidence and Meaning*. New York: Humanities Press.

FORTIN, C. R. (2007). *Indonesian Sluicing and Verb Phrase Ellipsis: Description and Explanation in a Minimalist Framework*. PhD thesis. University of Michigan.

FOX, D. (1999). 'Reconstruction, Binding Theory, and the Interpretation of Chains', *Linguistic Inquiry* 30: 157–96.

—— (2000). *Economy and Semantic Interpretation*. Cambridge, MA: MIT Press.

—— and H. LASNIK (2003). 'Successive Cyclic Movement and Island Repair: The Difference between Sluicing and VP-ellipsis', *Linguistic Inquiry* 34: 143–54.

—— and J. NISSENBAUM (1999). 'Extraposition and Scope: A Case for Overt QR', in S. Bird, A. Carnie, J. D. Haugen, and P. Norquest (eds), *Proceedings of the 18th West Coast Conference on Formal Linguistics*. Somerville, MA: Cascadilla Press, 132–44.

FRANCESCOTTI, R. M. (1995). '*Even*: The Conventional Implicature Approach Reconsidered', *Linguistics and Philosophy* 18: 153–73.

FRASCARELLI, M. and R. HINTERHÖLZL (2007). 'Types of Topics in German and Italian', in S. Winkler and K. Schwabe (eds), *On Information Structure, Meaning and Form*. Amsterdam: Benjamins, 87–116.

FRAZIER, L. (1978). *On Comprehending Sentences: Syntactic Parsing Strategies*. PhD book. University of Connecticut (published by Indiana University Linguistics Club, Westband, 1979).

—— and C. CLIFTON, JR. (1996). *Construal*. Cambridge, MA: MIT Press.

—— —— (2006). 'Ellipsis and Discourse Coherence', *Linguistics and Philosophy* 29, 315–46.

FREGE, F. L. G. (1879). *Begriffsschrift*. Reprinted: Hildesheim 1964.

—— (1919). 'Die Verneinung', *Beiträge zur Philosophie des Deutschen Idealismus* 1: 143–57. Reprinted in P. T. Geach and M. Black (eds), *Translations from the Philosophical Writings of Gottlob Frege*. Oxford: Blackwell, 117–35.

FREIDIN, R. (1986). 'Fundamental Issues in the Theory of Binding', in B. Lust (ed.), *Studies in the Acquisition of Anaphora, Vol. 1*. Dordrecht: Reidel, 151–88.

FREY, W. (2001). 'About the Whereabouts of Indefinites', *Theoretical Linguistics* 27 (2/3): 137–61.

—— (2003). 'Syntactic Conditions on Adjunct Classes', in E. Lang, C. Maienborn, and C. Fabricius-Hansen (eds), *Modifying Adjuncts*. Berlin: Mouton de Gruyter, 163–210.

FREY, W. (2004). 'The Grammar–Pragmatics Interface and the German Prefield', *Sprache, and Pragmatik 52*: 1–39.

FRIES, N. (1983). *Syntaktische und semantische Studien zum frei verwendeten Infinitiv und zu verwandten Erscheinungen im Deutschen.* Tübingen: Narr.

GAERDENFORS, P. (1994). 'The Role of Expectations in Reasoning', in M. Masuch and L. Pólos (eds), *Knowledge Representation and Reasoning Under Uncertainty.* Berlin and New York: Springer, 1–16.

GÄRTNER, H.-M. (2001). 'Bound Focus and Assertionality: Evidence from V2-relatives', in A. Benz (ed.), *Proceedings of Formal Pragmatics.* Berlin: ZAS.

—— (2002). 'On the Force of V2-Declaratives', *Theoretical Linguistics 28*: 33–42.

GAZDAR, G. (1979). *Pragmatics.* New York: Academic Press.

GEURTS, B. (1998). 'The Mechanisms of Denial', *Language 74*: 274–307.

GIANNAKIDOU, A. (1998). *Polarity Sensitivity as (Non)Veridical Dependency.* Amsterdam: Benjamins.

—— (2007). 'The landscape of EVEN', *Natural Language and Linguistic Theory 25*: 39–81.

GILBOY, E., J. SOPENA, C. CLIFTON, and L. FRAZIER (1995). 'Argument Structure and Association Preferences in Spanish and English Compound NPs', *Cognition 54*: 131–67.

GIORGI, A. and F. PIANESI (2004). 'Complementizer Deletion in Italian', in L. Rizzi (ed.), *The Structure of CP and IP. The Cartography of Syntactic Structures, Vol. 2.* Oxford: Oxford University Press, 190–210.

GÓMEZ TXURRUKA, I. (2003). 'The Natural Language Conjunction *And*', *Linguistics and Philosophy 26*: 255–85.

GOODALL, G. (1987). *Parallel Structures in Syntax.* Cambridge: Cambridge University Press.

GREWENDORF, G. (1990). 'Verbbewegung und Negation im Deutschen', *Groninger Arbeiten zur Germanistischen Linguistik 30*: 57–125.

GRICE, M., S. BAUMANN, and R. BENZMÜLLER (2005). 'German Intonation in Autosegmental-Metrical Phonology', in S.-A. Jun (ed.), *Prosodic Typology: The Phonology of Intonation and Phrasing.* Oxford: Oxford University Press, 55–83.

GRIMSHAW, J. (1997). 'Projection, Heads, and Optimality', *Linguistic Inquiry 28*: 373–422.

GROAT, E. and J. O'NEILL (1996). 'Spell-out at the LF Interface: Achieving a Unified Syntactic Computational System in the Minimalist Framework', in W. Abraham, S. D. Epstein, H. Thráinsson, and J.-W. Zwart (eds), *Minimal Ideas: Syntactic Studies in the Minimalist Framework.* Philadelphia: Benjamins, 113–39.

GROENENDIJK, J. and M. STOKHOF (1984). *Studies on the Semantics of Questions and the Pragmatics of Answers.* PhD book. University of Amsterdam.

GROHMANN, K. and R. ETXEPARE (2003). 'Root Infinitives: A Comparative View', *Probus 15*: 201–36.

GROOTVELD, M. (1994). *Parsing Coordination Generatively.* Dordrecht: HIL.

GROSU, A. (1985). 'Subcategorization and Parallelism', *Theoretical Linguistics 12*: 231–40.

GROSZ, B. J., A. K. JOSHI, and S. WEINSTEIN (1995). 'Centering: A Framework for Modeling the Local Coherence of Discourse', *Computational Linguistics 21*: 203–26.

GUERZONI, E. (2004). 'Even-NPIs in Yes/No Questions', *Natural Language Semantics 12*: 319–43.

GUSSENHOVEN, C. (1983). *On the Grammar and Semantics of Sentence Accents.* Dordrecht: Foris.

HAEGEMAN, L. (1985). 'INFL, COMP and Nominative Case Assignment in Flemish Infinitivals', in P. Muysken and H. van Riemsdijk (eds), *Features and Projections.* Dordrecht: Foris, 123–37.

—— (1992). *Theory and Description in Generative Grammar.* Cambridge: Cambridge University Press.

—— (1995). *The Syntax of Negation.* Cambridge: Cambridge University Press.

—— (2000). 'Negative Inversion, the Neg Criterion and the Structure of CP', in L. Horn and Y. Cato (eds), *Negation and Polarity.* Oxford: Oxford University Press, 26–69.

—— and J. GUÉRON (1999). *English Grammar: A Generative Perspective.* Oxford: Blackwell.

—— and R. ZANUTTINI (1991). 'Negative Heads and the NEG-Criterion', *Linguistic Review 8*: 233–52.

HAFTKA, B. (1994). 'Wie positioniere ich meine Position?', in B. Haftka (ed.), *Was determiniert Wortstellungsvariation?* Opladen: Westdeutscher Verlag, 139–59.

HAGSTROM, P. S. (1998). *Decomposing Questions.* PhD thesis. Cambridge, MA: MIT.

HAIDA, A. (2003). 'A Focus Semantics for Interrogatives', in P. Dekker and R. van Rooy (eds), *Proceedings of the 14th Amsterdam Colloquium.* Amsterdam: Universiteit van Amsterdam, 135–40.

—— (2007). *The Indefiniteness and Focussing of Wh-Words*, PhD thesis. Berlin: Humboldt University.

HAIDER, H. (1993). *Deutsche Syntax—generativ.* Tübingen: Narr.

—— (2004). 'Pre- and postverbal adverbials in OV and VO', *Lingua 114*: 779–807.

HALE, K. and S. J. KEYSER (1993). 'On Argument Structure and the Lexical Expression of Syntactic Relations', in K. Hale and S. J. Keyser (eds), *The View from Building 20: Essays in Linguistics in Honor of Sylvain Bromberger.* Cambridge, MA: MIT Press, 53–109.

HALLE, M. and A. MARANTZ (1993). 'Distributed Morphology and the Pieces of Inflection', in K. Hale and S. Keyser (eds), *The View from Building 20: Essays in Linguistics in Honor of Sylvain Bromberger.* Cambridge, MA: MIT Press, 111–76.

HAMBLIN, C. L. (1973). 'Questions in Montague Grammar', *Foundations of Language 10*: 41–53.

HAN, C.-H. (2000). *The Structure and Interpretation of Imperatives: Mood and Force in Universal Grammar.* New York: Garland Publications.

—— (2001). 'Force, negation, and imperatives', *The Linguistic Review 18*: 289–325.

—— and C. LEE (2007). 'On negative imperatives in Korean', *Linguistic Inquiry 38*: 373–95.

HANKAMER, J. (1971). *Constraints on Deletion in Syntax*. PhD thesis. New Haven, CT: Yale University.

—— (1973). 'Unacceptable Ambiguity', *Linguistic Inquiry 4*: 17–68.

—— (1979). *Deletion in Coordinate Structures*. New York and London: Garland Publications.

HARA, Y. (2006). *Grammar of Knowledge Representation: Japanese Discourse Items at Interfaces*. PhD thesis. University of Delaware.

—— and VAN ROOY (2007). 'Contrastive Topics Revisited: a Simpler Set of Topic-Alternatives', Paper presented at NELS 38. University of Ottawa.

HARDT, D. (1993). *Verb Phrase Ellipsis: Form, Meaning and Processing*. PhD book. University of Pennsylvania.

HARTMANN, K. (2000). *Right Node Raising and Gapping. Interface Conditions on Prosodic Deletion*. Amsterdam: Benjamins.

HASPELMATH, M. (1997). *Indefinite Pronouns*. Oxford: Oxford University Press.

HEGARTY, M. (1991). 'Adjunct Extraction without Traces', *Proceedings of West Coast Conference on Formal Linguistics 10*. Stanford, CA: Linguistic Association Stanford, 209–22.

—— (1992). *Adjunct Extraction and Chain Configuration*. PhD book. Cambridge, MA: MIT.

HENDRIKS, P. (2004). 'Coherence Relations, Ellipsis and Contrastive Topics', *Journal of Semantics 21*: 133–53.

HENRY, A. (1995). *Belfast English and Standard English: Dialect Variation and Parameter Setting*. Oxford: Oxford University Press.

HERBURGER, E. (2000). *What Counts: Focus and Quantification*. Cambridge, MA: MIT Press.

HEYCOCK, C. (1995). 'Asymmetries in Reconstruction', *Linguistic Inquiry 26*: 547–70.

HIGGINBOTHAM, J. (1987). 'Indefiniteness and Predication', in E. Reuland and A. ter Meulen (eds), *The Representation of (In)Definiteness*. Cambridge, MA: MIT Press, 43–70.

HINTERHÖLZL, R. (1999). *Restructuring Infinitives and the Theory of Complementation*. PhD book. University of Southern California, Los Angeles.

—— (2006). *Scrambling, Remnant Movement, and Restructuring in West Germanic*. Oxford: Oxford University Press.

HINTERWIMMER, S. and S. REPP (2008). 'Different Alternatives for Topics and Foci: Evidence from Indefinites and Multiple *wh*', in A. Grønn (ed.), *Proceedings of SuB12*, Oslo: ILOS.

HINTIKKA, J. (1978) 'Answers to Questions', in H. Hiz (ed.), *Question*. Dordrecht: Reidel, 279–300.

HOEKSEMA, J. (2006). 'Pseudogapping: Its Syntactic Analysis and Cumulative Effects on its Acceptability', *Research on Language & Computation 4*: 335–52.

—— (1983). 'Negative Polarity and the Comparative', *Natural Language and Linguistic Theory, 1*: 403–34.

HÖHLE, T. (1988). 'VERUM-Fokus', *Sprache und Pragmatik 5*: 2–7.

—— (1991). 'On reconstruction and coordination', in H. Haider and K. Netter (eds), *Representation and Derivation in the Theory of Grammar.* Dordrecht: Kluwer, 139–97.

—— (1992). 'Über Verum-Fokus in Deutschen', in J. Jacobs (ed.), *Information-sstruktur und Grammatik.* Linguistische Berichte Sonderheft 4/1991–1992. Opladen: Westdeutscher Verlag, 112–41.

HOLMBERG, A. and C. PLATZACK (1995). *The Role of Inflection in Scandinavian Syntax.* Oxford: Oxford University Press.

HORN, L. R. (1969). 'A Presuppositional Analysis of *Only* and *Even*', *Chicago Linguistics Society 5*: 97–108.

—— (1985). 'Metalinguistic Negation and Pragmatic Ambiguity', *Language 61*: 121–74.

—— (1989). *A Natural History of Negation.* Chicago: The University of Chicago Press.

—— (1996). 'Exclusive Company: *Only* and the Dynamics of Vertical Inference', *Journal of Semantics 13*: 1–40.

—— (1997). 'Negative Polarity and the Dynamics of Vertical Inference', in D. Forget, P. Hirschbühler, F. Martineau, and M.-L. Rivero (eds), *Negation and Polarity: Syntax and Semantics.* Amsterdam: John Benjamins, 157–82.

—— (2000). 'Pick a Theory (Not Just *Any* Theory): Indiscriminatives and the Free-Choice Indefinite', in L. Horn and Y. Kato (eds), *Negation and Polarity: Syntactic and Semantic Perspectives.* Oxford: Oxford University Press, 147–92.

HORNSTEIN, N. (1999). 'Movement and Control', *Linguistic Inquiry 30*, 69–96.

HUDSON, R. A. (1976). 'Conjunction Reduction, Gapping and Right-Node Raising', *Language 52*: 535–62.

—— (1987). 'Zwicky On Heads', *Journal of Linguistics 23*: 109–32.

—— (1996). 'What's a head?', in J. Rooryck and L. Zaring (eds), *Phrase Structure and the Lexicon.* Dordrecht: Kluwer, 35–70.

ITEN, C. (2000). '*Even if* and *even*: The Case for an Inferential Scalar Account', *UCL Working Papers 12*: 119–57.

JACKENDOFF, R. (1971). 'Gapping and Related Rules', *Linguistic Inquiry 2*: 21–35.

—— (1972). *Semantic Interpretation in Generative Grammar.* Cambridge, MA: MIT Press.

—— (1977). *X' Syntax: A Study of Phrase Structure.* Cambridge, MA: MIT Press.

JACOBS, J. (1982). *Syntax und Semantik der Negation im Deutschen.* München: Fink.

—— (1983). *Fokus und Skalen.* Tübingen: Niemeyer.

—— (1984). 'Funktionale Satzperspektive und Illokutionssemantik', *Linguistische Berichte 91*: 25–58.

—— (1986). 'The Syntax of Focus and Adverbials', in W. Abraham and S. de Meij (eds), *Topic, Focus and Configurationality.* Amsterdam: Benjamins, 103–28.

—— (1991). 'Negation', in A. von Stechow and D. Wunderlich (eds), *Semantik. Ein internationales Handbuch zeitgenössischer Forschung.* Berlin: de Gruyter, 560–96.

—— (1996). 'Bemerkungen zur I-Topikalisierung', *Sprache und Pragmatik 41*: 1–48.

JAYASEELAN, K. A. (1990). 'Incomplete VP Deletion and Gapping', *Linguistic Analysis 20*: 64–81.

JESPERSON, O. (1917). *Negation in English and Other Languages.* Copenhagen: Det Kgl. Danske Videnskabernes Selskab.

JOHANNESSEN, J. B. (1998). *Coordination.* New York and Oxford: Oxford University Press.

JOHNSON, K. (1988). 'Verb Raising and *Have*', *McGill Working Papers in Linguistics: Special Issue on Comparative German Syntax*, 156–67.

—— (1994). 'Bridging the Gap', Ms. University of Massachusetts at Amherst.

—— (1996/2003). *In Search of the English Middle Field.* Ms. University of Massachusetts at Amherst.

—— (2000). 'Few Dogs Eat Whiskas or Cats Alpo', in K. Kusumoto and E. Villalta (eds), *UMOP 23: Issues in Semantics and its Interface*, 59–82.

—— (2006). 'Gapping is not (VP) Ellipsis,' Ms. University of Massachusetts at Amherst.

JUNG, I. (1984). *Grammatik des Paez. Ein Abriß.* Unpublished PhD book. University of Osnabrück.

KADMON, N. and F. LANDMAN (1993). 'Any', *Linguistics and Philosophy* 16: 353–422.

KARTTUNEN, L. (1977). 'Syntax and Semantics of Questions', *Linguistics and Philosophy* 1: 3–44.

—— and S. PETERS (1979). 'Conventional Implicature', in C. K. Oh and D. Dinneen (eds), *Syntax and Semantics 11: Presupposition.* New York: Academic Press, 1–56.

KATO, Y. (2000). 'Interpretive Asymmetries of Negation', in L. R. Horn and Y. Kato (eds), *Negation, and Polarity: Syntactic and Semantic Perspectives.* Oxford: Oxford University Press, 21–61.

KAY, P. (1990). 'Even', *Linguistics and Philosophy* 13: 59–111.

KAYNE, R. S. (1984). *Connectedness and Binary Branching.* Dordrecht: Foris.

—— (1989a). 'Notes on English Agreement', *CIEFL Bulletin* 1: 40–67.

—— (1989b). 'Null Subjects and Clitic Climbing', in O. Jaeggli and K. Safir (eds), *The Null Subject Parameter.* Dordrecht: Reidel, 239–61.

—— (1994). *The Antisymmetry of Syntax.* Cambridge, MA: MIT Press.

—— (1998). 'Overt vs. Covert Movement', *Syntax* 1: 128–91.

KEENAN, E. (1972). 'On Semantically Based Grammar', *Linguistic Inquiry* 3: 413–61.

KEHLER, A. S. (1996). 'Coherence and the Coordinate Structure Constraint', in J. Johnson, M. L. Juge, and J. L. Moxley (eds), *Proceedings of the 22nd Annual Meeting of the Berkeley Linguistics Society.* Berkeley, CA, 220–31.

—— (2000). 'Coherence and the Resolution of Ellipsis', *Linguistics and Philosophy* 23: 533–75.

—— (2002). *Coherence, Reference, and the Theory of Grammar.* Stanford, CA: CSLI Publications.

KEMPSON, R., W. MEYER-VIOL, and D. GABBAY (1999). '*VP Ellipsis: Toward a Dynamic, Structural Account*', in S. Lappin and E. Benmamoun (eds), *Fragments. Studies in Ellipsis and Gapping.* Oxford: Oxford University Press, 227–90.

KENSTOWICZ, M. (ed.) (2001). *Ken Hale: A Life in Language.* Cambridge, MA: MIT Press.

KIM, D.-B. (1991). 'Metalinguistic Negation, Neg Raising, and Nun in Korean', *Papers from the 27th Regional Meeting of the Chicago Linguistic Society 2: The parasession on negation*, 125–39.

KIM, J.-B. and I. SAG (2002). 'Negation without Head-Movement', *Natural Language, and Linguistic Theory 20*: 339–412.

KIM, J.-S. (1997). *Syntactic Focus Movement and Ellipsis: A Minimalist Approach.* PhD thesis. University of Connecticut.

KISS, K. É. (1987). *Configuationality in Hungarian.* Budapest: Akadémiai Kiadó.

KITAGAWA, Y. (1986). *Subjects in Japanese and English.* PhD book. University of Massachussets.

KITIS, E. (2000). 'Connectives and Frame Theory: The Case of Hypotextual Antinomial "And" ', *Pragmatics and Cognition 8*: 357–409.

KLEIN, W. (1993). 'Ellipse', J. Jacobs, A. von Stechow, W. Sternefeld, and T. Vennemann (eds), *Syntax. Ein internationales Handbuch zeitgenössischer Forschung.* 1. Halbband. Berlin: Walter de Gruyter, 763–99.

—— (1994). *Time in Language.* London, New York: Routledge.

—— (1998). 'Assertion and Finiteness', in N. Dittmar and Z. Penner (eds), *Issues in the Theory of Language Acquisition. Essays in Honor of Jürgen Weissenborn.* Bern: Lang, 225–45.

—— and H. HENDRIKS (1995). 'Assertion Marking, Temporal Particles, and Resultative Verb Constructions in Chinese', Ms. Nijmegen: MPI.

KLIMA, E. (1964). 'Negation in English', in J. A. Fodor and J. J. Katz (eds), *The Structure of Language.* New York: Prentice Hall, 246–323.

KOENIG, J.-P. and B. BENNDORF (1998). 'Meaning and Context: German *Aber* and *Sondern*', in J.-P. Koenig (ed.), *Discourse and Cognition. Bridging the Gap.* Stanford, CA: CSLI Publications, 365–86.

KOIZUMMI, M. (1994). 'Layered Specifiers', in M. Gonzàlez (ed.), *Proceedings of NELS 24*: 255–69.

KOLB, H.-P. and C. THIERSCH (1991). 'Levels and Empty Categories in a Principles and Parameters Approach to Parsing', in H. Haider and K. Netter (eds), *Representation and Derivation in the Theory of Grammar.* Dordrecht: Kluwer, 251–302.

KÖNIG, E. (1985). 'Where Do Concessives Come From? On the Development of Concessive Connectives', in F. Fisiak (ed.), *Historical Semantics: Historical Word Formation.* Berlin: de Gruyter, 263–82.

KOOPMAN H. and D. SPORTICHE (1991). 'The Position of Subjects', *Lingua 85*: 211–58.

—— and A. SZABOCSI (2000). *Verbal Complexes.* Cambridge: MIT Press.

KORNFILT, J. (2000). *Directionality of Identical Verb Deletion in Turkish Coordination.* Jorge Hankamer WebFest. http://ling.ucsc.edu/Jorge

KOUTSOUDAS, A. (1971). 'Gapping, Conjunction Reduction, and Coordinate Deletion', *Foundations of Language 7*: 337–86.

KRATZER, A. (1978). *Semantik der Rede.* Königstein: Scriptor.

KRATZER, A. (1995). 'Stage-Level and Individual-Level Predicates', in G. Carlson and J. Pelletier (eds), *The Generic Book*. Chicago: Chicago University Press, 125–75.

——(1996). 'Severing the External Argument from its Verb', in J. Rooryck and L. Zaring (eds), *Phrase Structure and the Lexicon*. Dordrecht: Kluwer, 109–37.

KRIFKA, M. (1992). 'A Framework for Focus-Sensitive Quantification', *Proceedings of SALT II. Working Papers in Linguistics, 40*. Ohio State University, Columbus, 215–36.

——(1995). 'The Semantics and Pragmatics of Polarity Items', *Linguistic Analysis 25*: 209–57.

——(1997). 'Focus and/or Context: A Second Look at Second Occurrence Expressions', in H. Kamp and B. Partee (eds), *Context Dependence in the Analysis of Linguistic Meaning*. Proceedings of the Workshops in Prague, February 1995; Bad Teinach, May 1995.

——(1998). 'Scope Inversion under the Rise-Fall Contour in German', *Linguistic Inquiry 29*: 75–112.

——(1999). 'Additive Particles under Stress', *Proceedings of SALT 8*, Cornell University. Ithaca, NY: CLC Publications.

——(2004). 'Sprechakte und Satztypen'. Lecture Notes. Berlin: Humboldt-University Berlin.

——(2006). 'Association with Focus Phrases', in V. Molnar and S. Winkler (eds), *The Architecture of Focus*. Berlin: Mouton de Gruyter, 105–36.

KROCH, A. S. (1979). *The Semantics of Scope in English*. New York: Garland Publications.

KRUISINGA, E. (1931). *A Handbook of Present-Day English*, vol. 5. *English Accidence and Syntax I*. Groningen: P. Noordhoff.

KUNO, S. (1976). 'Gapping: A Functional Analysis', *Linguistic Inquiry 7*: 300–18.

——(1978). 'Japanese: A Characteristic OV Language', in W. P. Lehmann (ed.), *Syntactic Typology*. Austin: University of Texas Press, 57–138.

——(1997). *Binding Theory and the Minimalist Program*. Ms. Cambridge, MA: Harvard University.

KURODA, S.-Y. (1977). 'Description of Presuppositional Phenomena from a Non-Presuppositionist Point of View', *Lingvisticae Investigationes 1*: 63–162.

LADD, R. D. (1981). 'A First Look at the Semantics and Pragmatics of Negative Questions and Tag Questions', *Papers from the Seventeenth Regional Meeting of the Chicago Linguistic Society*, 164–71.

——(1996). *Intonational Phonology* Cambridge: Cambridge University Press.

LADUSAW, W. (1980). *Polarity Sensitivity as Inherent Scope Relations*. New York: Garland Publications.

——(1996). 'Negation and Polarity Items', in S. Lappin (ed.), *The Handbook of Contemporary Semantic Theory*. Oxford: Blackwell, 321–41.

LAHIRI, U. (1998). 'Focus and Negative Polarity in Hindi', *Natural Language Semantics 6*: 57–123.

LAKA, M. I. (1990). *Negation in Syntax: On the Nature of Functional Categories and Projections*. PhD book. Cambridge, MA: MIT.

LAKOFF, R. (1971). 'If's, And's and But's about Conjunction', in C. J. Fillmore, and D. T. Langendoen (eds), *Studies in Linguistic Semantics*. New York: Holt, Rinehart, and Winston, 114–49.

LAMBRECHT, K. (1990). 'What, Me Worry?'—"Mad Magazine" Sentences Revisited', *Proceedings of the Sixteenth Annual Meeting of the Berkeley Linguistics Society*. Berkeley: University of California, 215–28.

LANDAU, I. (2000). *Elements of Control: Structure and Meaning in Infinitival Constructions*. Dordrecht: Kluwer.

—— (2006). 'Chain Resolution in Hebrew V(P)-fronting', *Syntax 9*: 32–66.

LANG, E. (1977). *Semantik der Koordinativen Verknüpfung*. Berlin: Akademie Verlag.

—— (1984). *The Semantics of Coordination*. Amsterdam: Benjamins.

—— (1991). 'Koordinierende Konjunktionen', in A. von Stechow and D. Wunderlich (eds), *Semantik. Ein internationales Handbuch zeitgenössischer Forschung*. Berlin: de Gruyter, 597–623.

—— (2001). 'Kontrastive vs. Implikativ I: Interpretationseffekte intonatorischer Distinktionen bei Koordination', *Linguistische Arbeitsberichte 77*: 113–38.

—— (2002). 'Kontrastiv vs. implikativ II: Interpretationseffekte einer intonatorischen Distinktion bei elliptischen Sprichwörtern', *Linguistische Arbeitsberichte 79*: 187–212.

—— (2003). 'Adversative Connectors on Distinct Levels of Discourse: A Re-Examination of Eve Sweetser's Three-Level Approach', in B. Kortmann and E. Couper-Kuhlen (eds), *Cognitive and Discourse Perspectives on Cause, Condition, Concession, and Contrast*. Berlin, New York: de Gruyter.

—— (2004). 'Schnittstellen bei der Konnektoren-Beschreibung', in E. Breindl *et al.* (eds), *Brücken schlagen*. Berlin: de Gruyter.

—— and M. ADAMÍKOVA (2007). 'The lexical content of connectors and its interplay with intonation. An interim balance on sentential connection in discourse', in A. Späth (ed.), *Interfaces and Interface Conditions*. Berlin: de Gruyter, 199–32.

—— and C. UMBACH (2002). 'Kontrast in der Grammatik: spezifische Realisierungen und übergreifender Konnex', *Linguistische Arbeitsberichte 79*: 145–86.

LARSON, R. (1990). 'Double Objects Revisited: Reply to Jackendoff', *Linguistic Inquiry 21*: 589–632.

LASNIK, H. (1972). *Analyses of Negation in English*, PhD thesis. Cambridge, MA: MIT.

—— (1995). 'Verbal Morphology: Syntactic Structures Meets the Minimalist Program', in P. Kempchinsky and H. Campos (eds), *Evolution and Revolution in Linguistic Theory: Essays in Honor of Carlos Otero*. Washington, DC: Georgetown University Press, 251–75.

—— (1998). 'Some Reconstruction Riddles', *University of Pennsylvania Working Papers in Linguistics 5*: 83–98.

LASSER, I. (1997). *Finiteness in Adult and Child German*. PhD book. City University of New York. Published in MPI Series in Psycholinguistics.

LAW, P. (1993). *On the Base Position of Wh-Adjuncts and Extruction*. Paper presented at the 67th Annual Meeting of the Linguistic Society of America. Los Angeles.

LEBEAUX, D. (1988). *Language Acquisition and the Form of the Grammar.* PhD book. University of Massachusetts at Amherst.

—— (1991). 'Relative Clauses, Licensing and the Nature of the Derivation', in S. Rothstein (ed.), *Syntax and Semantics 25: Perspectives on phrase structure.* New York: Academic Press, 209–39.

—— (2000). *Language Acquisition and the Form of the Grammar.* Amsterdam: Benjamins.

LEDGEWAY, A. (1998). 'Variation in the Romance Infinitive: The Case of the Southern Calabrian Inflected Infinitive', *Transactions of the Philological Society 96*: 1–61.

LEE, H.-Y. (1998). *Ellipsen in Satzkoordinationen: Syntaktische und semantische Untersuchungen in einer unifikationsbasierten Grammatik.* Frankfurt: Peter Lang.

LEHMANN, W. P. (1974). *Proto-Indo-European Syntax.* London: Austin.

LERNER, J.-Y. and W. STERNEFELD (1984). 'Zum Skopus der Negation im komplexen Satz des Deutschen', *Zeitschrift für Sprachwissenschaft 3*: 159–202.

LEVIN, N. S. and E. F. PRINCE (1986). 'Gapping and Causal Implicature', *Papers in Linguistics 19*: 351–64.

LI, M. D. (1988). *Anaphoric Structures of Chinese.* Student Book Co., Ltd., Taipei.

LI, Y.-H. A. (1998). 'Argument Determiner Phrases and Number Phrase', *Linguistic Inquiry 29*: 693–702.

LIN, V. (2001). 'A Way to Undo A-Movement', in K. Megerdoomian and L. A. Bar-el (eds), *WCCFL 20 Proceedings.* Somerville, MA: Cascadilla Press, 358–71.

—— (2002). *Coordination and Sharing at the Interfaces.* PhD thesis. Cambridge, MA: MIT.

LINEBARGER, M. C. (1987). 'Negative Polarity and Grammatical Representation', *Linguistics and Philosophy 10*: 325–87.

—— (1991). 'Negative Polarity as Linguistic Evidence', *Papers from the 27th Regional Meeting of the Chicago Linguistic Society 2: The parasession on negation*, 165–88.

LOBECK, A. (1995). *Ellipsis.* Oxford: Oxford University Press.

LÖBNER, S. (1990). *Wahr neben falsch. Duale Operatoren als die Quantoren natürlicher Sprache.* Tübingen: Niemeyer.

LOHNSTEIN, H. (2000). *Satzmodus—kompositionell. Zur Parametrisierung der Modusphrase im Deutschen.* Berlin: Akademie Verlag.

—— and S. TRISSLER (eds) (2004). *The Syntax and Semantics of the Left Periphery.* Berlin: de Gruyter.

—— and A. WÖLLSTEIN-LEISTEN (2001). *Status als Aspektmarker.* Ms. University of Cologne.

LÓPEZ, L. (1995). *Polarity and Predicate Anaphora.* PhD book. Ithaca, NY: Cornell University.

—— and S. WINKLER (2003). 'Variation at the Syntax–Semantics Interface: Evidence from Gapping', in K. Schwabe and S. Winkler (eds), *The Interfaces: Deriving and Interpreting Omitted Structures.* Amsterdam: John Benjamins, 227–48.

LÖTSCHER, A. (1983). *Satzakzent und Funktionale Satzperspektive im Deutschen.* Tübingen: Niemeyer.

LYCAN, W. (1991). '*Even* and *Even If*', *Linguistics and Philosophy 14*: 115–50.

Maas, U. (2004). ' "Finite" and "Nonfinite" from a Typological Perspective', *Linguistics 42*: 359–85.

McCawley, J. (1982). 'Parentheticals and Discontinuous Constituent Structure', *Linguistic Inquiry 13*: 91–105.

—— (1991). 'Replace Negation and Metalinguistic Negation', *Papers from the 27th Regional Meeting of the Chicago Linguistic Society 2: The parasession on negation*, 189–206.

McDowell, J. P. (1987). *Assertion and Modality*. PhD dissertation, University of Southern California.

Mahajan, A. (1990). 'LF Conditions on Negative Polarity Licensing', *Lingua 80*: 333–48.

Malchukov, A. L. (2004). 'Towards a Semantic Typology of Adversative and Contrastive Marking', *Journal of Semantics 21*: 177–98.

Mann, W. and S. Thompson (1988). 'Rhetorical Structure Theory: Towards a Functional Theory of Text Organization', *TEXT 8(2)*: 243–81.

Marantz, A. (1984). *On the Nature of Grammatical Relations*. Cambridge, MA: MIT Press.

Marušič, F. and R. Žaucer (2006). 'On the Intensional Feel-Like Construction in Slovenian', *Natural Language & Linguistic Theory 24*: 1093–159.

Meinunger, A. (2004). 'Verb Position, Verbal Mood, and the Anchoring (Potential) of Sentences', in H. Lohnstein and S. Trissler (eds), *The Syntax and Semantics of the Left Periphery*. Berlin: de Gruyter, 312–42.

Merchant, J. (2001). *The Syntax of Silence. Sluicing, Islands, and the Theory of Ellipsis*. Oxford: Oxford University Press.

—— (2004). 'Fragments and Ellipsis', *Linguistics and Philosophy 27*: 661–738.

—— (2006). 'Why No(t)?' *Style 20*: 20–3. Special issue edited by W. Salmon and C. Kalpakidis as a Festschrift for Haj Ross.

—— (2008). 'An Asymmetry in Voice Mismatches in VP-Ellipsis and Pseudogapping', *Linguistic Inquiry 39*: 169–79.

Merin, A. (1996). *Die Relevanz der Relevanz. Fallstudie zur formalen Semantik der englischen Konjunktion* but. Unpublished Habilitation Book. Stuttgart University.

Moltmann, F. (1992a). *Coordination and Comparatives*. PhD book. Cambridge, MA: MIT.

—— (1992b). 'On the Interpretation of Three-Dimensional Trees', *Proceedings of SALT II. Working Papers in Linguistics 40*. Ohio State University, Columbus, 261–82.

Moritz, L. and D. Valois (1994). 'Pied-Piping and Specifier-Head Agreement', *Linguistic Inquiry 25*: 667–707.

Muadz, H. (1991). *A Planar Theory of Coordination*. PhD thesis. Tucson: University of Arizona.

Müller, G. and W. Sternefeld (1993). 'Improper Movement and Unambiguous Binding', *Linguistic Inquiry 24*: 461–507.

Munn, A. B. (1987). 'Coordinate Structure and X-bar Theory', *McGill Working Papers in Linguistics 4*: 121–40.

—— (1993). *Topics in the Syntax and Semantics of Coordinate Structures*. PhD thesis. University of Maryland.

MUNN, A. B. (1999). 'First Conjunct Agreement: Against a Clausal Analysis', *Linguistic Inquiry 30*: 643–68.

MURASUGI, K. (1992). 'Locative/Temporal vs. Manner/Reason Phrases', *Papers in English Linguistics and Literature*. Department of English Literature, Kinjo Gakuin University, 153–70.

MUSAN, R. (1997). *On the Temporal Interpretation of Noun Phrases*. New York: Garland.

NEIJT, A. (1979). *Gapping*. Dordrecht: Foris.

NISSENBAUM, J. (1998). 'Movement and Derived Predicates: Evidence from Parasitic Gaps', *MIT Working Papers in Linguistics 25*: 247–95.

—— (2000). 'Covert Movement and Parasitic Gaps', *Proceedings of NELS 30*. GLSA, University of Massachusetts at Amherst.

NUNES, J. (1995). *The Copy Theory of Movement and Linearization of Chains in the Minimalist Program*. PhD Dissertation. University of Maryland. College Park.

—— (2000). 'Erasing Erasure', *Revista de Documentação de Estudos em Lingüística Teórica e Aplicada (D.E.L.T.A.) 16*: 415–29.

—— (2001). 'Sideward Movement', *Linguistic Inquiry 32*: 303–44.

—— (2004). *Linearization of Chains and Sideward Movement*. Cambridge: MIT Press.

—— and J. URIAGEREKA (2000). 'Cyclicity and Extraction Domains', *Syntax 3*: 20–43.

OCHI, M. (1999). 'Multiple Spell-Out and PF Adjacency', *Proceedings of the North Eastern Linguistic Society, 29*. University of Massachusetts at Amherst.

OEHRLE, R. T. (1987). 'Booelan Properties in the Analysis of Gapping', in G. J. Huck and A. E. (eds), *Syntax and Semantics 20. Discontinuous Constituency*. San Diego, CA: Academic Press, 203–40.

OUHALLA, J. (1990). 'Sentential Negation, Relativized Minimality and the Aspectual Status of Auxiliaries', *Linguistic Review 7*: 183–231.

OVERSTEEGEN, E. (1997). 'On the Pragmatic Nature of Causal and Contrastive Connectives', *Discourse Processes 24*: 51–85.

PARTEE, B. (1973). 'Some Structural Analogies Between Tenses and Pronouns in English', *Journal of Philosophy 70*: 601–9.

PAUL, W. (1999). 'Verb Gapping in Chinese: A Case of Verb Raising', *Lingua 107*: 207–26.

PAYNE, J. R. (1985). 'Negation', in T. Shopen (ed.), *Language Typology and Syntactic Description 1*. Cambridge: Cambridge Univesity Press, 197–242.

PENKA, D. and A. VON STECHOW (2001). 'Negative Indefinita unter Modalverben', in R. Müller and M. Reis (eds), *Modalität und Modalverben im Deutschen. Linguistische Berichte, Sonderheft 9*. Hamburg: Helmut Buske Verlag, 263–86.

PESETSKY, D. (1982). *Paths and Categories*. PhD thesis. Cambridge, MA: MIT.

—— (1992). *Zero Syntax*. Cambridge: MIT Press.

—— (1998). 'Some Optimality Principles of Sentence Pronunciation', in P. Barbosa, D. Fox, P. Hagstrom, M. McGinnis, and D. Pesetsky (eds), *Is the Best Good Enough?* Cambridge, MA: MIT Press.

—— and E. TORREGO (2000). 'T-to-C Movement: Causes and Consequences', in M. Kenstowicz (ed.), *Ken Hale: a Life in Language*. Cambridge, MA: MIT Press, 355–426.

PHILIPPAKI-WARBURTON, I. (1987). 'The Theory of Empty Categories and the Pro-Drop Parameter in Modern Greek', *Journal of Linguistics 32*: 289–318.

PIERREHUMBERT, J. (1980). *A Phonology and Phonetics of English Intonation*. PhD thesis. Cambridge, MA: MIT.

PIÑON, C. J. (1991). 'Presupposition and the Syntax of Negation in Hungarian', *Papers from the 27th Regional Meeting of the Chicago Linguistic Society 2: The parasession on negation*: 246–62.

PLATZACK, C. and I. ROSENGREN (1998). 'On the Subject of Imperatives: a Minimalist Account of the Imperative Clause', *The Journal of Comparative Germanic Linguistics 1*: 177–224.

POLLOCK, J.-Y. (1989). 'Verb Movement, Universal Grammar, and the Structure of IP', *Linguistic Inquiry 20*: 365–424.

—— (1997). 'Notes on Clausal Structure', in L. Haegeman (ed.), *Elements of Grammar. Handbook of Generative Syntax*. Dordrecht: Kluwer, 237–80.

PORTNER, P. (1997). 'The Semantics of Mood, Complementation, and Conversational Force', *Natural Language Semantics 5*: 167–212.

—— and K. YABUSHITA (2001). 'The Semantics and Pragmatics of Topic Phrases', *Linguistics and Philosophy 21*: 117–57.

POSTAL, P. (1974). *On Raising*. Cambridge, MA: MIT Press.

—— (1997). *Strong Crossover Violations and Binding Principles*. Paper presented at the ESCOL '97, Yale University.

POTSDAM, E. (1995). 'Phrase Structure of the English Imperative', *The Proceedings of the Sixth Annual Meeting of the Formal Linguistics Society of Midamerica*. Bloomington: Indiana University Linguistics Club Publications, 143–54.

—— (1997). 'NegP and Subjunctive Complements in English', *Linguistic Inquiry 28*: 533–41.

—— (1998). *Syntactic Issues in the English Imperative*. New York: Garland Publications.

PRISCIAN (1981). 'De institutione Grammaticae' in H. Keil (ed.), *Grammatici Latini*. Vol. II. Hildesheim: Olms.

PROGOVAC, L. (1994). *Negative and Positive Polarity: A Binding Approach*. Cambridge: Cambridge University Press.

—— (1997). 'Slavic and the Structure for Coordination', in M. Lindseth, and S. Franks (eds), *Proceedings of 1996 Formal Approaches to Slavic Linguistics (FASL)*. Ann Arbor: Michigan Slavic Publications, 207–24.

—— (1998). 'Structure for Coordination', *Glot International 3(7)*: 3–6 (Part I) and *Glot International 3(8)*: 3–9 (Part II).

PUSCH, L. F. (1976). 'Über den Unterschied zwischen *aber* und *sondern* oder Die Kunst des Widerspruchs', in R. Kern (ed.), *Löwen und Sprachtiger*, 127–43.

QUIRK, R., S. GREENBAUM, G. LEECH, and J. SVARTVIK (1985). *A Comprehensive Grammar of the English Language*. London: Longman.

RAMCHAND, G. (2004). 'Two Types of Negation in Bengali', in V. Dayal and A. Mahajan (eds), *Clause Structure in South Asian Languages*. Dordrecht: Kluwer.

RAPOSO, E. (1987). 'Case Theory and Infl-to-Comp: the Inflected Infinitive in European Portuguese', *Linguistic Inquiry 18*: 85–109.

—— (1989). 'Prepositional Infinitival Constructions in European Portuguese', in O. Jaeggli and K. J. Safir (eds), *The Null Subject Parameter*. Dordrecht: Kluwer, 277–305.

REICHENBACH, H. (1947). *Elements of Symbolic Logic*. Reprint, New York: Free Press, 1966.

REINHART, T. (1981). 'Pragmatics and Linguistics. An Analysis of Sentence Topics', *Philosophica 27*, 53–94.

—— (1991). 'Elliptic Conjunctions—Non-Quantificational LF', in A. Kasher (ed.), *The Chomskian Turn*. Oxford: Blackwell, 360–84.

—— (1998). '*Wh*-in-Situ in the Framework of the Minimalist Program', *Natural Language Semantics, 6*: 29–56.

REIS, M. (1977). *Präsuppositionen und Syntax*. Tübingen: Niemeyer.

—— (2000). 'On the Parenthetical Features of German Was...W-Constructions and How to Account for Them', in U. Lutz, G. Müller, and A. von Stechow (eds), *Wh- Scope Marking*. Amsterdam: Benjamins, 359–407.

—— (2002). 'On the Form and Interpretation of German Wh-Infinitives', *Journal of Germanic Linguistics 15*: 155–201.

—— (2003). *Wie fängt der deutsche Satz an?* Talk given at the Humboldt University Berlin, June.

REPP, S. (2005). 'Interpreting Ellipsis. *The Changeable Presence of the Negation in Gapping*,' PhD thesis. Berlin: Humboldt University.

—— (2006). '¬(A&B). Gapping, Negation and Speech Act Operators', *Research on Language and Computation 4*: 397–423. Special Issue on Ellipsis edited by J. Spenader and P. Hendriks.

—— (to appear). 'When the Negative Goes Missing: The Role of the Information Structure in Gapping Coordinations with *but*,' in A. Steube (ed.), *The Discourse Potential of Underspecified Structures: Event Structure and Information Structure*. Berlin: Walter de Gruyter.

RIEBER, S. (1997). 'Conventional Implicatures as Tacit Performatives', *Linguistics and Philosophy 20*: 51–72.

RIVERO, M.-L. (1994). 'Negation, Imperatives and Wackernagel Effects', *Rivista di Linguistica, 6*: 91–118.

—— and A. TERZI (1995). 'Imperatives, V-Movement and Logical Mood', *Journal of Linguistics 31*, 301–32.

RIZZI, L. (1990). *Relativized Minimality*. Cambridge, MA: MIT Press.

—— (1991). 'Residual Verb Second and the Wh Criterion. *Technical Reports in Formal and Computational Linguistics 2*. Faculté des Lettres, Université de Genève. [Republished in A. Belletti and L. Rizzi (eds) (1995). *Parameters and Functional Heads: Essays in Comparative Syntax*. Oxford: Oxford University Press. 63–90.]

—— (1994). 'Argument/Adjunct (A)Symmetries', in G. Cinque, J. Koster, J.-Y. Pollock, L. Rizzi, and R. Zanuttini (eds), *Paths towards Universal Grammar. Studies in Honor of Richard S. Kayne*. Washington, DC: Georgetown University Press, 361–76.

—— (1997). 'The Fine Structure of the Left Periphery', in L. Haegeman (ed.), *Elements of Grammar: Handbook in Generative Syntax*. Kluwer: Dordrecht, 169–337.

ROBERTS, C. (1996). 'Information Structure in Discourse: Towards an Integrated Formal Theory of Pragmatics', in J. H. Yoon and A. Kathol (eds), *OSU Working Papers in Linguistics 49: Papers in Semantics*, 91–136.

ROBERTS, I. (1985). 'Agreement Parameters and the Development of English Modal Auxiliaries', *Natural Language and Linguistic Theory 3*: 21–58.

—— (2004). 'The C-System in Brythonic Celtic Languages, V2, and the EPP', in L. Rizzi (ed.), *The Structure of CP and IP. The Cartography of Syntactic Structures*, Vol. 2. Oxford: Oxford University Press, 251–97.

—— and A. ROUSSOU (1998). 'The EPP as a Condition on the Tense Dependency', in P. Svenonius (ed.), *Subjects, Expletives, and the EPP*. Oxford: Oxford University Press, 125–55.

ROMERO, M. and C.-H. HAN (2004). 'On Negative Yes/No Questions', *Linguistics and Philosophy 27*: 609–58.

ROOTH, M. (1985). *Association with Focus*. Ph.D. book. University of Massachusetts at Amherst.

—— (1992). 'A Theory of Focus Interpretation', *Natural Language Semantics 1*: 75–116.

ROSS, J. R. (1969). 'Auxiliaries as Main Verbs', in W. Todd (ed.), *Studies in Philosophical Linguistics*. Series one. Evanston, OH: Great Expectations Press, 77–102.

—— (1970). 'Gapping and the Order of Constituents', in M. Bierwisch and K. Heidolph (eds), *Progress in Linguistics*. The Hague: Mouton, 249–59.

ROUSSOU, A. (2001). 'Control and Raising', in A. Ralli and M-L Rivero (eds), *Comparative Syntax of Balkan Languages*. Oxford: Oxford University Press, 74–104.

ROWLETT, P. (1998). *Sentential Negation in French*. Oxford: Oxford University Press.

RUDOLPH, E. (1996). *Contrast: Adversative and Concessive Relations and Their Expressions in English, German, Spanish, Portuguese on Sentence and Text Level*. Berlin: de Gruyter.

RULLMANN, H. (1995). *Maximality in the Semantics of Wh-constructions*. PhD thesis. University of Massachusetts at Amherst.

—— (1997). 'Even, Polarity, and Scope'. *Papers in Experimental and Theoretical Linguistics 4*: 40–64.

—— (1998). 'Book Review. Liliane Haegeman, The Syntax of Negation', *The Journal of Comparative Germanic Linguistics 1*: 157–76.

RUPP, L. (2003). *The Syntax of Imperatives in English and Germanic: Word Order Variation in the Minimalist Framework*. Basingstoke: Palgrave Macmillan.

SABEL, J. (1998). *Principles and Parameters of Wh-Movement*. Habilitation thesis. University of Frankfurt.

256   *References*

Sæbø, K. J. (2003). 'Presuppposition and Contrast: German *Aber* as a Topic Particle', in M. Weisgerber (ed.), *Proceedings of Sinn und Bedeutung 7.* Arbeitspapier Nr. 114, FB Sprachwissenschaft Universität Konstanz, 257–71.

Safir, K. (1999). 'Vehicle Change and Reconstruction in A-Bar-Chains', *Linguistic Inquiry 30*: 587–620.

Sag, I. (1976). *Deletion and Logical Form.* PhD Thesis. Cambridge, MA: MIT.

—— (1978). 'Floated Quantifiers, Adverbs, and Extraction Sites', *Linguistic Inquiry 9*: 146–50.

—— (1980). *Deletion and Logical Form.* New York: Garland Publishing.

—— (to appear). 'Rules and Exceptions in the English Auxiliary System', *Journal of Linguistics.*

—— G. Gazdar, T. Wasow, and S. Weisler (1985). 'Coordination and How to Distinguish Categories', *Natural Language and Linguistic Theory 3*: 117–71.

Saito, M. (1985). Some Asymmetries in Japanese and their Theoretical Consequences. PhD thesis. Cambridge, MA: MIT.

—— (1987). 'Three Notes On Syntactic Movement in Japanese', in T. Imai and M. Saito (eds), *Issues in Japanese Linguistics.* Dordrecht: Foris, 301–50.

Sauerland U. (2000). 'Obligatory Reconstruction and the Meaning of Traces', *Arbeitspapiere des SFB 340, Bericht Nr. 153.* Tübingen: Tübingen University.

—— and P. Elbourne (2002). 'Total Reconstruction, PF-Movement and Derivational Order', *Linguistic Inquiry 33*: 283–31.

Schachter, P. (1977). 'Constraints On Coordination', *Language 53*: 86–103.

Schmitt, B. M. (1997). *Lexical Access in the Production of Ellipsis and Pronouns.* PhD thesis. Nijmegen: MPI.

Schütze, C. T. (1997). *INFL in Child, and Adult Language: Agreement, Case and Licensing.* PhD book. Cambridge, MA: MIT.

Schwabe, K. (2000). 'Coordinative Ellipsis and Information Structure', in K. Schwabe and N. Zhang (eds), *Ellipsis in Conjunction.* Tübingen: Niemeyer, 247–69.

Schwarz, B. (2005). 'Scalar Additive Particles in Negative Contexts', *Natural Language Semantics 13*: 125–68.

Schwarzschild, R. (1997). *Why Some Foci Must Associate.* Ms. Rutgers University.

—— (1999). 'GIVENness, AvoidF and Other Constraints on the Placement of Accent', *Natural Language Semantics 7*: 141–77.

Searle, J. (1969). *Speech Acts.* Cambridge: Cambridge University Press.

—— and D. Vanderveken (1985). *Foundations of Illocutionary Logic.* Cambridge: Cambridge University Press.

Selkirk, E. (1984). *Phonology and Syntax: The Relation between Sound and Structure.* Cambridge, MA: MIT Press.

—— (1995). 'Sentence Prosody: Intonation, Stress, and Phrasing', in J. Goldsmith (ed.), *Handbook of Phonological Theory.* Oxford: Blackwell, 550–69.

Seuren, P. M. A. (1988). 'Presupposition and Negation', *Journal of Semantics 6*: 175–226.

SHAER, B. and W. FREY (2004). 'English and German Left-Peripheral Elements', Proceedings of the Workshop *Dislocated elements in discourse: Syntactic, semantic and pragmatic perspectives.* ZAS Berlin, 465–503.

SIEGEL, M. E. A. (1984). 'Gapping and Interpretation', *Linguistic Inquiry* 15: 523–30.

—— (1987). 'Compositionality, Case, and the Scope of Auxiliaries', *Linguistics and Philosophy* 10: 53–76.

SOHN, K.-W. (1994). 'On Gapping and Right Node Raising', in Y.-S. Kim *et al.*, *Explorations in Generative Grammar.* Seoul: Hankuk Publishing Co., 589–611.

SPERBER, D. and D. WILSON (1986). *Relevance: Communication and Cognition.* Oxford: Blackwell.

SPROUSE, J. (2003). 'The Presence of Negation and the Absence of Neg°', Ms. University of Maryland.

STEEDMAN, M. J. (1990). 'Gapping as Constituent Coordination', *Linguistics and Philosophy* 13: 207–63.

STENIUS, E. (1967). 'Mood and Language Game', *Synthese* 17: 254–74.

STEPANOV, A. V. (2001). *Cyclic Domains in Syntactic Theory.* PhD book. University of Connecticut.

STILLINGS, J. T. (1975). 'The Formulation of Gapping in English as Evidence for Variable Types in Syntactic Transformations', *Linguistic Analysis* 1: 247–73.

STOWELL, T. (1981). *Origins of Phrase Structure.* PhD book. Cambridge, MA: MIT.

—— (1982). 'The Tense of Infinitives', *Linguistic Inquiry* 13: 561–70.

—— (1996). 'The Phrase Structure of Tense', in J. Rooryck and L. Zaring (eds), *Phrase Structure and the Lexicon.* Dordrecht: Kluwer, 277–91.

SVENONIUS, P. (1992). 'The Extended Projection of N: Identifying the Head of the Noun Phrase', *Working Papers in Scandinavian Syntax* 49: 95–121.

SZABOLCSI, A. (2004). 'Positive polarity—negative polarity', *Natural Language and Linguistic Theory.* 22: 409–52.

—— and F. ZWARTS (1993). 'Weak Islands and an Algebraic Semantics for Scope Taking', *Natural Language Semantics* 1: 235–85.

TAGLICHT, J. (1984). *Message and Emphasis. On Focus and Scope in English.* London: Longman.

TAKANO, Y. (1995). 'Predicate Fronting and Internal Subjects', *Linguistic Inquiry* 26: 327–40.

TANG, S.-W. (2001). 'The (Non-)Existence of Gapping in Chinese and its Implications for the Theory of Gapping', *Journal of East Asian Linguistics* 10: 201–24.

TE VELDE, J. R. (2006). *Deriving Coordinate Symmetries. A Phase-Based Approach Integrating Select, Merge, Copy and Match.* Amsterdam: Benjamins.

THOMPSON, S. A. and A. MULAC (1991). 'The Discourse Conditions for the Use of the Complementizer that in Conversational English', *Journal of Pragmatics* 15: 237–51.

THRÁINSSON, H. and S. VIKNER (1995). 'Modals and Double Modals in the Scandinavian Languages', *Working Papers in Scandinavian Syntax* 55: 51–88.

TOVENA, L. (1998). *The Fine Structure of Polarity Sensitivity.* New York: Garland Publications.

Travis, L. de Mena (1984). *Parameters and Effects of Word Order Variation*. PhD book. Cambridge, MA: MIT.

Tsoulas, G. (1995). 'The Nature of the Subjunctive and the Formal Grammar of Obviation', in K. Zagone (ed.), *Grammatical Theory and Romance Languages*. Amsterdam: Benjamins, 293–306.

Uhmann, S. (1991). *Fokusphonologie. Eine Analyse deutsche Intonationskonturen im Rahmen der nicht-linearen Phonologie*. Tübingen: Niemeyer.

Umbach, C. (2001). 'Contrast and Contrastive topic', in I. Kruijf-Korbayová and M. Steedman (eds), *Information Structure, Discourse Structure and Discourse Semantics*, 2–13.

—— (2005). 'Contrast and Information Structure: A Focus-Based Analysis of *But*', *Linguistics 43*: 207–32.

Uriagereka, J. (1999). 'Multiple Spell-Out', in S. Epstein and N. Hornstein (eds), *Working Minimalism*. Cambridge, MA: MIT Press, 251–82.

van den Wyngærd, G. (1998). *Gapping, Verb Raising, and Small Clauses*. Ms. Katholieke Universiteit Brussel.

van der Auwera, J. (1985). 'Only If', *Logique et analyse 28*: 61–74.

van der Heijden, E. (1999). *Tussen Nevenschikking en Onderschikking. Een Onderzoek naar Verschillende Vormen van Verbinding in het Nederlands*. LOT. The Hague: Holland Academic Graphics.

van der Sandt, R. (1988). *Context and Presupposition*. London: Routledge and Kegan Paul.

—— (1991). 'Denial', *Papers from CLS, 27(2). The parasession on negation*, 331–44.

—— and E. Maier (2003). *Denials in Discourse*. Ms. University of Nijmegen.

van der Wouden, T. (1997). *Negative Contexts: Collocation, Polarity, and Multiple Negation*. London: Routledge.

van Kuppevelt, J. (1995). 'Discourse Structure, Topicality and Questioning', *Linguistics 31*: 109–47.

—— (1996). 'Inferring from Topics', *Linguistics and Philosophy 19*: 393–443.

van Oirsouw, R. (1987). *The Syntax of Coordination*. London: Croom Helm.

—— (1993). 'Coordination', in Jacobs, J., A. von Stechow, W. Sternefeld, and T. Vennemann (eds), *Syntax. Ein internationales Handbuch zeitgenössischer Forschung*. 1. Halbband. Berlin: Walter de Gruyter, 748–63.

van Riemsdijk, H. (1981). 'The Case of German Adjectives', in J. Pustejovsky and V. A. Burke (eds), *Markedness and Learnability*. University of Massachusetts Occasional Papers in Linguistics 6, 148–73.

Vanderveken, D. (1990). *Meaning and Speech Acts. Volume I: Principles of Language Use. Volume II: Formal Semantics of Success and Satisfaction*. Cambridge: Cambridge University Press.

Verkuyl, H. (2003). 'On the Semantics of Complementizers', in J. Koster and H. van Riemsdijk (eds), *Germania et alia. A Linguistic Webschrift for Hans den Besten*. http://www.let.rug.nl/~koster/DenBesten/contents.htm

VIKNER, S. (1995). *Verb Movement and Expletive Subjects in the Germanic Languages*. Oxford: Oxford University Press.

VON FINTEL, K. (1994). *Restrictions on Quantifier Domains*. PhD book. Cambridge, MA: MIT.

VON STECHOW, A. (1991a). 'Current Issues in the Theory of Focus', in A. von Stechow and D. Wunderlich (eds), *Semantik. Ein internationales Handbuch zeitgenössischer Forschung*. Berlin: de Gruyter, 804–25.

—— (1991b). 'Focusing and backgrounding operators', in W. Abraham (ed.), *Discourse Particles*. Amsterdam: Benjamins, 35–84.

—— (1992). *Intensionale Semantik—eingeführt anhand der Temporalität*. University of Konstanz. Fachgruppe Sprachwissenschaft, Arbeitspapier Nr. 40.

WASOW, T. (1979). *Anaphora in Generative Grammar*. Ghent: Story Scientia.

WEBELHUTH, G. (1992). *Principles and Parameters of Syntactic Saturation*. Oxford: Oxford University Press.

WECHSLER, S. (1990). 'Verb Second and Illocutionary Force in Swedish', in E. Engdahl, M. Reape, M. Mellor, and R. Cooper (eds), *Parametric Variation in Germanic and Romance. Edinburgh Working Papers in Cognitive* Science, 229–44.

—— (1991). 'Verb Second and Illocutionary Force', in K. Lefel and D. Bouchard (eds), *Views on Phrase Structure*. Dordrecht: Kluwer, 177–91.

WEIß, H. (2002). 'Three Types of Negation: A Case Study of Bavarian', *Syntactic Microvariation*: 305–32. www.meertens.knaw.nl/books/synmic

WESCHE, B. (1995). *Symmetric Coordination. An Alternative Theory of Phrase Structure*. Tübingen: Niemeyer.

WEUSTER, E. (1983). 'Nicht-eingebettete Satztypen mit Verb-Endstellung im Deutschen', in K. Olszok and E. Weuster (eds), *Zur Wortstellungsproblematik im Deutschen*. Tübingen: Narr, 7–88.

WIJNEN, F. (1997). 'Temporal Reference and Eventivity in Root Infinitives', *MIT Occasional Papers in Linguistics 12*: 1–25.

WILDER, C. (1994). 'Coordination, ATB and Ellipsis', in C. J. W. Zwart (ed.), *Minimalism and Kayne's Asymmetry Hypothesis. Groninger Arbeiten zur Germanistischen Linguistik 37*. Groningen: Rijksuniversiteit Groningen, 291–329.

—— (1995). 'Some Properties of Ellipsis in Coordination', *Geneva Generative Papers 2*: 23–61. Also in A. Alexiadou and T. A. Hall (eds), *Studies on Universal Grammar and Typological Variation*. Amsterdam: Benjamins, 59–107.

—— (1996). 'V2-Effekte: Wortstellungen und Ellipsen, in E. Lang (ed.), *Deutsch typologisch*. Berlin: de Gruyter, 142–80.

—— (1999). 'Right Node Raising and the LCA', in S. A. C. Bird, J. Haugen, and P. Norquest (eds), *WCCFL 18 Proceedings*. Somerville, MA: Cascadilla Press, 586–98.

WILKINSON, K. (1996). *The Scope of Even. Natural Language Semantics, 4*: 193–215.

WILLIAMS, E. (1977). 'Discourse and Logical Form', *Linguistic Inquiry 8*: 101–39.

—— (1978). 'Across-the-Board Rule Application', *Linguistic Inquiry 9*: 31–43.

—— (1997). 'Blocking and Anaphora', *Linguistic Inquiry 28*: 577–628.

WILSON, D. (1975). *Presuppositions and Non-Truth-Conditional Semantics*. New York: Academic Press.

WINKLER, S. (1997*a*) *Focus and Secondary Predication*. Berlin and New York: Mouton de Gruyter.

——(1997*b*). *Ellipsis and Information Structure in English and German: The Phonological Reduction Hypothesis*. Arbeitspapiere des SFB 340, Nr. 121.

——(2005). *Ellipsis and Focus in Generative Grammar*. Berlin: de Gruyter.

WINTER, Y. and M. RIMON (1994). 'Contrast and Implication in Natural Language', *Journal of Semantics* 11: 365–406.

WÖLLSTEIN, A. (2004). 'Complementizer Selection and the Properties of Complement Clauses in German', in H. Lohnstein and S. Trissler (eds), *The Syntax and Semantics of the Left Periphery*. Berlin: de Gruyter, 489–518.

WURMBRAND, S. (2001). *Infinitives. Restructuring and Clause Structure*. Berlin: Mouton de Gruyter.

YEOM, J. (1998). *A Presuppositional Analysis of Specific Indefinites*, New York: Garland.

YOSHIMURA, K. (to appear). 'Scope Theory vs. Polarity Theory: Analysis of Japanese Focus Particle *Sae*', *CLS 40*.

ZAEFFERER, D. (2001). 'Deconstructing a Classical Classification: A Typological Look at Searle's Concept of Illocution Type', *Revue Internationale de Philosophie 217*: 209–25.

ZANUTTINI, R. (1991). *Syntactic Properties of Sentential Negation: A Comparative Study of Romance Languages*. Ph.D. thesis. Philadelphia, University of Pennsylvania.

——(1994). 'Speculations on Negative Imperatives', *Rivista di Linguistica* 6: 119–41.

——(1996). 'On the Relevance of Tense for Sentential Negation', in A. Belletti and L. Rizzi (eds), *Parameters and Functional Heads: Essays in Comparative Syntax*. New York: Oxford University Press, 181–207.

——(1997). *Negation and Clausal Structure: A Comparative Study of Romance Languages*. Oxford: Oxford University Press.

——(2000). 'Sentential Negation', in M. Baltin and C. Collins (eds), *The Handbook of Contemporary Syntactic Theory*. Oxford: Blackwell, 511–35.

ZEIJLSTRA, H. H. (2004). *Sentential Negation and Negative Concord*. Utrecht: LOT Publications.

——(2006). 'Don't Negate Imperatives! Imperatives and the Semantics of Negative Markers', in C. Ebert and C. Endriss (eds), *Proceedings of Sinn und Bedeutung 10*. Berlin: ZAS, 453–68.

ZHANG, N. (1997). 'Verb Gapping in Chinese', *ZAS Papers in Linguistics 9*: 145–64.

——(2000). 'On Chinese Verbless Constructions', in K. Schwabe and N. Zhang (eds), *Ellipsis in Conjunction*. Tübingen: Niemeyer, 157–78.

ZHANG, S. (1991). 'Negation in Imperatives and Interrogatives: Arguments against Inversion', *Chicago Linguistics Society 27*: 359–73.

ZIMMERMANN, M. (2004). 'Zum *Wohl*': Diskurspartikeln als Satztypmodifikatoren. *Linguistische Berichte 199*: 253–86.

—— (2008). 'Discourse Particles in the Left Periphery', in B. Shaer, P. Cook, W. Frey, and C. Maienborn (eds), *Dislocated Elements in Discourse: Syntactic, Semantic, and Pragmatic Perspectives*. Oxford: Routledge.

ZOERNER, C. E. (1995). *Coordination: The Syntax of &P.* PhD thesis. University of California-Irvine.

—— and B. AGBAYANI (2000). 'Unifying Left-peripheral Deletion, Gapping and Pseudogapping', *Chicago Linguistic Society 36*: 549–61.

ZWART, J. W. (1993). *Dutch Syntax: A Minimalist Approach.* PhD thesis. University of Groningen.

—— (1997). *Morphosyntax of Verb Movement. A Minimalist Approach to the Syntax of Dutch.* Dordrecht: Kluwer Academic Publishers.

ZWICKY, A. (1985). 'Heads', *Journal of Linguistics 21*: 1–30.

—— and G. PULLUM (1983). 'Cliticization vs. Inflection: English *n't*', *Language 59*: 502–13.

—— and J. SADOCK (1975). 'Ambiguity Tests and How to Fail Them', in J. Kimball (ed.), *Syntax and Semantics*. New York: Academic Press, 1–36.

Index

OXFORD STUDIES IN THEORETICAL LINGUISTICS